The Risk of Reading

The Risk of Reading

How Literature Helps Us to Understand Ourselves and the World

Robert P. Waxler

BLOOMSBURY

NEW YORK · LONDON · NEW DELHI · SYDNEY

Bloomsbury Academic
An imprint of Bloomsbury Publishing Inc

1385 Broadway	50 Bedford Square
New York	London
NY 10018	WC1B 3DP
USA	UK

www.bloomsbury.com

Bloomsbury is a registered trade mark of Bloomsbury Publishing Plc

First published 2014

© Robert P. Waxler, 2014

Library of Congress Cataloging-in-Publication Data
Waxler, Robert P., 1944- author.
The risk of reading : how literature helps us to understand ourselves and the
world / Robert Waxler.
pages cm
Includes bibliographical references and index.
ISBN 978-1-62356-357-8 (paperback) – ISBN 978-1-62356-106-2 (hardback)
1. Fiction. 2. Books and reading. 3. Literature–Philosophy.
4. Self-actualization (Psychology) I. Title.
PN3341.W39 2014
809.3'927–dc23
2014009513

ISBN: HB: 978-1-6235-6106-2
      PB: 978-1-6235-6357-8
      ePub: 978-1-6235-6815-3
      ePDF: 978-1-6235-6060-7

Typeset by Newgen Knowledge Works (P) Ltd., Chennai, India
Printed and bound in the United States of America

To Linda, Jeremy, and Jonathan

Contents

Acknowledgments

I have dedicated this book to my wife, Linda, and my sons, Jeremy and Jonathan. They are always with me, and I am forever grateful for that. Special thanks to Jeremy, though. He read the manuscript more often than anyone else and always found a kind word to say about it.

I also want to thank the thousands of students at UMass Dartmouth who have graced my classrooms over the years. They have significantly contributed to my love and understanding of literature. The participants in the Changing Lives Through Literature program (judges, probation officers, and probationers) have also made a difference. Their insights and spirited conversation shared around the seminar table have offered me endless joy and surprise.

While writing this book, I have found particularly helpful the intense and ongoing response from David Sarles, Carl Schinasi, Jim Marlow, David Sherman, Howard Senzel, David Beckman, and Jim Nee. Their suggestions (often pointed and critical) and their encouragement (always welcome) were valuable and important to me.

Haaris Naqvi, my editor at Bloomsbury, gave direction and guidance to this project. I thank him for that and for his generous spirit, always an inspiration.

I also appreciate the work of Hugh Cowling (his cover design captures an important dimension of this book) and the service of Paige Gibbs, at the UMass Dartmouth library, whose devotion to scholarship and reading stands as a shining example for all of us.

Thanks to Sue Demers, who typed the first draft of my original handwritten document, miraculously turning it into an electronic text, and to Mark-Anthony Lewis, Sloan Piva, and Cassandra Quillen, whose comments and search for references will always be remembered.

I am grateful, as well, to Dennis Greene, Tom Dargan, Susan Newman, Mickey Loewenstein, Adrienne and Joel Rosenblatt, Richard Larschan, William Nelles, Bob Gormley, Raphael Kanter, Jerry Blitefield, Jerry Waxler, and Wendy Robertson. They are friends and colleagues, and their comments on the manuscript meant a lot to me.

An earlier version of Chapter 1 appeared in *Journal of Arts and Humanities*, Vol. 1, No. 2 (2012) and a significantly different version of Chapter 8 appeared in *Journal of Popular Culture*, Vol. 29, No. 3 (1995).

1

Story and Real Life

Why should we be concerned about the fate of literature as we move from a book culture to a screen culture in the digital age? Not primarily because we are losing our sense of story, but because we are losing our sense of the central importance of linguistic narrative. There is a difference. The technologies creating the digital revolution devalue language and increasingly do away with boundaries, celebrating instead speed and boundless exhilaration. The visual trumps the linguistic, while the image and the screen trump the word and the book. As a result, we no longer seem to engage deeply with others or ourselves. We are beginning to move, in other words, from "a reading brain" to "a digital brain" (Wolf 4), from a brain capable of deep reading and deep thinking to a brain increasingly addled by spectacle and surface sensation. We are losing our standing as linguistic beings.

In 1994, Sven Birkerts coined the term "deep reading." As he said: "Reading, because we control it, is adaptable to our needs and rhythms. We are free to indulge our subjective associative impulse. The term I coin for this is deep reading: the slow and meditative possession of a book. We don't just read the words, we dream our lives in their vicinity" (Birkerts 146). Birkerts argued that the change from a print culture to an electronic culture was flattening out human identity, threatening our understanding of the complexity and wonder, the interior depths of both our emotional and conceptual lives.

Dreaming our lives through linguistic narrative, as Birkerts indicated, was an important way to explore the unknown territory in the interior of the embodied self, to connect with the tacit knowledge that we can best experience and understand through literature. The deeper we journey into ourselves through deep reading, the more we learn about who we are and where we are located in the midst of the complexities of the world. Unlike watching television or engaging in other types of screen entertainment, Birkerts suggested, deep reading is not an escape from the confusions of daily life but a way of discovering meaning in that life through linguistic narrative. Deep reading is a risky but rewarding encounter with our rhythms and needs, our own feelings and emotions, and it offers a way of making sense of that encounter. Through such reading, we discover how we are all connected to others and to our own evolving stories. We experience our own plots and stories unfolding through the imaginative language and voice of others, and we desire to move on.

Unlike electronic images that often seem to invite us to manipulate them, to possess or consume them, somehow to quickly reduce them, literary language can be lived in, as if it embraces us as we embrace it. The rich texture of literary language calls to our imagination, beckoning us to question, to quest on, to doubt our fixed assumptions, to recognize the complexity and sense of the mystery of the human experience that we share with it. As Socrates knew, every answer is temporary, evoking another question. Literary language encourages us in the same direction.

Jacques Lacan once put it this way: "Language is not to inform but to evoke" (Lacan 63). It is through the rich texture of language, rather than through the digital image, that we have the best chance of finding what we seek: the response of the other whom we have questioned in order to find out something about ourselves. This kind of linguistic exchange drives us on, accounts for our desire to know ourselves and to engage with others. As Lacan indicates, this is the fundamental rhythm of human desire itself: "To put it in a nutshell, nowhere does it appear more clearly that man's desire finds its meaning in the desire of the other . . ." (Lacan 31).

This fundamental rhythm sets the human journey in motion and helps account for the relationship between narrative telling and deep reading, a relationship that we want to explore throughout this book. Like an adventurous journey, both narrative telling and deep reading are always questing, stirring desire and reflection, revealing and concealing, moving us backward and forward, in an attempt to deepen understanding of both our uniqueness and our connectivity as human beings.

Several years after Birkerts's discussion of deep reading, Nicholas Carr (2010) took up this argument, expanding its implications for our digital age. For Carr, we were already living in a fragmented and flattened-out world ("the shallows"). As he put it: "The Net seizes our attention only to scatter it" (Carr 118). The more often we used the Web (and other electronic devices), the more distracted we became. We were losing our ability to sustain attention and focus. As Carr claimed, instead of remembering, we were learning to forget.

The digital culture today has become the mainstream culture, creating a revised sense of time (a fragmented sense of the present without past or future) and a revised sense of space (everywhere experienced as nowhere). It has hollowed out the human self, privileging surfaces (the shallows) and celebrating the digital image (to be consumed like a commodity as fast as possible).

Like Carr, Paul Virilio (2010) sounds a similar warning. For him, all the boundaries of the world are collapsing, suppressing both the depth of our experience as temporal beings as well as the depth of our connections with the world that surrounds us. "The whole world stage is turned upside down . . . to the point where 'representations' gradually lose their pertinence . . . What is promoted instead is 'presentation', an untimely out-of-place presentation that suppresses the depth of time for shared reflexion every bit as much as the depth of field of action and its displacement" (Virilio 6).

For Virilio, we live in an endless NOW, even the present moment has become hallucination. When we journey out on an electronic screen, we forget our "conscious interiority" (Virilio 6), the narrative and historical sense of self rooted in the depths of our embodied experience. Instead, we crave instant gratification to the detriment of the tacit knowledge of organic and vital life. Refusing the challenge of slow and thoughtful discovery, we become instinctual nodes in a network, thinly connected, at best, to other nodes flickering on the screen.

We can call this experience of an endless present the new electronic unconscious replacing the linguistic unconscious. It is an experience flowing without access to origins or horizons, devoid of the traditional human sense of temporal duration or spatial rootedness. As we naturalize this new electronic consciousness, we, too, begin to float in cybertime and cyberspace. In such a process, we lose the common ground of our human nature, our embodied connection to ourselves and other mortal human beings. When we walk we no longer feel our feet on the ground but focus on the tablet in front of us. When we talk, we no longer look at the eyes or the wrinkles of the face before us but focus on pixels on a screen demanding recognition. Slowly we are becoming disembodied selves floating at the surface of the electronic grid. As the world grows curiouser and curiouser, we are no longer curious about our beginnings or our end.

The digital age increasingly collapses the boundary between illusion and reality, the original and the copy, fiction and ordinary life, and in the process, it also celebrates electronic consciousness as the new human consciousness, naturalizing it and privileging it, reinforcing its mainstream success. The "online life" becomes the favored model for "offline life." We begin to behave as if we were always surfing on the screen all the time, and we begin to believe that intelligence is best judged not by wisdom but by technological know-how, not by the depth of human knowledge but by the quick acquisition of transient skills.

Bits and bytes, tweets and visuals, provide us with information to be manipulated, data to be possessed and consumed. But to manipulate things is to give up living in them (Virilio 78). If we want to risk the journey to know ourselves, we need more than bytes and bits, more than data and information. As Walter Benjamin once put it: "The value of information does not survive the moment in which it was news. It lives only at that moment; it has to surrender to it completely and explain itself to it without losing any time" (Benjamin 90). Believing in information short-circuits the journey to know ourselves in the same sense that we begin to foreclose on the question: "What is a human being?"

As Jaron Lanier, the father of virtual reality technology observes: "Being a person is not a pat formula, but a quest, a mystery, a leap of faith" (Lanier 5). But that quest, that risky journey, has been significantly reduced by information, by the very databases that electronic technology celebrates. We cannot count on information exchange to evoke what we desire: the desire of the desire of the other. This is what Lacan indicated as well. "If I now place myself in front of the other to question him, there is no cybernetic computer imaginable that can make a reaction out of what the response will be" (Lacan 63).

"Information systems need to have information in order to run, but underrepresent reality…" (Lanier 69). There is no mystery in a digital image, no originality, no human surprise, as Lanier suggests: "A digital image captures a certain limited measurement of reality within a standardized system that removes any of the original source's unique qualities" (Lanier 134). One of the central assumptions of this book is that language, especially language shaped into narrative, helps to restore those unique qualities, the qualities that make us all human.

This book argues that language is a way into the interior of ourselves as well as a way out into the human community that surrounds us. It is the best way we have to discover our singularity (our individual self) and our commonality (our social self), our strangeness and our familiarity. Grappling with linguistic narrative allows us to connect to the past and to the future. Entering the depths of literary narrative, we risk ourselves, but we are also offered the opportunity to encounter unknown connections between our own self and the world that stretches before us. Language is a gift to us as unique individuals; it gives us the human world to consider, if we dare to. In this regard, literature offers an ethical engagement for those willing to take the risk.

Hans-Georg Gadamer explains it this way: "Language is not one of man's possessions in the world but on it depends the fact that man has a world at all . . . Language has no independent life apart from the world that comes to language within it. Not only is the world 'world' only insofar as it comes into language, but language, too, has its real being only in the fact that the world is presented in it" (Gadamer 401). Human beings are linguistic beings existing in a finite universe. Language grounds us and keeps us human. We are limited in our knowledge of self and the world, finite and mortal, unable to grasp the ultimate secret, but, as mortal beings, we have a journey to make, a responsibility to know the truth as linguistic beings can know it. Literary language remains the best pathway to that kind of mortal truth, to the kind of understanding that promises the possibility of knowing ourselves and the world that surrounds us.

This book does not argue that we should give up mobile devices or abandon the screen culture, but rather suggests that living a life more attentive to words than images, more engaged with narrative knowledge than with bits and bytes of fragmented information, is a way of establishing a crucial counterculture, a culture serving as a contrary to the dominant mainstream culture. It is a way of keeping dialogical relationships fresh and in motion. Deep reading of literary narrative today is necessary to bring us back to the complexity and ambivalence of our own identity and to a recognition of the worth of other linguistic beings, mortal beings who desire to share in the enduring quest to expand and discover what it means to be human—"to know thyself" (as Socrates insisted).

The journey to gain human knowledge is the fundamental journey of life. It is a complex and troubling journey, filled with fear and fascination, an ongoing and embattled quest to know the meaning of our mortal human self and our place in the world that surrounds us. All great writers address this journey as do all human beings who innately desire to know the secrets of mortal human existence. Language shaped into story leads the way to an understanding of the ambiguities and contradictions of our mortal existence. That way calls to us, and deep reading is the ethical response to that challenging call. Literature offers an ethical engagement for those willing to take the risk.

*

When we talk about linguistic narrative (stories shaped by language), we always appear to contradict ourselves. We make ourselves known to ourselves and to others through these stories, but, at the same time, these stories distance us from ourselves and others. There is always a gap between our everyday unstoried experience (the contingent and chaotic events of our everyday experiences), what we sometimes call "real life," and the stories we tell about those "real life" experiences. Sometimes we even insist, because the gap is so noticeable, that the story we have told is "fiction." In this book, though, I want to suggest that all stories are "fiction," to one degree or another, and this is our good fortune.

The gap that opens up between our "real life" and our stories—between the contingent events of our everyday lives and the narratives that shape those chaotic events—rouses us, excites desire, invites us to further recreate ourselves in pursuit of knowing ourselves. Telling stories to ourselves and to others sets us on the most important journey of our lives.

We always exist in the present moment, our sensuous body interacting with the world surrounding it. But it is language that offers us the best opportunity to understand ourselves in relation to that world. In an important sense, it is language that creates that world for us and makes us who we are. As Lacan insists: "It is the world of words which creates the world of things—the things originally confused in the *hic* and *nunc* of the all-in-the-process-of-becoming—by giving its concrete being to their essence, and its ubiquity to what has been from everlasting . . ." (Lacan 39). Through language, we try to create coherence for our "real life" by shaping the past and making it a part of us and by projecting future possibilities for ourselves. In this sense, the metaphoric function of language, especially language shaped into narrative, is a gift that allows us to become conscious of who we are, where we have been, and where we are headed. Linguistic narrative is an especially rich way of making meaning for ourselves in the world and a way of making the world human.

Linguistic narrative offers an embodied sense of time and space through the sensuous and complex associations of language given to the reader to experience. Extended narratives demand that we slow down, that we enter the rich storehouse of language itself, that we feel the systolic and diastolic rhythms of that language on our pulse, and that we reflect on that language, making it our own. That kind of language carries with it traces of the past and possibilities for the future. It evokes memory and desire. Such narrative excites the imagination as well, through its auditory and visual power and through the movement readers experience when they are engaged with the rhythm and intensity of the unfolding of the language. In this context, literary narrative has an affective, conceptual, and somatic quality. It invites us into the interior of ourselves, opening us to empathy and reflection.

We also need to emphasize, though, that literary narrative always has a dual function, a doubleness about it. When we engage with a story, the story engages us. We are in dialogue with it. If a story reinforces the mainstream culture, it also puts that culture into question. If we locate ourselves in a story, that story also urges us to question that location. If a story seems familiar, it also seems strange. As a result, stories offer temporary stability and coherence, but they simultaneously make us feel unstable. When we live in a story, the story also lives in us. As we read it, it reads us. As we experience it, we question it. So we are always questing for our relationship to that story, which is another way of saying that we journey through stories to discover not only our singularity, our uniqueness, our strangeness, but also our connection to others, our home in the world. Linguistic narrative offers us a way into our conflicted identity as both unique individuals and social beings.

How else can we say what linguistic narrative does, how it behaves when we engage it? Language, especially in its literary form, gives us "the ground, the soil in which to strike root and stand" (Heidegger 90). But it also puts us into exile, sends us into the wilderness, as someone like Maurice Blanchot (1999) seems to believe. Language allows us to glimpse a potential home, a place to root ourselves in and to stand in the midst of the confusion and chaos of the world, but that home is always envisioned at a distance, a place that we do not yet fully know, and so it also reminds us of the strangeness of the real world that we presently live in. It makes us anxious. Language reminds us that we lack the fullness of our being, that we are ambiguous and ambivalent human beings, incomplete mortal selves. We are wounded beings on a quest for wholeness.

When we engage with linguistic narrative, it excites our desire and imagination to want to know more, to seek our beginnings and to pursue our ends, to discover the secret that we cannot grasp. As Michael Burke says: "I believe that the imagery produced while reading literature is so powerful, in part, because it is fundamental to who we are as individuals and where we come from. The meaning that participants and indeed locations and activities carry in the mental imagery of literary readers appears to be bound to those three fundamental questions: Who are we? Where did we come from? Where are we going?" (Burke 58). Literary narrative transports us back toward the depths of our beginning and projects us forward toward our end. But it can never fully make explicit that beginning or that end anymore than we can articulate the experience of our birth or our death.

We might imagine the importance of literary narrative in the following way:

1. "Real life" is a series of mostly contingent events, primarily chaotic and infused with anxiety and intimations of death. As mortal beings we

are often thrown about by these troubling events, leaving us with little sense of our origins or our end.

2. That moment-by-moment experience of contingent events can be made into a life story, envisioned both as a linear narrative from birth to death and as a series of concentric circles (or expanding loops) taking us deeper and deeper into our interior self and out into the depths of the external world. That journey, shaped by the rich texture of language, transports us through an emotional, somatic, and conceptual arc of human meaning and purpose.

3. This journey, a person's life story, always intermingles with the stories of others, thus helping human beings to create a sense of identity through time and also helping them to create meaning and location for their lives.

4. Language, especially when shaped into story, is likely the most crucial development in giving the mortal body human purpose and direction on this life journey. Through the rich texture of literary narrative, in particular, human beings appreciate the deep and enigmatic complexity of the human experience and become self-reflective.

5. Story evokes story, further deepening the reading experience and the human quest for further knowledge of the self. Reading and discussing stories, then, also enhances the significance and interactivity of human community. Such a process inspires a rejuvenated and ongoing sense of the individual self and offers a glimpse of genuine democracy.

In this context, we might agree that human experience is only possible within a world that is already linguistically articulated. As Kristen Dietrich Balisi says: "Human speech does not create or bring elements of lifeforms into being; it does not establish a physical order within the cosmos. Rather it creates linguistic 'beings' and a grammatically ordered realm within which the terms relate to each other; a secondary humanly constituted vision of reality layered upon the physical and cosmological order" (Kass 78–79n). This is the world as we know it: the way the world becomes human and meaningful as we experience it through language and story. We are linguistic beings.

*

Seeking to create a life story, we live in dialogical relation with ourselves and with others, with our stories and with the stories of others. As Alasdair MacIntyre says: "I can only answer the question: 'What am I to do?' if I can answer the prior question: 'Of what story or stories do I find myself a part'?" (MacIntyre 216). We need story to contextualize our contingent experiences, and we need that imagined context to create and interpret the ongoing story of our "real lives."

Some people today have no story; they have no context and seem to have nothing to say. They cannot rely on themselves, so they cannot be relied on. They live without perspective, so they have trouble being self-reflective. They live in an endless present, without apparent goals or direction. They appear to have no future, no promise to fulfill. They have become zombies, the walking dead.

But, as human beings, we have an ethical responsibility to acknowledge others, to listen to their stories, and to offer stories to them. The exchange of stories is an ethical response to a most natural human demand. That demand, never fully satisfied, nevertheless obligates us. Through the telling of stories and the listening to stories, human beings begin to acknowledge each other's desire. Within that linguistic environment, they create and enter into what Emmanuel Levinas calls, "a curvature of intersubjective space" (Levinas 291). Within that space (or gap), they make themselves vulnerable to each other, and, at the same time, protect themselves from the direct glare of their own mortality. They sense their connectivity to others by creating a shared space and a common horizon, and yet they acknowledge their difference, their singularity. In this way, the exchange of stories becomes an act of human love, a way to bring compassion into the world. It allows us to glimpse our imperfections, our shared mortal wounds.

Through the experience of language shaped into story, we not only feel empathy and compassion for the other, but we also acknowledge the strangeness of the other. That is why stories are said to "infect" us (Tolstoy), shake us up (Kafka), and also give us "a habitation and a name" (Shakespeare). Such stories drive us forward into the future as a promise would; they signify that a promise has been kept, a covenant secured. Stories give us hope, which allows us to return to the series of contingent events in our daily lives with fresh perceptions and renewed possibilities, but they also remind us that we are necessarily mortal and vulnerable beings, limited and incomplete, strangers in the world. Stories give us a sense of familiarity, but also remind us of our strangeness.

As Stanley Cavel suggests, stories allow us to temporarily leave behind our confusions, the chaos of our everyday existence, even the distractions that pull us away from ourselves. By moving us to acknowledge our strangeness in that everyday world of distraction, stories can inspire us to strike out in a new direction, to find a new beginning. As Cavel says: "The first step in attending to our education is to observe the strangeness of our lives, our estrangement from ourselves, the lack of necessity in what we profess to be necessary" (Cavel 55). The strangeness of the story opens a gap for us to enter, invites us to sense our mortality and our vulnerability, what we lack. But, then, with our desire aroused, it also offers us compassion, the human desire to connect, the promise to continue on with others in our quest to discover ourselves in the midst of the chaos.

*

Encountering literature is always risky business. It reminds us of what we have and what we do not have, what we are and what we are not, what is familiar to us and what is strange to us. It also makes an ethical demand on us. As Arnold Weinstein claims: "Literature endows us and teaches us to endow other living human beings who cross our path, not only in books, but in the world that we live in, with consciousness. This is an ethical injunction; for it moves from self to world" (Weinstein 6). Literature teaches us to recover our own story and also teaches us that others have (at least potentially) a story to tell.

As Weinstein indicates, language is the best means we have "for chronicling and choreographing that huge realm of feeling and fantasy that is one's ultimate real estate" (Weinstein 6). That "real estate" is our home, the capacious scaffolding of the complexity and depth of our human identity, the embattled and troubled mortal being articulated as a linguistic self. It is our home, but also an enigma, a riddle, a knot that cannot be fully untied until its story ends and we become a corpse.

Like mortal life, language has its limits, hinting at that which we desire but cannot fully grasp. Language takes us to the threshold of this boundary, to the edge of this ultimate strangeness, but no further. In the human world, language makes the strange somewhat familiar, and the familiar somewhat strange, giving us stability, at times, and shaking us up, at other times. But it cannot carry us over the threshold into the direct experience of death (or the direct experience of God). Language can perhaps give us a glimpse of this mysterious experience. But, as linguistic beings, we cannot fully articulate that experience anymore than we can experience our own death and then name it.

In "real life," we move through contingent events, what we usually consider chaotic experience and chance occurrence. As story tellers, though, we move back through those chance events, giving them shape and meaning, a sense of necessity. We are like the detective working backward from effects to causes, from clues to detection; like the doctor working from symptoms to the primary cause; or like Heidegger working from the fact of death to life, from nonbeing to being, from end to beginning. As human beings, we quest for the knowledge of "real life" experience, revealed and concealed through linguistic narrative. We seek for the answer to the riddle of "real life," the secret embodied only in the story itself.

The story we tell, though, is always somewhat of a deception, a covering that hints at, but also protects us from full exposure to the ultimate mystery, the secret of our singularity, our uniqueness. Yet, that fiction also invites us to reconnect with our lived past experience and create imagined meaning for the future. Story projects us backward and forward in this way; it gives us imagined coherence and keeps us alive. It is the truth of our mortal lives, whether it actually happened or not. By contrast, once the mystery is unveiled, the secret fully revealed, we collapse. As Foucault says: "That which hides and envelops, the curtain of night over truth, is paradoxically, life; and death, on the contrary, opens up to the light of day the black coffer of the body" (Foucault 166).

Without story, we have neither meaningful life nor meaningful death, at least in terms of human identity. As unstoried beings, we are conflicted bodies without conscious knowledge or understanding of the rich contradictions of mortal life. Without story, we are, at best, endlessly distracted, often by what is insignificant, by indifference, by carelessness, by the contingencies of existence. We refuse to embrace our uncertainty or the necessity of our mortality. We exist in endless illusion. Michael Roemer puts it well: "If we can accept our uncertainty, even though we cannot trust it as we once trusted God, story may regain its credibility, and, by affirming rather than distracting us from necessity, recover its ancient, persuasive and telling role. For what we call 'fiction' embodies a reality we cannot afford to face in life, and what we call 'reality' is, in fact, a fiction that allows us a measure of consciousness without casting us into despair. It may well be the reality and contradictions we can face only in fiction that gives our lives meaning and shape" (Roehmer 386).

There is a sense, then, that story is sturdier than we might expect. It makes us aware of how narrow the boundary between life and death, being and nonbeing, our uniqueness and our commonalities, fiction and "real life" experience, is: how strong and how vulnerable we all are.

Literature in particular creates a bounding line for us, and so helps us to keep the shifting sense of difference between contingency and necessity in place (as blurry and unclear as that place might be). Literature reminds us, as Gregory Jusdanis says, "of the boundary we draw between what we experience and what we imagine" (Jusdanis 59). In that context, it is a social practice, and more than any other social practice, it "accentuates the threshold between itself and other spaces" (Jusdanis 59). As Jusdaris indicates, literature watches over these boundaries, but in order to do that, it must also "retain its own distance from reality" (Jusdanis 61). Through its linguistic inventions, it helps us recognize the boundary between contingent experience and "fiction." As a result: "It brings light to the gap between fiction and reality because it needs this gap to live" (Jusdanis 61). Literature guards a crucial border that accentuates a sense of difference, that fortunate gap that allows us to continue on, to create an imagined meaning and purpose for our everyday experiences (commonly called "real life").

Unlike the abstract language of scientism (the ironic attempt to use distinct and efficient language as a means to an instrumental and practical end), the imaginative language of story offers us sensuous experience, an embodied language shaped into narrative (or poetic forms), expressing personal knowledge open to reflection. Literary language binds us to that experience, but also inspires us to movement and agency. It grants us both sensuous experience to immerse ourselves in and the perspective to distance ourselves from that experience so that we can make sense of the experience and begin to create our own story. It allows us to acknowledge that we are mortal bodies experiencing the world and that we can reflect on that embodied experience. In this way, we recognize how the story we are reading is similar to our own story and so we are able to recognize how we are connected to other mortal human beings. Another's story is our story as well. But we also recognize our difference from this story, our difference from others. Another's story is not quite our story after all. In this way, we know what we are and what we are not. We acknowledge the self and the other, our life and our death.

Since we cannot experience our own singular death and then name it, we can never say all that we are any more than we can know what the mute body would say. But linguistic narrative can remind us that we are more than the mute body. We are both similar and different from others. Within the depth of language, we connect to others, giving us a sense of community, and, at the same time, we sense our mortality, our fragility, even our death. Story embodies the enigma of our mortal human identity.

*

My hope is that the close reading of the linguistic narratives offered in this book will take you back to the stories themselves and then out again to your "real life," and so enhance your own journey. The readings are based on years of puzzling over these stories and endless, often heated, discussions with students in many of my university classes and in the Changing Lives Through Literature program. In addition to rereading and discussing these stories over the years, I have also found the voice of countless critics of considerable value at different times in the reading process. Given the approach to reading literary narrative that I am advocating here, though, I want to mention a few critics who especially have resonated with my own reading over the years and with the conversations I have had with my many students. No doubt, these exceptional critics have influenced my own thoughts (both consciously and unconsciously) about the narratives discussed in this book. Their work often seems to follow a path similar to the one I have been on for some time, and although at times I arrived at their work after formulating readings of my own, I always found their own analysis probing, their voices helpful and encouraging. I am thinking, in particular, of Peter Brooks and J. Hillis Miller, especially their discussions of *The Heart of Darkness*, and Brooks's discussion of *Frankenstein*. Wendy Steiner's comments on *Alice in Wonderland* and Leon B. Kass's commentary on the Creation story in *Genesis* also stand out for me in this context.

I believe that deep and close reading of literature can help us to understand ourselves and the world around us, that we need fiction to give our so-called real life meaning, and that reading narrative fiction remains crucial to the making of a humane and democratic society. We are linguistic beings, and language, especially language shaped into narrative, is central to our quest for identity. Reading literature is one of the best opportunities we have today to maintain a coherent human identity and remain self-reflective individuals in a world that seems particularly chaotic and confusing.

Most chapters in this book take up a well-known work of nineteenth- or twentieth-century literature in order to discuss more fully these issues, exploring, in particular, the notion of life as a journey or quest and the crucial relationship between language and our contingent everyday existence. Of particular interest along the way is the question of what literary narrative can teach us about our mortality and how stories offer opportunities to reflect on the ambivalent and profound meaning of mortal knowledge.

I begin the journey with the story of Adam and Eve. Approached as literary narrative, that story reminds us that we all repeat their journey in our own way. It is a story about Creation, about the mortal world, about language and finitude, about freedom and necessity, about life and death, about the complex contradictions embodied in human experience. We want to follow it in great detail, because, like all important stories, it is our story, whether it happened or not.

2

The Creation Story

We start with the Creation story (*Genesis* 1–3), a story that seems to know nothing about reading or writing. It is a quintessential story about language and knowledge, though, and it has survived all the myths and tales it draws upon, indicating its central importance as a story about the meaning of mortal human life, especially within the Western World.

Interestingly, Adam and Eve are only mentioned once in the Hebrew Bible after the Creation story, and this has led some commentators to suggest that this story has no importance. Harold Bloom (1990) sees it, for example, as little more than a children's story, at best a tale of family romance. By contrast, Elaine Pagels (1989) argues that the story does have importance, but much of the meaning and interpretation of the story comes from the development of the Church and the Christian West: the story of Jesus fulfilling the work begun by Adam, especially on issues of sexuality; Jesus's birth and resurrection allowing for the redemption of Adam's fall into mortality and sin. Of equal significance for us, though, is the reminder that the writers of this admittedly short, but richly textured narrative—the Priestly writer (P) and the Jahwist writer (J), as well as the redactor who wove the strains of the various Hebrew texts together—never refer to the "Fall" or to "Sin." No doubt much of the importance of the Creation story is based on how it has lived through the centuries, taking on new meaning and depth as it continually unfolds through time.

It is not quite right to say that we are our stories as those stories have developed through history and time; nor is it accurate to claim that there is no Creation text, only discussions and interpretations of that text. The Creation story resonates for us today, first and foremost, because it narrates through language something important about our origins, our identity, our sexuality and death, our freedom and our limitations as mortal human beings. Like most significant stories, it does not offer solutions, but raises crucial questions, worthy of our attention precisely because it is a story that arouses our desire to know, to continue the ongoing quest for the secret that seems just beyond our grasp.

Genesis 1–3 is a story we want to wrestle with because it helps us shape our own story and helps us locate ourselves in the midst of all the other stories that we hear and know. With its mystery and depth, it has inspired great artists and poets—including John Milton whose *Paradise Lost* stands as one of the most imaginative interpretations and extensions of this story—as well as philosophers and theologians. Its appeal transcends politics or cultural correctness as it calls to us across the centuries as a narrative bounded by language, but language that is always moving and alive, always overflowing its apparent boundaries, and returning us to "real life."

Although we are reading this story in translation, part of the significance of the story may also be the movement of the language itself. Thorleif Boman claims that Hebrew language and knowledge are critically different than Greek language and knowledge. Just as an Orthodox Jew in prayer is always moving his body in rhythm with the language, the Greek thinker stays still, reflecting and contemplating, distancing himself from the body in motion (Boman 205). Hebrew thought, in this context, is embodied and in ongoing motion; Greek thought bends to reflection and stasis. We read *Genesis* 1–3 with both dimensions in mind.

Genesis 1–3 confronts us with a nearly insurmountable series of difficulties, ranging from how to experience the Creation story as text (are we getting two versions of the same story or two separate and incompatible versions?) to how to make this story our own (are we reading from a Jewish context, a Christian context, a secular context, and so on?). If this story evokes "the beginning of wisdom," as Leo Kass (2003) suggests, then is it also true that in our beginning is our end? How deep does this story go? How capacious is it? How does it shape us as we shape it?

We start with the P text, *Genesis* I, approaching it not as a religious text, but as a literary narrative, a story shaped by a Priestly narrator, whose primary purpose seems to be to evoke the awesome act of God's Creation. P wants us as readers to know God through his acts, not through his attributes. Unlike the Jahwist narrator, J, whose irony and humor will allow for complex character development in *Genesis* 2, P focuses on God the Creator, the origin of all things. God is complete before the beginning of the beginning of Creation itself. He is what He is before the beginning and after the end. As readers, we are invited by P to apprehend God as a secret, a mystery that can be glimpsed but never fully known. For P, we sense God through the awesomeness of His acts of Creation.

P is not speaking in the language of God but in the language of man. He cannot do otherwise. Through his linguistic narrative, though, he is attempting to create an after-effect in the consciousness of the reader, a penumbra of the mystery of the Creation story that he is shaping. Bounded by the temporal and spatial limits of human speech, P tells the story of the seven days of Creation so that we, as readers, will experience the human meaning of Creation, make it part of our human identity. *Genesis* I offers us finite knowledge of the Creation and a space for reflection through language that says more than it knows.

In the Creation story, the language of God is timeless, not only bringing elements and lifeforms into being, but actually being as one with those elements and lifeforms. By contrast, as Dietrich Balisi puts it: "Human speech does not create or bring elements or lifeforms into being; it does not establish a physical order within the cosmos. Rather it creates linguistic beings and a grammatically ordered realm with which the terms relate to each other, a secondary humanly constituted vision of reality layered upon the physical and cosmological order" (Kass 77n). This human vision of the Creation gives us an opportunity to situate ourselves within the world, a beginning for our own journey.

"In the beginning God created the heavens and the earth" (1.1 NIV), P tells us as his narration starts. That beginning, majestic in its declarative style and tone, refers not to God's beginning (which cannot be articulated by the mortal P), but to what we can know of Him according to His acts. P cannot take us to the actual moment of the Creation (the beginning before the beginning of the world). He can only render the Creation in human language, bound in temporal terms (using "created"—the past tense, for example). He can only refer to what we, as human beings, assume to be spatial locations ("heavens" and "earth"). It is our journey that P speaks about, an earthly journey at that.

P tells us about the elements of earth, water and air, but does not mention fire, apparently a gift given to human beings after the Creation (thanks to Prometheus?). God sees, but we do not see him. His spirit hovers over the dark and deep waters, a mystery that we cannot grasp. Then, through the language of P, we hear God's voice directly for the first time: "Let there be light" (1.3). As narrator, P has no other choice than to suggest that God's command causes the effect of the light that we now see. But we might assume that God's articulation of "light" is light; from God's perspective (if He had one), His language moves as "light," language and act being one. In the human vision, though, we experience the Creation as linguistic beings, a grammatically ordered realm, a humanly constituted vision of reality through P's narrative, syntactically structured in sequence. God does not use a temporal grammar. He does not say, "There is light" or "There will be light" or "There was light." He says, "Let there be light," just as He says, on the second day, "Let there be a vault between the waters to separate water from water" (1.6).

God's Creation appears to the reader to proceed by cause and effect and His acts of naming appear to proceed by division, but that is our own way of envisioning the Creation, not His. He calls the light "day" and the darkness "night." He separates the water under the vault from the water above it. He calls the dry ground "land" and the gathered waters "seas." And, according to P, when God sees these acts He acknowledges that they are "good."

As readers, we might wonder how P knows what God saw and why God "saw that it was good" (1.10). God does not say that it was good; P does. We trust the truth of the narration here precisely because we experience the story as P creates it. Perhaps we sense the Spirit of God hovering over the movement of the linguistic narrative and the Presence of His voice in His declarative commandments, but it is the human vision that we are responding to, the vaulting of the language itself, the arching and jumping movement that seems to create a horizon of possibilities as the story connects with our own internal expanse.

God manifests Himself through His Creation, but it is P's linguistic narrative that makes known to us what was unknown before. On the third day, the land produces vegetation, fruit with seed in it, plants, and trees, according to their kind. If there is division, there is also multiplication, as the narrative unfolds. Stars, the moon and the sun, planets are all created in the vault of the sky. According to P, God's voice is creating the material world, externalizing His language for the world to experience. But it is actually P who is drawing us into his creation; it is his narrative that we begin to experience and believe. P's narrative becomes our narrative as well.

As Thorleif Boman suggests, P is not concerned with a visual description of the world, but with the wonder of that world as it manifests itself through metaphorical speech. He is not trying to describe God as a set-designer to be seen at a distance, but rather he is asking us to experience the creative movement of his language in its metaphoric richness. P invites us to sense the magnificence of the light of the stars, for example, and to wonder at their creation. The stars are not elements in the sky at a distance to be visualized; rather P wants us to enact the creation of those stars through his metaphoric language; he wants us to know those stars are as much inside us as outside in the cosmos (Boman 132–133). Boman best explains the difference between the metaphoric and the visual in terms of the Hebrew language. Citing lines from Isaiah 66, Boman points out that "when Jahveh says: 'Heaven is my throne and the earth is my footstool,' it does not mean that Jahveh sits in heaven with his feet upon the earth, but that the whole earth has no more value for Him than a footstool for an earthly king" (Boman 183). So, too, with P's text: P is not asking us to picture God placing stars in the vault of the sky, but rather to experience that kind of creative act, sense its wonder, its goodness and light. Read this way, the language of *Genesis* is not primarily visual, but like all literary narrative, it should be read through its metaphoric function.

On the fifth day, God creates lifeforms, birds to fly across the vault, and great creatures of the sea, and on the sixth day, He creates livestock and wild animals to move across the earth, all according to their kind. Then, in His longest declaration, God says, "Let us make mankind in our image, in our likeness, so that they may rule over the fish in the sea and the birds in the sky, over the livestock and all the wild animals, and over all the creatures that move along the ground" (1.26). P insists on repeating the crucial point:

"So God created mankind in His own image,
In the image of God He created them;
Male and female He created them." (1.27)

For P, and for the readers who have journeyed through the six days of Creation with him, this Creation is a gift from God to mankind who now rules over it just as the light from the stars govern the day and the night. But what does God mean when he declares that mankind is made "in our image," or as P puts it, "in the image of God He created them"? P cannot mean that mankind looks like God, or that God should now be visualized as mankind. Instead he must be suggesting that the elements and lifeforms of the Creation are manifestations of God brought into being by His voice, by His language. The Creation is an act of God, but it is not God. Mankind, both male and female equally (with no apparent sexual difference in P's version of the Creation) can glimpse God through experiencing the gift that it has been given. Like P himself, male and female can create the human vision of the Creation. Created in His image, we can make God's Creation our story as well. Through linguistic narrative, we can glimpse what was before the beginning and experience the after-effects that will continue to resonate through history and time. Those after-effects (the wonder of the story itself) help create the ongoing journey for all of us. Glimpsing the wonder of P's creation, we move back into the contingent events of the chaotic world of our everyday experiences.

On the seventh day, the heavens and the earth are completed, and God rests from all his work, blessing the seventh day and making it holy: that rest, as P suggests, is another gift for mankind: a time for reflection and respect for the work that has unfolded. When we leave this version of the Creation narrative, if we are fortunate, we know through the singular encounter with the story that we have gained something unknown to us previously, a dimension of our identity unfolding and a renewed sense of location in the world. We are stirred to read on.

Thanks to the redactor, what we read next is J's version of the Creation of the heavens and the earth, a version that focuses on the story of Adam and Eve and the one that has made the greater impact over the centuries. As Harold Bloom (1990) has pointed out, J is more of a literary writer than P, and he seems particularly interested in character development and the numerous twists and turns of human existence. J raises questions that stir the deepest dimensions of human consciousness, troubling and intriguing questions that will continue to haunt us throughout this book. J adds many details to the story of Creation, enhances the human drama significantly, and changes the sequence of the Creation itself. He seems less interested in the majesty of God and his Creation than in the journey of mankind, the existential reality of Adam and Eve, all of us in search of what we have lost, what we lack as mortal human beings, the gap in human existence.

Jack Miles (1996) offers a valuable literary reading of *Genesis* 2–3 in terms of J's narrative. Miles makes God Himself a literary character, further emphasizing J's psychological insights and his ability to develop rich and complex characters. God becomes a character in conflict with Himself, struggling for coherence and control despite significant inner turmoil. For us, though, especially having arrived at J's narrative through P's vision, Miles seems overextended. God's acts cannot be understood as any indication that God Himself experiences internal splitting. As we have already seen, God is what man knows of God; Miles fails to approach the internal splitting of God's character as J himself does. J understands that mankind is already split, lacking what God already knows. For J, the Creation story is a detailed account of the beginning of the quest for the knowledge of mortal identity. What does it mean to be a human being? What does it mean to be created in the image of God, but yet not to be God? Miles collapses a significant border that is purposely preserved by the story itself.

J offers a narrative perspective from the ground. He is less interested in God's majesty, the beginning before the beginning, than in the start and the end of mortal human identity. He is interested, in other words, in the gap, the wound that human beings share. J starts with barren earth (dust); then streams emerge to water the surface of the ground. There is no one to work the ground, so the Lord God forms "a man from the dust of the ground" and breathes "into his nostrils the breath of life," making the man "a living being" (2.7). The dust, perhaps clay, is the mute body of man in this rendering. It has no story, nor will it be able to tell its own story. God's breath, the spirit of God which hovered over the waters in P's narration, perhaps even the voice of God, certainly His language, inspires this dust, gives it movement and direction, desire and imagination as well. Man becomes "a living being" through the imaginative act of God, but yet the origins of man remain rooted in the dust.

In contrast to P's account, we have not yet heard the voice of God in J's account; we have only heard J's description of events. As readers, we are "the man," the living being amidst the watery ground. God then plants a garden in the East, in Eden, and puts the man alone in that garden with trees "pleasing to the eye and good for food" (2.9). It is as if God is beginning to give location to man just as J is beginning to create a sense of location for us as readers. If man is created in the image of God, we are being created through J's narrative. J seems purposefully puzzling, though, a sign of his literary genius. The Garden, in Eden, for example, is said to be in the East— but where is the East?— we are justified in asking. God does not need such direction, but we do.

To give us a still richer context to experience his story, J continues to enrich the descriptions of the landscape and location of the Garden of Eden. But why does he tell us specifically that the trees in the garden were "pleasing to the eye and good for food"? Is he already warning us that visual pleasure stirs temptation and excites desire in man? And is J using "good" here as P had used it—referring to the way God saw what he created and declared it "good"—or is J being ironic, implying that not all trees are equally "good for food"? J is not simply inviting us into the Garden, he is insisting that we quest through his story, acknowledge this troubling story as our own. He is giving us a story to experience and to question.

J next enriches our environment with the crucial description of the two trees set in the middle of the garden: the tree of life and the tree of the knowledge of good and bad (a better translation from the Hebrew than the more familiar "good and evil"). Both trees must be "pleasing to the eye," but, as the story unfolds, only one gains our primary attention. The tree of life offers immortality, God knows, but the tree of knowledge gains the focus in J's story and becomes the subject of God's first command: "You are free to eat from any tree in the garden, but you must not eat from the tree of the knowledge of good and bad, for when you eat from it you will certainly die" (2.16–17).

This is certainly not the language of God that we heard from P. It is J's language, carrying an impulse to human consciousness, an enactment of law implying its own transgression. Man is free to eat from any tree, but he cannot eat from the tree of knowledge. Again, we need to reflect: What is the meaning of these apparent contradictions?

We might assume that if man eats from the tree of life, he will know God, but that is incorrect because we already know that man cannot know God the way that God knows Himself. If man is created in the image of God, he must also, according to J, already feel uncertain, an anxiousness, a sense of alienation from the ground of his own existence. He has been given freedom, but also warned with a death sentence. If he chooses to act with unfettered freedom, he will "certainly die." Like us, he must already sense that he is in the midst of a riddle.

Man does not know God through abstraction or metaphysical speculation, but through his experience of His acts, through the flourishing of the garden and the majestic flow of the river watering the garden, now separated into four headwaters winding out into the entire land beyond Eden. In conventional terms, man is in Paradise, moved there by God from the vast barren ground. He is apparently innocent (without the knowledge of good and bad), although he seems anxious, already feeling alone and alienated. We might question how he understands what death is ("you will certainly die") if he does not sense such intimations. Perhaps his connection with dust fuels such beginnings, connects him to his own unique strangeness.

Then, for the first time, God acknowledges that something in His Creation "is not good" (2.18). The man is alone. Again, we imagine that what is "not good" must be "bad." It is not "bad" for God, but for the man. God will make a helper suitable for the man so that he will not be alone.

Just as God created the man out of dust, he now "forms" all the wild animals and all the birds in the sky. He brings them to the man, "and whatever the man called each living creature, that was its name" (2.20). We do not hear the voice of God, nor do we hear the voice of the man. J summarizes: "So the man gave names to all the livestock, the birds in the sky and all the wild animals" (2.20). This is man acting in the image of God, creating the human vision as linguistic movement. But, unlike God's language ("Let there be light"), man's language is spoken in time, rich in ambiguity, fraught with pitfalls and limitations. The gift of speech enriches man's internal experience of what God is like, but it is not God. It stirs man on his journey in time as it unfolds man's temporal meaning. Naming the living creatures not only grants man dominion over them, but it also creates an understanding of his difference from them. If God is like man, then man is like the animals. As readers, we acknowledge the connection, but it is hierarchical (vertical). On the ground the earthman seems on the edge of an existential crisis, seeking an intimacy that he cannot discover.

For the first time, J calls the man "Adam" and tells us that despite Adam's naming of the living creatures, Adam is still alone: "But for Adam no suitable helper was found" (2.20). Adam's naming apparently creates the ambiguous human vision, sharpening not only the sense of connection between man and other living creatures, but also the sense of difference between them. Most importantly, the familiar intimacy that the man desires remains unfulfilled; it cannot be named anymore than the mute body (the dust) can name itself.

J's literary genius, keenly attuned to these intimations of anxiety and internal struggle, responds to the growing intensity of the human drama beginning to unfold. Adam (originally named by whom exactly we are uncertain) has been given the gift of speech. He has been taken from barren ground and placed in Paradise. We can assume, as is customary, that he is innocent, without memory of his formation before entering Eden, especially since he was then without language. He is in Paradise but there is already signs of restlessness, rhythmic impulse, an undefined gap between his need for connection and his need for differentiation. J is offering to us, as readers, our own story, the beginning of earthly man.

We credit the redactor for where we are in terms of our experience of the Creation story so far. We have moved, thanks to P, from a glimpse of God's Presence and the experience of His Creation through His language manifested as elements and living creatures; we have glimpsed His wonder enacted for us by P's narrative. We do not know God Himself, but, now thanks to J, we also know more fully the beginning of mankind's story, the story of Adam created in the likeness of God. We are experiencing, as Balisc put it, the "secondary humanly constituted vision of reality layered upon the physical and cosmological order" (Kass 78n). Such an experience puts us in dialogue with the text and with ourselves. It enacts the creation of linguistic beings.

Despite the profound gift of speech, the ability to name the living creatures, Adam remains restless, unable to find the intimacy he seeks, a suitable helper to alleviate his loneliness. "So the Lord God caused the man to fall into a deep sleep; and while he was sleeping, he took one of the man's ribs and then closed up the place with flesh" (2.21).

With J, God's actions seem more direct than with P, although more puzzling. God does not say, for example, "Let there be trees in the Garden";

according to J, God plants trees in the Garden. God does not say, "Let us make mankind"; instead, he forms Adam from dust and takes one of the man's ribs to make a woman. Why does He cause the man to fall into a deep sleep, though? There is certainly a sense of interiority here, an entry through the flesh (the surface) into unknown territory (the deep), perhaps echoing P's opening lines: "Darkness was over the surface of the deep, and the Spirit of God was hovering over the waters" (1.1). God must open the flesh to take the rib, since, according to J, He subsequently "closed the place with flesh" (2.21). Man is wounded. But we, as readers, are not to experience this literally, but metaphorically, and not from God's vision, but in time through our earthly existence. It is as if the man dreams his own desire and need, an unknown dimension of his own self, and when he awakes, he finds that his dream has come true (as the poet Keats once suggested). What was inside has been brought outside; it will now be made into a woman for the man to know.

The man does not witness God's Creation of the woman (another beginning before the beginning), but once God brings her to the man, we hear the man speak for the first time. Adam has already exercised the human power to name other living creatures, but only after he sees the woman, stirred by desire, we imagine, does he speak directly through the unfolding narrative:

"This is now bone of my bones
and flesh of my flesh;
She shall be called 'woman'.
For she was taken out of man." (2.23)

The name "woman"—rooted in "man" ("ishi" and "ishier" in Hebrew)—binds the man and woman, evoking mankind, male and female. United as man and wife, "they become one flesh" (2.24), J tells us, although his language is again perplexing, suggesting that this is the reason that a man leaves his father and mother. To become one flesh resonates for us, with the wonder of ultimate intimacy fully embodied, the Paradisial consciousness in the Garden, but it also carries traces of leaving, a lack (or a loss) already troubling mankind on an endless quest for the secret, the mystery that human beings cannot fully name.

Up to this moment in the narrative, we have no indication of any difference between Adam and his wife. They are both naked, but they feel no shame. If their eyes are open to the pleasures of sight, they are not open wide. In Christian terms, we are now at the dawn of the Fall, although we might prefer to think of it as the beginning of the movement from innocence to experience, the expanding journey into the depths of human consciousness and out into the world.

In the Garden of Eden, Adam has named the animals and been given a help-mate, bone of his bone, flesh of his flesh, a counterpart to him, suggesting that human beings are social animals, sexual and connected. Together Adam and Eve appear to have all they need to satisfy their appetite, not only to survive but to flourish. Their nakedness is not yet of any consequence to them: "They were both naked, the man and the woman, and they felt no shame" (2.25). They seem, though, to have little interest in, or desire for the tree of life, apparently not thinking about immortality because they are essentially unaware of death itself. They are similar to God but they are not God. They have the power of human speech and the ability to listen; they are dialogical. Like God, they have the ability to name, but, unlike God, their naming cannot create the elements or living creatures. They are earth bound, although capable of experiencing the wonder of God.

When J introduces the serpent, the serpent immediately speaks to the woman: "Did God really say, 'You must not eat from any tree in the garden'?" (3.1) The serpent is clearly different from "any of the wild animals the Lord God had made" (3.1). He is apparently upright when he speaks, and we might question how he has learned to speak. As readers, we have assumed God granted the gift of speech to Adam and Eve, but to no other living creature. (The poet Milton suggests that the serpent has already eaten from the tree of knowledge.) The serpent is a strange character, but we expect this kind of narrative development from J. The serpent is a smooth talker, interested in drawing Eve in, engaging her in dialogue. Its question—"You must not eat from any tree in the garden?"—is, at best, indirect, a ploy for discussion and deception. God did not say what the serpent claims He said, but the serpent must know this. It is not asking for information, but calling for a response from the woman.

The woman corrects the serpent: "We may eat fruit from the trees in the garden" (iii.2). But then she focuses on what the crafty serpent has anticipated, the law that has already been internalized through language and the transgression implied in that language. "God did say, 'You must not eat fruit from the tree that is in the middle of the garden" (3.2), she explains. From J, we know there are two trees in the middle of the garden, but the woman feels no need to name the one she is talking about. For her, the tree of knowledge seems to have captured her full attention. It will become the primary desire of human beings: to know thyself. Intensifying the intrigue, the woman now expands on what God said, "You must not touch it or you will die" (3.3). To touch is not to eat, however, and there is no previous indication that God explicitly commanded mankind not to touch "it" (tree or fruit). Her fascination with the tree must come from her sensual longing for it, the pleasure of what she sees, set in motion by her original experience of God's command (the law). That fascination is fueled by her desire to transgress and by her fear of the consequences of that transgression ("You will die"). Like Adam, she, too, is a conflicted and ambivalent mortal being.

As the dialogue between the serpent and the woman develops, we, as readers, experience its expansive movement as much from the inside as from the outside. It is the woman's struggle with herself; our own struggle as conflicted human beings. Neither the serpent nor the woman lie outright, but their language now unfolds as half-truths, experienced as finite knowledge, incomplete and, at times, corrupted, but always in motion, subject to revision and the deepening of possibilities.

When the woman claims that God said, "You will die," the serpent quickly responds with an emphatic counterclaim, "You will certainly not die" (3.4), echoing God's original certainty which the woman has interestingly toned down. The language is slippery like human speech itself, ambiguous and nuanced. It demands further narration.

As it turns out, Adam and Eve will die, but the immediate implication is that, according to God, they will die as soon as they eat the fruit. That does not happen. Through human language, the serpent is creating instability, but he is also enriching the texture of the human vision, arousing desire that will further shape the complexity of human consciousness.

The serpent next explains, "For God knows that when you eat from it your eyes will be opened, and you will be like God, knowing good and bad" (3.5). As we soon discover, God does know this (as far as we can tell). When Adam and Eve eat the forbidden fruit (as it is customarily called), they see what they have not seen before, or, more accurately, they are awakened to unknown dimensions of themselves and the world, gaining personal knowledge through embodied experience (the ingesting of the fruit that pleased their eye). Through that experience, as the serpent says, they "will be like God" (3.5), although they will still not be God. They will know good and bad, which we understand not as a statement about morality, but one about the nature of human identity, its embodiment of sexuality and death, disease and alienation, pain and suffering—but also its ability to glimpse Paradise and wholeness, health, and shining wonder.

To know good and bad is to experience Creation, the way Adam and Eve might have experienced it. But when reading their story, it is also to know the depth of meaning of that experience through literary language, to sense its ambiguity and complexity, its twists and turns, its temporal movement. That kind of language activates in us, as Michael Wood puts it: "A knowledge that is often so intimate and so immediate that it scarcely feels like knowledge at all because it feels like something we have always known" (Wood 62). But then such tacit and intuitive knowledge demands further reflection, as we return to the story to find out what happens next.

The woman takes some of the fruit, eats it, and then gives some to her husband, who also eats it. Then the eyes of both of them are opened wide. They have given human meaning to God's law because they have now transgressed that law. They will forever know the meaning of "yes" because they have said "no" through their actions. Desiring to gain knowledge, they have chosen to exercise their freedom, for better and worse, for good and bad. They do not know this yet, but we know it, thanks to J. Unlike Adam and Eve, we are not only experiencing the events but also helping to create the story through the gift of J's language.

As the man and woman move from innocence to their newly discovered experience, J suggests to the reader that the couple grows increasingly self-conscious, self-aware. With their eyes wide open, "they realized they were naked" (3.7). Apparently it is not nakedness that causes their shame, but the realization of this nakedness. Experiencing the story, we ask about the implications.

Before they gained such knowledge, the man and woman shared an intimacy, essentially "one flesh," a feeling of belonging, a sense of Paradise (which will now always linger in memory, if not in deed). The emphasis was on their social being, the harmony of their communal connection, a sense of empathy and compassion deep down in the bones. Gaining knowledge of their nakedness does not change them from God's perspective (as if He had one); rather, their emerging knowledge must make them aware of the way they experience themselves and each other. They realize they are naked, and they hide. They are not only bodies, but they acknowledge that they have bodies. They are one flesh, but they are two different human beings. They are dust, and each one will return to dust.

It will be helpful for us, in this context, to make a further distinction about this emerging mortal identity, conflicted within itself and anxious in its relationship to what appears external to it. The mortal self, as a social being, is empathetic and compassionate, desiring intimacy. But the mortal self also desires differentiation, individual being, the uniqueness of self, its singularity. Why, then, do the man and the woman make coverings for themselves by sewing fig leaves together?

It is not that the man sees his own nakedness, but that he now sees the nakedness of the woman, the other, knowing that nakedness as different from his. The same must be true for the woman. They experience each other for the first time as incomplete doubles of themselves, recognizing the sexual difference, their own vulnerability and needs exposed to each other. They are conscious of what they lack.

To open the eyes in this way is not only to see the other, but to begin to acknowledge that the other sees you, recognizing your limitations. Adam knows he is naked not by looking at Eve, but by realizing Eve can see him as he reflects on himself and his difference. Neither the man nor the woman is complete, but rather in need. They are conflicted and limited, anxious and ashamed. They are becoming human beings. Out of the pain of their vulnerability comes the first signs of their ability to create their own common ground, the sewing of leaves for a covering, the initial rendering of both their fear and their fascination with their mortal existence, what can be seen and not seen, hidden and revealed. We might also be reminded that they have the gift of creation, human speech, and invention. Created in the image of God, they could imagine their own story, as we are imagining theirs, give it a sense of continuity and being in time: a past, present, and future.

When the man and his wife hear the Lord God walking in the Garden in the cool of the day, J tells us, they hide from Him among the trees. J seems at his comic best here, better than Beckett himself. God appears willing to participate in the absurd game of hide and seek. Unless He has blindfolded Himself, He certainly knows where they are. Of course, He does know. God is; mankind has blindfolded itself.

Man now hears God, but it is as if he hears God through his own embodied consciousness. "Where are you?" (3.9), God asks. The man answers, "I heard you in the garden, and I was afraid because I was naked; so I hid" (iii.10). This is the human language of vulnerability, of fear and instability. It is not a lie, but a corruption, a half-truth. The man is afraid; trying to hide, he is vulnerable. But it is what he doesn't say that is crucial; his exposure is in the telling. What he doesn't say reveals what he prefers to keep concealed (that he has eaten from the tree of knowledge).

God moves the man on, though, not through harsh command, but through further questions: "Who told you that you were naked? Have you eaten from the tree that I commanded you not to eat from?" (3.11).

The blame game now begins. The man blames the woman, who gave him the fruit, and indirectly God who put the woman in the garden with him. Then, confronted by God, the woman blames the serpent. Neither human being is willing to take responsibility for their act of freedom. Their great refusal to obey now looks like pride and deception as the complexity of the human vision in the mortal world continues to unfold through the acts of God's living creatures: Adam, Eve, and the serpent.

The instability felt intensifying through the emotional curve of J's narrative significantly contrasts with P's narrative, the harmonious and unified sense of mankind within the heavens and earth. It is as if Adam, Eve, and the serpent are all connected with a sentiment of being within God's dominion, but they are also incomplete enactments of God's language, split dimensions of the human self.

That sense of instability, emotional splitting and chaos, deepens the anxiety and longing for its contraries, stability, and wholeness. In the world of human experience, questioning gives way to sentencing, transgression is met with punishment, the super-ego struggles for control of the id. J's narrative, however, embodies all these dimensions in its language, concealing and revealing the human experience as it unfolds through J's telling.

God does not question the serpent after he hears the woman's confession: "The serpent deceived me, and I ate" (3.13). He moves to depreciate the serpent with language that Adam and Eve can understand. In the future, the serpent "will crawl" (iii.14) on his belly and will eat dust. As readers, we are reminded that Adam was created from dust. His flesh and bones are dust. He will return to dust. Man is not the serpent, but he is implicated with the serpent. He is similar and he is different. Like the woman, the serpent will have offspring, we are now told, a future fraught with enmity and conflict between mankind—male and female—and the serpent, within and without.

Human beings desire what they do not have, a desire experienced both as lack and overflow. That desire shaped through human language gives shape, in turn, to the human vision as an ongoing and dialectical journey, at times stabilized temporarily through the metaphorical function, but always open to further possibilities. God's judgment of the woman ("still not named in J's" narrative) and of Adam is also their judgment of themselves, a manifestation of their shame and guilt brought on by their belief that they were independent rather than interdependent, autonomous and wholly individualized, boundless and totally free.

God now says to the woman that her pains in childbearing will be very severe; she will give birth with painful labor. To the woman, God addresses directly issues of birth. But, by implication, He is also discussing with her the knowledge of good and bad, the sexual act, the acknowledgment of sexual difference, the longing for profound intimacy, an intimacy not to be fully satisfied but to be pursued and embodied within the conflicted human self. If there is pain here, intimations of profound loss, there is also hope, a sense of the future, birth. It is as if sex and death anxiously commingle within the vulnerable mortal consciousness.

To the man, God says the ground itself is now cursed because of his transgression, and he will suffer through painful toil, producing thorns and thistles by the sweat of his brow. God says that the man will return to the ground: "for dust you are and to dust you will return" (3.19).

J's mention of "dust" brings us back to the beginning, God's Creation of Adam, and it throws us into the future as well, Adam's mortal death. It does not close off Adam from God, though, nor does it indicate that Adam has closed himself off, that he will spin endlessly in his own despair. By contrast, the serpent will eat dust all the days of its life. Human beings are earth walkers, more than dust; they have the ability to shape human desire, give it direction and purpose, duration and continuity, a sense of history as time unfolds through their naming, through their generative narrative.

Once Adam is told about his beginning and end, it is as if the glimpse of his own death evokes his own ongoing naming process. He now names the woman: "Adam named his wife Eve, because she would become the mother of all the living" (3.20). Through human language, Adam and Eve gain a temporary moment of stability, a sense of the future, both the good and the bad, and they are again open to the wonder of the acts of God as they experience such acts. God makes "garments of skin" (3.21) for Adam and his wife, clothing them, easing their unbearable anguish and despair, their otherwise unbearable existential loneliness, their vulnerability and shame. Those garments do not hide the knowledge of their nakedness, but teach them something about humility and the risk of boundless desire. God's graciousness here is the graciousness of art within human experience; it reveals as much as it conceals, stirring desire, shaping the purpose and direction of the ongoing human narrative.

Experienced as literary narrative, *Genesis* 1–3 gives us, as readers, the beginning of the human journey, the movement from innocence to experience, the shaping of the human person, the creation of the meaning of mortal identity. In this beginning, we also glimpse our end. "The man has now become like one of us, knowing good and bad" (3.22), God says: health and disease, pleasure and pain, life and death, experienced inside and out, through human existence; the meaning of such knowledge granted to us through J's capacious narrative.

J has not forgotten what we, as readers, have half forgotten, the other tree, the tree of life, which must also linger in the distant memory of

Adam and Eve. According to J, God now says about the man, "He must not be allowed to reach out his hand and take also from the tree of life and eat, and live forever" (3.22). The tree of life in the middle of the Garden is very much that other secret, the one that can perhaps be glimpsed but never grasped by mortal beings, the one we continue to quest for in dreams and possibilities. Given freedom, Adam and Eve chose the tree of knowledge, desiring to transgress the law, but they did not choose the tree of life. They are blocked from it. They are like God, but they do not know God. They remain alienated from the fullness of their own transcendent meaning.

The memory of the tree of life lingers in human consciousness, though, just as the dream of immortality does, the hope of perfection, imagined but not experienced. That Adam and Eve would now desire to eat from that tree, to know God as God knows Himself, is not surprising. The pursuit of immortality will become the subject of great literature. But the satisfaction of such desire is now impossible. This is God's judgment, but it appears to be mankind's judgment as well.

To assure that the man and the woman continue their journey, but do not achieve their dream of being God, the Lord God not only banishes Adam and Eve from the Garden to work the ground, but also guards the way back to the tree of life by placing at the Garden's entrance cherubim and a flaming sword flashing back and forth. Adam and Eve are granted the world to experience and a Garden, with its tree of life, to dream. The couple remain conflicted mortal human beings as they set out to journey east of Eden.

It is not incorrect to read *Genesis* 1–3 as a tragedy or as a family romance with moments of comic absurdity, nor is it incorrect to read it as a story about sin and redemption or crime and punishment. It is better than most mystery stories, though, because it is our story. We know it is true each time we read it, whether it actually happened or not.

3

Frankenstein

Mary Shelley's *Frankenstein* is a literary narrative with three storytellers. The three stories are closely connected, they overlap, and they play off each other. Victor Frankenstein's story seems central, and, from one perspective, it is. But Captain Walton's story leads us in and out of Frankenstein's story, and the Monster's story appears as if it were "the inside story" of Frankenstein's tale, calling that tale into question. The three stories, like the three storytellers, are similar but also different. They remind us of the complex and contradictory meanings embodied in linguistic narrative and human identity. The three stories are connected through Mary Shelley's own language, the book called *Frankenstein*. It is the literary narrative of the book as a whole that brings these stories into meaning. As a book, *Frankenstein* offers us a riddle as profound as *Genesis* itself. It calls to the reader to question the human journey, to wonder about the beginning and the end. We need to follow the details of this narrative to make what we can of our own lives.

When the book opens, we are with Walton, a sea captain heading to the North Pole. He is on edge, having already journeyed with his crew out toward the margins of the known world, but he still feels a connection to family (writing letters to his sister) and a responsibility (tentative as it becomes) to his crew. As he journeys further north, pursuing his childhood dream of exploration, "the want of a friend" (18) intensifies.

Then Frankenstein suddenly appears out of the distressed ocean onto the deck of Walton's ship. He is half-dead, emaciated by fatigue and suffering. Unlike Walton, he is at the end rather than the beginning, crazed by the choices he has already made throughout a tumultuous journey. A stranger in wretched condition, Frankenstein faints on deck, almost a corpse. He is quickly brought back to life, though, by his gracious host with brandy and with the warmth of blankets and fire in the kitchen stove. It is as if the warmth of human sentiment animates the corpse, and after two days of this kind of nurturing, the body of the stranger slowly begins to speak. If he is a stranger, he quickly becomes a speaking body and familiar friend, "a brother" (25) to Walton.

When Victor begins to speak, he evokes compassion from Walton, who, in turn, empathizes with Victor's story of grief and loss, acknowledging Victor's admirable capabilities and eloquence. According to Victor, though, his fate is already sealed; by contrast, Walton is just beginning his journey: "You have hope, and the world before you, and have no cause for despair. But I—I have lost everything, and cannot begin life anew" (25). If Frankenstein cannot start over, Walton apparently can. Victor will tell his story with this in mind.

As readers, we are about to hear—apparently through the letters of Walton, edited from his journal, which are, at times, further edited by Victor himself—Victor's story of his journey from the beginning, the contingent events of his "real life" shaped into linguistic narrative. If Victor is telling his story for Walton (and us), though, he is also telling it for himself. He needs to come to terms with his life before the end sets in.

Victor needs to tell his story, to voice his journey as he has experienced it, and Walton needs to listen to this strange tale, much as we (the readers) do. Walton's act of listening is our act as well. It indicates his (and our) sense of curiosity, but also his sense of connectiveness, his need for others. That Victor is compelled to tell his story, a kind of confession and warning, resonates with his profound guilt, but it also suggests his ongoing need to reconnect with the human community. He is not yet ready to die, at least not until he acquires some interpretative distance on his own life, especially distance from the horror he has experienced. As Victor Frankenstein begins his story, we, in turn, listen, as Walton must be listening. Like Walton, we are not at the end, but at the beginning of our lives, and Frankenstein has something to tell us about that.

Frankenstein starts with tales about his family and childhood, his benevolent father and mother, and his good friend Henry Clerval. He tells about the arrival of Elizabeth, his "cousin"—"more than sister" (35), suggesting that his harmonious and nurturing childhood, filled with goodness and domestic love, carried with it darker emotions as well. In Frankenstein's telling of his childhood, we sense undertones of the haunting ambiguity of compassion, the danger of an intensified love, a passion troubled by sexual desire and the incest taboo ("more than sister"). His early relationship with Elizabeth seems also to have been troubled by the death of his mother, highlighted by his mother's extraordinary affection for Elizabeth whose sickness ironically caused his mother's own infection and death.

With Walton, we also learn what inspired Victor at the beginning, and seems to have unhinged him in the long run: a chance discovery of "a volume of the works of Cornelius Agrippa" (39), an event that clearly excited enthusiasm and imagination for the medieval alchemists who searched for the "philosopher's stone" (to change lead to gold) and "the elixir of life" (to continue life without end). Exposed to these alchemists in his youth, Frankenstein's goal was a noble one and a costly one: "To banish disease from the human frame, and render man invulnerable to any but a violent death!" (40).

Such dreams of the alchemists might seem like "sad trash" (38), as Victor's father suggests, or "chimerical" (47), as Victor himself later claims, but the ambitious vision of the goal itself, its spiritual nobility, and endless possibilities, rarely seem in doubt for Victor. When he goes to the university in Ingolstadt, he is inspired once again, by M. Waldman this time, who dismisses the "philosopher's stone" and "the elixir of life" as nonsense, but who recontextualizes the ancient alchemist's vision into the progressive vision of modern science and technology. These "modern philosophers, whose hands seem only made to dabble in dirt, and their eyes to pour over the microscope or crucible, have indeed performed miracles," Waldman insists. "They penetrate into the recesses of nature, and show how she works in her hiding places. They ascend into the heavens; they have discovered how the blood circulates, and the nature of the air we breathe" (47).

If these new philosophers start where the original Adam started ("hands . . . dabble in dirt"), they now—apparently through the pleasure of what they can see—"can command the thunders of heaven, mimic the earthquake, and even mock the invisible world with its own shadows" (47). Penetrating the depth of nature, these modern men are the new gods, seeking the secrets of the universe. At the time, Victor pursues such vision with abandonment. It is as if he, too, can achieve more than the original Adam did.

We might remember that in *Genesis* 1–3, the language of God was enacted through the creation of the natural world, and Adam could, at best, only glimpse the wonder of that world, the penumbra of that secret mystery. Adam could not know God directly. By contrast, Victor has come to believe otherwise: that secret can not only be revealed indirectly, but grasped, reenacted by mortal beings who apparently can make visible what was invisible, give light to what was previously only shadows. Not only has the language of God collapsed into the language of man, but mankind, fueled by his own imagination, has, in essence, become God. Victor has not only eaten from the tree of knowledge, he is determined to act directly on that knowledge. It is as if he believes that the gates of the

Garden of Eden have been reopened for him: not only can he discover the beginning before the beginning, the origins of life itself, but embody that knowledge within the human frame, incorporate it within the physical condition of the mortal body. As readers, we might wonder if we should be drawn to Victor's capacious vision. Was he blind then to the menacing undercurrents creeping now into his linguistic telling? If he was inspired by such vision originally, he seems now to be telling Walton (and us) about how he was undone by that vision—isn't he? Yet, he continues on.

Pursuing such knowledge in vaults and charnel houses, Victor closely observes the minute changes "from life to death, and death to life" (52), until he "becomes capable of bestowing animation upon lifeless matter" (53). It is as if "buried with the dead" (53), he is reborn into a new world that he can shape and move. Or, at least, he believes he can do this. He is convinced that he can bring life out of death.

It is a remarkable moment of hubris, but, at first, for Victor, it is only a belief, a dream that, according to his narrative, has not yet been made real. We, as readers, are caught in the excitement of Victor's story as he is telling it. We want to know what happens next, but Victor now halts his narration as if to warn Walton (and us). It is a gesture of self-reflection: "Learn from me, if not by my precepts, at least by my example, how dangerous is the acquirement of knowledge, and how much happier that man is who believes his native town to be the world than he who aspires to become greater than his nature will allow" (52).

Victor has barely started his story, but he now makes clear that he will not speak about the secret that he knows, the secret that we, his interlocutors, desire to know but cannot know because, if we did know it, we, too, would then become undone. Frankenstein will continue to tell his story, shaping the contingent experiences of his life through human language, but his story apparently will not be about the triumph of the visionary imagination, but about the existential crisis of mortal beings. As Victor claims, he had hoped "in process of time" to "renew life where death had apparently devoted the body to corruption" (53), but now, having attempted to make such a bold dream into reality, he knows that that kind of dream can result in a kind of trauma. The body can be given purpose and direction through the imaginative workings of human language, he seems to be saying, but human beings cannot defeat time itself anymore than the body can defeat death. There is always a gap that cannot be crossed in the imperfect mortal world. Attempting to cross that gap puts human beings in mortal danger.

With this warning, Victor returns to his story. Deciding to enact his dream, he begins to work in "a solitary chamber" (52). He becomes increasingly alienated from family and friends as he continues his labor, "the creation of a human being" (52). From dissecting rooms and slaughter houses, he gathers material, falling into acute anxiety and unremitting sickness, as he cobbles together his gigantic man. He had chosen each part for its beauty, but, as Victor says: "The different accidents of life are not so changeable as the feeling of human nature" (56). He has cobbled together the contingencies of life, but he has not breathed the soul of life into what otherwise is mere accident. As a result, when he has completed his work and looks at it, he seems instantly to judge that his Creation is not good but bad, a wretch that evokes not the beauty of his dream (or "the feeling of human nature"), but breathless horror and disgust ("the different accidents of life"). We imagine that he has not created something from the depths of human sentiment and care, but from the contingencies of time and place. When he sees his Creation, Victor does not say a word. Inarticulate himself at the moment, without language, he runs from his Creation, falling on his bed into a disturbing sleep. It is as if the birth of his Creation has traumatized not only the child itself but the father as well.

We wonder about the existential complexity that Victor has entangled himself in. What has he actually created? Why does he run from it? What is he avoiding? In his sleep, he dreams about Elizabeth, his cousin and soul mate, walking in the streets of Ingolstadt. He attempts to kiss her, but, as he does, her lips become "livid with the hue of death." Her sensuous body changes into the corpse of his dead mother, her clothes into "a shroud crawling with grave-worms" (57), as if love and sexuality are giving way to death itself. Then, awakening from this nightmare, Victor again sees "the miserable monster," as Victor now calls him, in front of him. The monster's eyes are fixed on Victor. The wretch mutters inarticulate sounds, trying to detain him. If he speaks, Victor does not hear him. Refusing to respond to his living Creation, Victor instead runs out into the street, fleeing "the demoniacal corpse" (57). Apparently Victor Frankenstein has entered a hell of his own making.

As readers, we have moved with Victor from an innocent and nurturing world, the ordinary and familiar world of family and friends, to a strange world, a world of corpses. He has become ghoulish in his quest for the unknown. He has attempted to imitate, perhaps mimic, God by trying to create a human being without help, without a helpmate, without a woman, without human sentiment, without compassion itself. Lacking a mother, the Creation is well-proportioned in terms of its bones, but it is an obvious forgery, an inauthentic copy of a human being, made up of fragments of corpses, disordered in terms of flesh and breath, a cobbled together accident. Its eyes are notably watery and menacing to Frankenstein, as if he cannot see beyond the surface of his Creation, cannot look deeply into the heart of his own Creation.

When the wretch first opened his eyes, it must have seen Frankenstein looking down at him from above. Frankenstein did not embrace him, but shamed him then. Instead of taking responsibility for his Creation, instead of listening to him and acknowledging him, instead of talking to him, Victor runs. Like Adam and Eve, he wants to hide from his own vulnerability, but he cannot escape the nightmare that will now haunt him, the shame of his own contingent condition made intensely visible by his obsessive act. Like Adam and Eve, his transgression has led him into the world of sexuality and death, but his obsession has closed him off from the complexity and ambiguity of that world of experience, making him the monster he has created. The wretch is a disjointed corpse never nurtured by the body of the mother, disconnected from sexual origins, and unacknowledged by his creator. He is a product of "the accidents of life," lacking the origins of human connectivity, the warmth of the human bond, apparently outside the flow and exchange of human language.

Entangled in a world of his own making, Frankenstein is now unable to experience the bliss of a kiss, the touch of lips, the beauty of the sensuous body (Elizabeth's, in particular). He acknowledges only the ugliness and deterioration of the flesh (his mother's corpse, for example), the loss of the warmth of the womb, the familiar turned toward death. It is as if the origin of mortal creation, the mother of humankind, the Eve figure, the other who is also us, has now become the alienated stranger, the tomb. Unable to embrace the other in himself, that stranger who needs him and is also a part of him, Victor is alienated from himself and overwhelmed with guilt.

This is the dark underside of Frankenstein, revealed more fully to Walton as Victor's narrative continues to unfold, but it is not the whole story. Abandoning the Monster, Frankenstein hopes to forget what he has created (if he only could), and relieve his growing anxiety and instability by hiding from it. If he is fragmented, torn apart, traumatized, he would prefer not to think about it.

Wandering the streets of Ingolstadt, Frankenstein now meets his childhood friend Clerval, who nurses him back to health, and he reinvigorates his connection with family through an exchange of letters with Elizabeth. His health and joy appear to improve, resonating with the budding natural environment that now surrounds him, and bolstered further by lively conversations with his familiar friend, the affable and literary Clerval: "We returned to our college on a Sunday afternoon: the peasants were dancing, and every one we met appeared gay and happy. My own spirits were high, and I bounded along with feelings of unbridled joy and hilarity" (68).

It takes almost two years for Frankenstein to regain his sense of stability, but he then begins to plan a trip back to his native town, Geneva, to visit family. In terms of his narrative, Victor makes no mention of his thinking about the monster during this time, and we, as readers, might assume that his wound has sufficiently healed and that he has regained health and balance. But, then, a letter arrives from his father, announcing another disaster: William, his youngest brother, has been murdered, and Justine Moritz, a beloved friend of the family, has been accused of the crime and awaits trial. The grieving family is understandably fraught with despair, especially Elizabeth (Victor's "more than sister") who blames herself for the murder. As his father's letter explains: "She told me, that that same evening William had teased her to let him wear a valuable miniature that she possessed of your mother. This picture is gone, and was doubtless the temptation which urged the murderer to the deed" (70). That picture of the mother has been found in the clothing of Justine. As readers, listening (as Walton is) to Frankenstein's telling, we might wonder if the trauma that Victor has apparently repressed for two years has been displaced onto Justine as well.

In the context of the narrative, Victor is clearly shaken by this new twist, this tale of crime and punishment, which opens the well-springs of grief within the context of family romance and reopens the wound within the depths of the vulnerable mortal body. No one in the family can believe that Justine has committed such an unspeakable act, but the physical evidence, slight as it is, the image of the dead mother, points to the accused. Hesitant, Victor begins his journey home.

But Victor can never really return home, and he knows it. In the shadow of Mont Blanc, in "the environs of Geneva," Victor, before seeing his family, decides to visit "the spot where my poor William had been murdered" (72). He is the criminal returning to the scene of the crime. Once at the crime scene, though, the sky, stormy with bolts of lightning and thunder, elevates his spirits. It is as if he is hallucinating, experiencing a "noble war" in the heavens played out for William, a dear angel: "This is they funeral, this they dirge" (73). For a moment, he seems beside himself, transported as he looks out into the gloom and suddenly sees "a figure which stole from behind a clump of trees." The figure seems "more hideous than belongs to humanity" (73), Victor claims, and then he quickly concludes that it is this shadowy figure, not Justine, who must have killed his brother: "He was the murderer. I could not doubt it. The mere presence of the idea was an irresistible proof of the fact" (73).

As we listen to Victor's story, we might imagine that he is impulsively jumping to conclusions now, but we suspect that he is right despite the evidence gathered by the judicial system. It is the Monster, not Justine, who has committed the vicious act of murder, although we also need to remind ourselves that Victor is wrestling with his own ongoing trauma as well. Victor's intimate knowledge of the crime goes far deeper than any visible evidence could possibly reveal. Unlike the reasoning of a judicial system (or the law), Victor's judgment takes place, as he puts it, "nearly in the light of my own vampire, my own spirit let loose from the grave, and forced to destroy all that was dear to me" (74). If that vampire is really the Monster, Victor's Creation, it is also his own "vampire spirit let loose from the grave," his own trauma, the strangeness that he cannot come to terms with, the Monster who is also himself.

At the time it happened, such a moment of vampirish horror apparently evoked Victor's obsession and fear. Seeing the Monster at the crime scene, a decided embodiment of his own shame, a reminder of his trauma, he could not speak. It was as if he were hallucinating then. As he rationalizes it now to Walton: "I well knew if any other had communicated such a relation to me, I should have looked upon it as the ravings of insanity" (74). As readers, we might conclude that he was hiding then from himself and that his act of silence was monstrous (it cost Justine her life), but what if he confessed then? Would it have a made a difference? As Victor indicates, referring to the Monster, "the strange nature of the animal" may very well elude all pursuit (74). The Monster that he has created may very well be beyond all human comprehension, before the beginning and after the end of the limits of mortal knowledge. We are with Victor, deep within his narrative.

Victor's anguish at the time that he experienced these events is not in doubt, but it is the tension in his narrative that is significant for us, the telling now shaping through language the experience then. That narrative tension allows us (and Walton) to experience the complexity of the existential dilemma that Victor, and all of us, now find ourselves in. As we discover Victor, Victor is discovering himself through his telling, locating himself in relation to the world around him. He is the wretch that he has created, the other that is himself (his double), but to grasp this other may very well be a sentence of death, or, as likely, an impossibility. The strange nature of this other eludes all pursuit.

After Justine is executed, the Frankenstein house becomes "a house of mourning" (88). The family retreats to the countryside, calming and soothing their grief, and then Victor, alone, climbs to the summit of Montanvert, again in sight of Mont Blanc. "My heart, which was before sorrowful, now swelled with something like joy," Victor tells Walton: "I exclaimed—Wandering spirits, if indeed ye wander, and do not rest in your narrow beds, allow me this faint happiness, or take me, as your companion away from the joys of life" (94).

As it has before, such sublime incantation once again evokes the presence of the wretch bounding over the icy heights, and now for the first time Victor speaks directly to his Creation, not with soothing words of parental concern, though, but "with words expressive of furious detestation and contempt" (94). His contemptuous tone is not surprising, obsessed as he is with the Monster. Seeking revenge, refusing to acknowledge his own strangeness, Victor has become a wrathful god demanding punishment for the crime committed by his wicked offspring.

"Devil," Victor calls the wretch. "Vile insect," "Diabolic murderer" (95)—a series of epithets that could easily provoke further violence. By contrast, the demon's response is not violent, but measured, resonating with a self-reflecting knowledge acquired through his own experiences in time. As readers, we know about the demon's creation, his abandonment, his apparent killing, but we do not yet know his story, although we now realize the he, too, must have a story. The Monster can speak, and he can be self-reflective, as he suggests to Victor:

> I expected this reception. All men hate the wretched; how then must I be hated, who am miserable beyond all living things; yet you, my creator, detest and spurn me, my creator, to whom thou art bound by ties only dissoluble by the annihilation of one of us. (95)

The Monster admits that he is "wretched," and with that knowledge, he appeals not to Victor's compassion, but to his sense of responsibility and parental duty. He wants a covenant with Victor, bound by obligation, if not by blood. "I ought to be thy Adam," the Monster says. But, instead, "I am rather the fallen angel, whom thou drives from joy for no misdeed. . . . I was benevolent and good; misery made me a friend. Make me happy, and I shall again be virtuous" (96).

The Monster's "wretchedness" is complex and deeply ambiguous, raising more questions than answers to the riddle of the Monster himself. Is the Monster "wretched" like Adam, anxious and alone, fraught with the knowledge of contradiction? Or is he more like the "fallen angel," rebellious and fiery, consistently disobedient, but capable of benevolence and virtue? Or, perhaps, more like the Devil itself, not just "bad" but truly "ugly"?

When accused, Justine Moritz had thought she was "wretched" (84) because everyone appeared to have called her guilty. She began to believe that she was a monster, internalizing the story of others, accepting it as her own. Such a belief turned the world upside down for her, forcing her to confess to a crime that she did not commit. Only the support of Elizabeth and Victor kept her from utter ruin, from complete unhinging. "How sweet is the affection of others to such a wretch as I am!" she had said to Elizabeth at the time. "It removes more than half my misfortune and I feel as if I could die in peace, now that my innocence is acknowledged by you, dear lady, and your cousin" (84).

Unlike Justine, the Monster has no one to support him. We might at first assume that if someone did acknowledge his familiarity, his link with the human community, then he, too, could overcome his sense of wretchedness, his otherness that seems so strange and ugly. But, without exception, everyone who sees him recoils from what they see: the apparent ugliness of mere contingency, the accidental body itself. From William to Walton, the human eye seems to judge the Monster as a strange being, outside the boundaries of the human community, beyond human language and understanding.

Is this a condition that could be resolved if Victor (and others) embraced the stranger, the other? Or is it a condition that indicates that there is always a Monster lurking out there, the other that cannot be embraced within human boundaries? Frankenstein raises such questions through his narrative; the narrative cannot answer them for us, though—although it can embody the contradictions. Like all narratives, it does not so much offer solutions but raise questions, putting us as readers into question as well, creating further desire in us to continue our quest.

Peter Brooks (1993), our best reader of *Frankenstein*, reminds us about much of this, especially that the Monster desires what we all desire: what Jacques Lacan would say is the desire of the other, the desire of the one before us (Brooks 199–220). The Monster makes an ethical demand on Frankenstein, just as Frankenstein makes an ethical demand on Walton (and on us). The Monster needs a listener for his story (and he deserves one). He hopes to convince Frankenstein, through the telling of his story, that they are bound together as beings desiring the desire of the other. If they are different from each other, they also share similarities. They may look different, but they speak the same language. Their experiences are unique, but they are both linguistic beings. The Monster now hopes for such recognition.

The Monster demands that his story be heard, and Frankenstein now is urged by curiosity and the stirrings of compassion to "comply with his demand" (97). But what the Monster is asking for may very well be beyond anyone's capability to provide. As Brooks puts it: "What is finally desired by the speaker is 'the desirer in the other'. That is that the speaking subject himself be 'called to as desirable'. The Monster's unconscious desire may most of all be for unconditional hearing, recognition, love from his parent. Its absolute requital could only take the form of handing over the mother, which in this case is barred not only by the law of castration but more radically still, since this mother does not exist and has never existed" (Brooks 210). The Monster without a name, without a mother, may have to settle for a helpmate. As a second Adam, he needs a second Eve. But, if so, would that second Eve be sufficient?

As listeners, we are now ready to hear the story of the Monster as if it is "the inside story" of Victor told to Walton (apparently through the letters sent by Walton to his sister). No doubt, it is deep in the subconscious rhythms of the narrative experience. We follow along.

Just as Victor began his story with his early childhood days, the Monster tells first about his early development in nature, his pain and his pleasure, his moments of rejection and his moments of joy. Central to his story is his well-developed observations of the DeLacey family, their own story of family romance, woven into the Monster's own educational development in terms of language and reading and the growing sense of empathy and importance of family ties.

As readers ourselves, it is difficult not to empathize with the Monster as his narrative unfolds and as he enriches his understanding of the meaning of his own identity through his felt observations of the DeLacey family saga and his own literary pursuits.

When the Monster moves from observation to interaction with the DeLacey family, we also move with him, pleased with the initial generosity of the blind old man, the elderly father in the DeLacey household, who first encounters the Monster directly. In response to the Monster's confession that he fears becoming "an outcast in the world forever," the old man, alone with the Monster in his cottage, is kind and generous to him. He encourages the Monster.

> Do not despair. To be friendless is indeed to be unfortunate; but the hearts of men, when unprejudiced by any obvious self-interest, are full of brotherly love and charity. Rely, therefore, on your hopes, and if these friends are good and amicable, do not despair. (128)

The contingent events of life seem quickly to trump the old man's language, though. The younger family members rush into the scene, seeing what the blind man has not seen, and quickly and violently attack the Monster. Without further conversation (and without language to shape the moment), the Monster is driven back to his hovel, permanently cut off from this family. It is as if the contingencies of "real life" experience have overwhelmed human language, but, as readers, we feel the shame of the event through the linguistic narrative: the limitations of the characters, sympathy for the Monster. The tension in the narrative, its doubleness, creates a residue of desire in us, as readers, although we also sense the near impossibility of resolving the existential dilemma, the trauma, in this particular narrative, evoked from the birth of the Monster itself. There is no simple solution for the complexity, the human riddle that the linguistic narrative embodies and articulates.

As a result of these events, the Monster is abandoned by the DeLacey family, and so now decides to pursue his own father. As he tells Victor: "... you were my father, my creator; and to whom could I apply with more fitness than to him who had given me life?" (133). Seeking his father in Victor's native town, Geneva, the Monster, again by chance, confronts an innocent young boy, hoping for a friend and companion. The boy responds immediately to the horrifying sight: "Hideous monster! Let me go . . . You are an ogre. Let me go, or I will tell my papa" (136).

The boy turns out to be William, and once he mentions the name Frankenstein, the Monster's story becomes a story of revenge. We might imagine that the Monster is an uncle of William's (more than uncle just as Elizabeth is more than sister to Victor), but the Monster's experience (if not his narrative) drives him next not to the contemplation of family bonds, but to "something glittering" on the dead boy's breast, "a portrait of a most lovely woman" (136). We have already encountered that "lovely woman." She is the elusive mother, the origin of the mortal body, the cause and the effect of the trauma that both Frankenstein and the Monster seem to be wrestling with. At the moment, for the Monster, that portrait is a reminder of the womb he has been permanently deprived of, the empty tomb of his strange existence. In a rage, the Monster, again by chance, impulsively grasps the glittering image. He does not destroy it, though, but eventually hides it in the folds of the clothing of a passing young woman (Justine).

The Monster's story moves Victor, as his emotions ebb and flow with compassion for the Monster and with the fear that if he acts with that compassion and fulfills the promise that the Monster demands (the creation of a female companion for the Monster in exile), then this further act will only multiply the malice and corruption that he has already created.

As readers, we, too, experience the ebb and flow of the multiperspectives of the narrative language, as the story unfolds and loops upon itself, the affections of sensitive beings arousing our sympathy, but also calling for judgment. Like Victor and the Monster, we, too, are vulnerable mortal bodies, hoping to find identity and location in the world, purpose and direction through language. We are driven by the narrative to further questioning: Should Victor create a female counterpart for the Monster? How far out should a mortal being travel? Is there any way for Victor to resolve the dilemma he finds himself in?

To answer those questions implies a judgment, and judgment always ultimately ends in a death sentence, ending dialogue and conversation within the world of contingent experience. But the after-effect of stories can return us to living experience, the desire to continue our own story. Death cannot do that. Engaged deep within the narrative, we desire to read on, to keep the conversation going. We reserve judgment, knowing that it is the questions, not the solutions, that keep us alive, that invite us to quest on.

Motivated by the Monster's story, Victor, in the third and final section of *Frankenstein* can now more fully contextualize his own contingent experience, shape his narrative for Walton (and for us). It will become his final opportunity to offer the meaning of his life as an exemplum for those willing listeners to experience.

Victor tells us that he now decided to marry Elizabeth: "My future hopes and prospects are entirely bound up in the expectation of our union" (144). They will marry in Geneva, his native town, surrounded by the affection of family and friends. But first, he: "must perform" his other "engagement" (145), fulfill his promise to create a female being for the Monster. Not wanting to reveal this to his father, however, he insists that he must travel for two years before his marriage to restore his tranquillity. Clothing his secret motives in deception, he is engaged both to Elizabeth and his Monster. A slave to his Creation, he has nevertheless rekindled sexual romance.

Accompanied by Clerval, his familiar guide and giver of temporary joy, Victor arrives in London to gather information and scientific instruments for his work. Clerval is no doubt a good friend, "formed in the very poetry of nature" (149). He is the poetic imagination "chastened by the sensibility of his heat" (149). Unlike Frankenstein he needs no instruments to penetrate the natural world, to recreate that natural world in his own image. Instead, he expands his vision through conversation and literature, through the linguistic imagination. Clerval is Victor's benevolent self; the Monster is his wretched destiny.

Eventually, Victor heads far north, to "the remotest of the Orkneys" (156), a barren and desolate place, wretched as his original miserable laboratory back at the university. Haunted by the absence of the Monster, unbalanced again by the geographic and psychic limits of his existential condition, he reflects on his Creation and the potential results of repeating that act again in the shape of a female being: "Moved by the sophisms of the being I had created . . . now for the first time, the wickedness of my promise burst upon me" (161). Such revelation of wicked consciousness again evokes the presence of the daemon at the casement of his window. Seeing the Monster (located as much inside his empty heart as outside at the casement), Victor "tears to pieces the thing" (161) on which he is engaged. The Monster vanishes, but not for long. Like trauma itself, the Monster returns quickly, now with full vengeance and a powerful curse: "I will be with you on your wedding-night" (161). Victor's destiny is fixed, he is convinced.

With the curse securely in place—a transgression of weddings and family romance—Victor's life becomes increasingly toxic. It is as if it is polluted by the collapse of all boundaries: dream and reality, the self and the other, the linguistic narrative and the contingent events of "real life," all flowing in and out of each other. Deep sleep, even double doses of laudanum, cannot protect Victor from such haunting: it is as if the truth can only emerge from the unfolding narrative itself—the truth that Victor's life was an illusion until he began to tell his story.

The Monster has no mother, and he has, in essence, lost his father (except as a revenant to be haunted to death). Having now abandoned hope for a female companion, he has no future. As a mortal being, human or otherwise, his condition has become increasingly clear: he is now caught in an endless present, the hellish and isolated tomb. With nothing left to lose, he travels the earth as a dangerous corpse.

What about Victor? When he wakes from his deep and drugged sleep, and returns to civilization, Victor discovers that Clerval has been murdered and that he is the accused. He is innocent of the specific crime, but he knows that he is a guilty man. Locked in prison and still delirious, Victor now confesses, not only to the killing of his friend but to the death of Justine and William as well. Through the intervention of his father, though, he is declared innocent (an ironic juxtaposition to Justine's own case), and, as if again "awakening from a dream" (169), he is then liberated from his two-month confinement in prison, surrounded by family and the possibilities of a wedding.

At least, this is the way it appears from the outside looking in. Unlike the Monster, Victor appears now to have a new horizon to look forward to, the wonder of romance that can make "real life" into a dream. But, as Victor tells Walton, the inside story is different. His "real life" has become a nightmare, a living hell: "For me the walls of a dungeon or a palace were alike hateful. The cup of life was poisoned for ever; and although the sun shone upon me, as upon the happy and gay of heart, I saw around me nothing but a dense and frightful darkness, penetrated by no light but the glimmer of two eyes that glared upon me" (174). His attempt to penetrate the natural world in pursuit of the secret of life has ended in the haunting gaze of a Monster fixed on him. He is possessed by his obsession, unhinged by the knowledge that he himself is death-in-life, a walking corpse of flesh and blood.

But what about the Monster's wedding curse? As a vampire (as Victor earlier called him), the Monster needs blood, but his curse—"I will be with you on your wedding-night!" (161)—is not directly aimed at Victor (despite Victor's own assumption), but at Elizabeth, his beloved. Elizabeth is the embodiment of compassion; she, like Victor's mother before her, is willing to sacrifice herself for Victor. She says as much in her letter to her beloved, discussing the prospects of marriage. Despite her overwhelming desire to marry Victor, she can only be happy in his happiness: "I confess to you, my friend, that I love you, and that in my airy dreams of futurity you have been my constant friend and companion. But it is your happiness I desire as well as my own, when I declare to you, that our marriage would render me eternally miserable, unless it were the dictate of your own free choice" (179). To rob Victor of such unconditional love by destroying that love may be the Monster's intention. That Victor believes the curse is directed at him, though, seems another indication of his hubris and his obsession.

Unconditional love embodied is Paradise, the genre of high romance, the bride and groom living happily ever after. It is the dream of Adam and Eve, the tree of life, the reason that God, with the weapon of a flaming sword, barred the first couple from the east gate of the Garden of Eden. It defeats death and the suffering of temporal human existence. But Victor's narrative is not about his dream, but about his nightmare. His pride drives him to think that his marriage to Elizabeth will protect her from the Monster who wants to kill him. "I will consecrate myself, in life or death, to the happiness of my cousin" (181), he tells his father, believing that his death at the wedding will free Elizabeth from the menace of the Monster. He is fooling himself. He remains engaged to the Monster, death not love, traumatized, imprisoned by his own undoing. The genre is not high romance, but gothic terror.

Right after the wedding, we, as readers, are offered a temporary glimpse of Paradise through Victor's narrative, the wonders of the world magically rejuvenated from the dome of Mont Blanc to the fish swimming in the clear waters. Elizabeth's voice resonates with that joy: "What a divine day! How happy and serene all nature appears!" (183). By nightfall, though, the sun sinking beneath the horizon, Victor again feels his fear revive, clasping him and clinging to him as if forever.

As readers, where are we now in this complex narrative? We might assume that the wedding night will bring climax, if not resolution, to

Victor's story. Perhaps the marriage will be consummated, although the Monster's curse will inevitably be enacted. If we are thoughtful, though, we also realize that Victor is still alive telling about the events of this wedding night to Walton. We experience the events with Victor, but we have distance on them, as does Victor as he is shapes them for Walton.

We might also be reminded now that near the start of Victor's narrative, he made clear to Walton that he had discovered the principle of life, the secret of nature, the beginning before the beginning. He had not only glimpsed it, but had tried to take control of it, act on that godlike knowledge, make it his own. Attempting to control it, it has gotten control of him. He will not tell Walton that unspeakable secret; like God's name, it cannot be made known. It is before the beginning of all mortal stories, and Victor, since the start of his narrative has not mentioned it again.

We understand that Victor's narrative, although inspired by that secret, the ultimate mystery, is not really about that secret, but about his Creation, the secret of his mortal self, unfolding first as contingent experience and then through linguistic narrative given meaning through Walton (and us). His narrative is an anguished attempt to know his mortal identity (to know himself) and to share that knowing with other human beings (his interlocutors). In delirium, he tried to confess this secret to his accusers at the time of Clerval's murder and later to his father, but those fragmented outbursts were dismissed as insane ravings. That Victor needs to tell his story is crucial to him and to us as readers as well.

Victor has promised to tell Elizabeth about his Creation on the day following their wedding night. We might ask why he doesn't tell her sooner, but the delay is typical of Victor. He apparently prefers to resolve his engagement with the Monster before he enters the bed-chamber of his bride: "I resolved that I would sell my life dearly, and not shrink from the conflict until my own life, or that of my adversary, was extinguished" (185).

At the advice of Victor, Elizabeth, alone, retreats to their bed-chamber. Victor seeks the Monster, hoping to shield Elizabeth from the terror to come. But is he again deceiving himself? By leaving Elizabeth by herself and by approaching the Monster, what is he avoiding? The Monster's curse, we recall, was not aimed at the wedding ceremony but at the wedding night, not at disruption of the vows of unconditional love, but at the disruption of sexual intimacy, the womb turned into the cold tomb, the experience of mortal creation with its full dialectical complexity, eros and thanatos, tragically reduced to death alone.

In this context, what, then, is the meaning of the bed-chamber? Victor's narrative at this point does not help us very much to answer that question, but clues to that secret have appeared throughout the narrative. As readers we know that Victor, godlike, attempted from the beginning to create a human being without the generative authority of the female body, without the sanction of the Eve figure, without the mother (or the womb) of mortal human life. After that botched creation, his dream of kissing the lips (the mortal flesh) of Elizabeth transformed into the nightmare of his mother's corpse. We know his own mother died, and the Monster has no mother and no female companion. In fact, it is difficult not to associate this bridal chamber with the primal scene itself, the secret location of birth, generative life, and inevitable death, the ultimate horizon of personal knowledge. That bed-chamber is not a part of the Monster's "real life" story, it will never be that, and it seems to be a sign that Victor will not consummate his marriage, either.

Traumatized by the birth of the Monster from the beginning, obsessed by the Monster now, Victor will not reenact that primal scene, nor will he generate a mortal family embodied for the future. He cannot rejuvenate such a beginning anymore than he can tell us about the secret of life that he supposedly discovered long ago. His only salvation now is the telling of his story, a story listened to by others inspired by the sensuous language of his overflowing desire. He is doing his best to account for himself.

We might be shocked, but not surprised, to hear first the screams of Elizabeth coming from the bed-chamber, and then, following Victor rushing into the room, to see Elizabeth there, "lifeless and inanimate, thrown across the bed, her head hanging down, and her pale and distorted features half covered by her hair" (186). The image resonates with sexual torment, a clear echo of Fuseli's erotic painting "Nightmare" with its undertones of erotic transgression, even rape. It is a linguistic rendering of the effect of a Monster penetrating the female body, violating the natural world, much as the instruments of modern science probe nature for her secrets. Only when Elizabeth has become a corpse, her breath ceasing to issue from her lips and her face covered with a handkerchief (186)—her human identity essentially gone—does Victor embrace her. Then, only the jeering grin of the Monster remains at the open window, a specter silently pointing with his finger back into the dreadful room.

With the narrative reenactment of the Monster's curse, Victor's story has reached its "acme" (188). Elizabeth's corpse has made visible the Monster's thwarted dream of a female companion as readily as the Monster's act makes clear Victor's radical egotism. Victor will now, as he tells Walton, conclude in a few words his "hideous narration" (188).

We might wonder if, for Victor, that "hideous narration" is really the linguistic narrative that he is shaping, or the fragmented and contingent events of his life, the absurd and monstrous experience of his "real life" before his narrative began. For Victor, that "real life" experience has become very much like the body of the fiend that he has created, but Victor's story is not the Monster's story anymore than the Monster's story is Victor's. Victor is and is not the Monster, and that is the truth of his story, whether it happened or not. If we want to know Victor, we must believe his story, acknowledge that this story could happen to us. Victor will eventually die, but his story and the Monster's story continue to live into the future, thanks to Victor. That is his modern Promethean gift to us, and our responsibility (and Walton's) is to stay open to it.

After the wedding night, Victor returns to his father and Ernest in his hometown (Geneva), but the remnants of his family are no longer enough to sustain him. He has been permanently unhinged, yet he still seeks revenge, and so attempts to tell his story to the criminal judge there, demanding that he be heard: "It is indeed a tale so strange, that I should fear that you would not credit it were there not something in truth which, however wonderful, forces conviction. The story is too connected to be mistaken for a dream, and I have no motive for falsehood" (189). Unlike the disjointed body of his Creation, seen as a Monster misshapen by the disconnected events of mortal experience, the accidents of time, Victor's story, motivated by the desire for human connection, shaped by language and breath, is not illusion but the truth of his identity, now embodied for others to experience and interpret through time.

Rejected by the criminal judge, Victor is now bound by revenge, an endless wanderer, in pursuit of the Monster who can never be named. With no hope from the law (and with the death of his father), he also becomes an eternal mourner, haunted by all "the spirits of the departed" (192), who can be felt but not seen. Stripped of all but the most fragile traces of human sentiment and connection, he has become a devil living in the hell of his own experience. He is driven on by the nightmare that he has created, the thing that he has experienced but cannot grasp.

Always staying ahead of Victor, the Monster leads him to the far North, the edge and limits of the geographic and psychic terrain. As readers, we are also led there, back to the beginning of the book (*Frankenstein*) where we first experienced Walton writing letters to his sister. We are back on board Walton's ship (a place we never actually left), the place where Victor's own narrative began and will end.

It has taken a week for Victor to tell his story to Walton. He has not engaged in the mortal conflict with the Monster as he had hoped, but he has told his story to Walton, a more meaningful victory. Walton has listened carefully, convinced more by the material evidence that he has seen (letters about the DeLacey household, the apparition of the Monster spotted early on from the ship), than by the narrative itself. But as Walton tells his sister, Victor's story has opened new possibilities for him: "His tale is connected, and told with an appearance of the simple truth" (199). Frankenstein refused to speak about "the particulars of his creature's formation" (199), although Walton cannot doubt the Monster's existence, or, more importantly, the truth of Victor's narrative. Victor's story has become a covenant between Victor and Walton, a promise that Victor now anticipates being passed from generation to generation, "down to posterity" (199). Although Victor assumed that he was creating "a hideous narrative" (188), he now appears (to Walton and himself) to have created an ennobling tragedy. "He seems to feel his own worth, and the greatness of his fall" (200), Walton tells his sister.

Victor does not end his life grappling in mortal combat with the wretch, his Creation, but, weary and fatigued, he dies on Walton's ship, his quest for revenge unsatisfied. His final advice to Walton, who is also struggling with the dilemma whether to journey further out (north) or to return home (south) with his crew, is as conflicted as Victor's life has proven to be. At one pole of consciousness, Victor urges Walton onward, exhorting him and his crew to fulfill his purpose: "Oh! Be men, or be more than men . . . Do not return to your families with the stigma of disgrace marked on your brows. Return as heroes who have fought and conquered, and who know not what it is to turn their backs on the foe" (204). At the other pole, though, Victor urges the pursuit of happiness, the familiar and nurturing life within the neighborhood of family and friends: "Seek happiness in tranquility, and avoid ambition even it be only the apparently innocent one of distinguishing yourself in science and discoveries" (204). It is just that kind of tension that *Frankenstein*, the book itself, embodies, but cannot resolve.

Victor dies as an exemplum of the richly complex and conflicted experience of the quest for human identity. He has no lesson to teach, although he claimed he did. His narrative raises more questions than it answers. Like the book itself, Victor is a riddle that keeps dialogue alive.

With Victor's death, the Monster once again returns, and it will be the Monster (through the language of Walton) who will get the last word. Seeing that Victor, his father, is dead, the Monster asks for forgiveness and explains to Walton what Victor has apparently not emphasized in his own narrative. "Think ye that the groans of Clerval were music to my ears?" he asks Walton. "My heart was fashioned to be susceptible of love and sympathy" (208), he tells him, but barred from the world of empathy and affection, he became a slave to his perverse impulses (the Monster claims). Like Victor, the Monster is also a riddle, a wretch without a name, but with a story that he has articulated. As readers, we empathize with him, but we are also repulsed by his horrifying acts of violence. He is no doubt the other, different from us, but whether that is our limitation or his is never resolved by the narrative. We might recognize our story in Victor's, but the Monster's story remains, in its details, unknown to us; it is perhaps too much for us to acknowledge, too much for us to endure. As the Monster says of Victor's story about the Monster's acts: ". . . in the detail which he gave you . . . he could not sum up the hours and months of misery which I endured, wasting in impotent passions . . . I desired love and fellowship, and I was still spurned" (210).

Walton turns south with his crew and heads home. The Monster springs from the cabin-window, "borne away by the waves, and lost in darkness and distance" (211). We might wonder if there is some middle way, but that, too, is not offered as a lesson but as another question. Desire and passion move us backward and forward, looping through time. Mary Shelley knows this. But she wants the reader to wonder: How far out should mortal beings travel?

4

Alice in Wonderland

One of the great delights of reading *Alice in Wonderland* is to be reminded that the human quest for knowledge, always a passage from innocence to experience, can be joyful and that such a journey is inevitably implicated with language and its relation to embodied acts of experience. Lewis Carroll's interest in word and number games adds to the playfulness of the reading experience, but his insights into the nature of language and its relation to human understanding strikes us as profound. In *Alice in Wonderland*, Carroll makes clear that language and "real life," linguistic narrative and contingent experience, metaphoric functioning and random events are in dialectical relation, open to each other, coinciding, but not to be confused with each other anymore than the language of God is to be confused with the language of man. "The idea that language controls reality and reality language" (Steiner 107), as Wendy Steiner suggests, is one way of understanding the novel. The natural world does not conform to linguistic narrative, and linguistic narrative does not conform to the natural world. But each needs the other if human beings are to expand knowledge of themselves. Alice's journey can be especially appreciated from this perspective, as a quest for the truth to be discovered not outside of time, but within it, through the temporal unfolding of language interpreted in its dialectical relation to the natural world. It is Alice's story, but it is our story as well. We experience it as long as we are in dialogue with it. We need to follow Alice and the White Rabbit down the rabbit-hole.

When we first see Alice, she has lost interest in her familiar and ordinary existence above ground. The book that her older sister is reading, and that Alice peeps into, seems dry and abstract, lacking the sensuous qualities of human voice or imaginative vision. It has no conversation or pictures in it, as Alice notes, and "what is the use of a book," she thinks, "without pictures or conversations?" (1). Sitting with her sister in the natural landscape, Alice believes that even the daisies that surround her are too familiar and common for her young and curious mind. Like us, Alice is in need of adventure and story, something to move her.

The sudden appearance of a White Rabbit in motion stirs desire in Alice, beginning her adventure. Somewhat like the serpent in the Garden of Eden, the Rabbit speaks: "Oh dear! Oh dear! I shall be late!" (1). Clothed in a waist-coat, he checks the time with a watch that he carries with him. He is a surprise, and as Alice pursues the Rabbit, we do, too.

From the start, though, we know more than Alice, with her impulsiveness and naïveté, knows. With the pleasure of the eye, Alice sees the White Rabbit moving at a distance, visible, above ground. But the Rabbit quickly becomes invisible, disappearing down a dark hole. As Alice pursues the invisible Rabbit, falling down what seems "to be a very deep well" (2), we, as readers, follow, destabilized as if entering a dream world, noticing cupboards and bookshelves, a jar labeled "orange marmalade" (2) (in reality empty), and wondering, with Alice, if we might fall forever, right through the earth.

Language cannot prevent Alice from falling, but, even while falling, she attempts to recover some stable sense of identity. First, she recalls her school lessons in "Latitude" and "Longitude." As Alice admits, they are "grand words to say" (2) but not very helpful in the present situation, although they do give her momentary support. Then she imagines a dialogue with others above ground, including her favorite cat, Dinah: language giving her hope until she thumps "upon a heap of sticks and dry leaves, and the fall was over" (3). She is underground, in Wonderland.

Such a fall into unknown territory disorients the self, sets it spinning, but although Alice is now in the dark and deep, pursuing her impulse, she clearly has memory of her past experience above ground to give her the texture of herself and language to preserve some sense of social connection and purpose. Landing in Wonderland, she is innocent and naïve, unaware of the risks and dangers in her fall, but language helps her along—at least until she moves to the edge of that language where the potential menace, the mortal possibility of collapse or breakdown always threatens. That there is a limit to her fall marks the limits of her language, though. The narrator will not let her die anymore than he will let her fall endlessly. He is not shaping a tragedy, but a slow and innocent story about the expansion of a young girl's consciousness as she continually adjusts to the experience she encounters. Alice is seeking the beginning of experience, not its end. Her journey focuses on creation rather than death.

For Alice, we are now told, "very few things were really impossible" (4). That sense of endless possibility is her charm and her wonder. When she finds a golden key that, to her great delight, fits a door leading from a dark hall into a small passage, she glimpses the loveliest garden, bright with colorful flowers and cool fountains. She cannot even get her head through the door, but she is convinced that she could, if she "only knew how to begin" (4).

Alice is not curious about discovering what was before the beginning, the origins of the natural world. She is interested in experiencing the felt moments of "real life" experience, the contingent moments that she can then take up and recreate as new meaning. She wants to find a way to make experience her own. In this way, she will become "one respectable person" (6), as she later says.

As a result, Alice invites adventure, seeing things she has not seen before, but she is far from understanding the relationship between language and the contingent events of her adventure. Finding a bottle labeled DRINK ME, she checks to see if "it's marked poison or not" (4); reassured that it will not disagree with her, she tastes it, eventually finishing it off. Whether the jar actually lacks a label that says "poison" is, of course, no guarantee that it isn't poison, anymore than the empty jar labeled "orange marmalade" in the rabbit-hole was guaranteed to have marmalade within it.

Words are not things, nor do they convey absolute truths, but they do interact with things and with the natural world of contingent experience. Words can give guidance and direction, shape the contingencies of mortal life, give that life some meaning. Alice seems to understand this. What Alice does not seem to have realized, yet, is that she has to make her language her own, give that language a voice. In her innocence, she is still too willing to accept the language already existing in the world without thinking it through and making it her own. She needs to articulate her experience in order to discover her human identity, both as an individual and as a social being. At the moment (still early in her journey), she has begun to question who she is; she has opened the quest for personal knowledge, a risk that demands courage and confidence, as she becomes "curiouser and curiouser" (7), experiencing dramatic fluctuations in body and thinking, She is an identity in motion, but one just beginning to take shape.

"Let me think: was I the same when I got up this morning? I almost think I can remember feeling a little different. But if I'm not the same, the next question is 'Who in the world am I'? Ah, that's the great puzzle" (8).

Alice senses that her identity consists of similarities and differences, categories determined, to a large extent, through language, but these categories, like experience itself, seem always to be changing. For the moment, she is perplexed and uncertain: ". . . her voice sounded hoarse and strange, and the words did not come the same as they used to do" (9). Wonderland is a strange place, the contrary of Alice's world above ground. When she thinks about the language and social relations above ground (even about her acquaintance Mabel whom she does not want to be), Alice gains comfort and security. They are known to her, and she understands them. By contrast, the underground world is strange to her, but is also a part of her, what she does not know or understand, the part that fascinates her, excites her curiosity. That strangeness makes her feel alone, split from herself and the known world. It is not surprising that, in the midst of her identity crisis, she longs for the old attachments above ground: "I do wish they would put their heads down! I am so very tired of being all alone here!" (10).

We begin to understand that Alice continually needs to adjust her language to the situation just as she needs to adjust her actions to the changing context. Fortunately, language is familiar to her and to all the other living creatures that she encounters, and that sense of familiarity gives her common ground with them, often turning strangeness into social bonding. When language drifts to the edge, though, the border of nonsense and breakdown, then dialogue becomes impossible. At such moments we, as readers, become nervous as does Alice. Such moments in Alice's journey, as Wendy Steiner suggests, "signal that the limit of thought has been reached, either logically . . . or existentially, as in the desire for knowledge about death, the ultimate unknown" (Steiner 130).

Both language and existential experience are significant dimensions of mortal identity, but what Alice needs to know is the similarity and difference between them. Language disconnected from experience is nonsense, but so is experience disconnected from language, especially language shaped into narrative. Alice often confuses the two. When the Mouse offers to tell Alice his history (his tale), Alice cannot understand its meaning because she visualizes his tail, misunderstanding the metaphoric function. If Alice understood that the Mouse was telling "a tale" rather than talking about "his tail" (16), then his story would evoke another story, further conversation, and dialogue. The mouse's tail will end in death not only because it an element of the material world, but also because Alice cannot shape it though language into a shared truth. She does not know enough to make it part of her own telling.

Alice is not curious about endings, but, as we have said, about beginnings, the intuitive knowledge carried through language that evokes desire and the possibility of a new meaning. The Caucus Race that Alice observes has no beginning or end, and she cannot find any meaning in it (who can?). She needs to write her own book, her own story, but she is not convinced yet that she can. "There ought to be a book written about me, that there ought!" she says when she realizes that she is now living the fairy tales she used to read but never believed in. "And when I grow up, I'll write one—but I'm grown up now" (21). For Alice, only grown-ups have the ability to name the world, to find the voice that gives contingent experience its meaning. At the moment, it's only her body that seems to be growing. Language is as confusing as her experience in Wonderland.

The dialectic between language and the body, voice and dust, inevitably creates slippage; we never are who we think we are or who we seem to be. This is certainly true for Alice. When a blue caterpillar, sitting atop a mushroom, asks Alice: "Who are you?" her reply is not surprising: "I—I hardly know, Sir, just at present—at least I know who I was when I got up this morning, but I think I must have been changed several times since then" (27). It is difficult to know if the blue caterpillar, smoking a long hookah, is hallucinating, or as likely, that Alice herself is hallucinating. As readers, we acknowledge Alice's increasing confusion and ongoing feelings of strangeness. If she is growing, she is showing few signs that she believes in herself, that she can find language capable of giving purpose and direction to what is happening to her. "I can't explain myself, I'm afraid, Sir," she says to the caterpillar, "because I'm not myself, you see" (28). Her challenge is to make meaning from the nonsense that she seems to be experiencing as chaos and disorder. She needs to find her own way of saying things.

Despite her naïve lack of confidence, Alice does seem to be progressing on her journey by the time she has encountered the blue caterpillar. In one sense, the voice of the caterpillar is as much the internal voice of Alice as it is the external voice of the caterpillar—not surprising since we were told early in the narrative that "this curious child was very fond of pretending to be two people" (6). When the caterpillar explains the secrets of the mushroom to Alice, "One side will make you grow taller, and the other side will make you grow shorter" (33), he appears to have offered a meaningless fragment of discourse with no understandable reference to the material world. But it is as if Alice is already internalizing this floating discourse, trying to make sense of it.

"One side of what? The other side of what?" Alice logically thinks to herself. "Of the mushroom," said the caterpillar, just as if she had asked it aloud; and in another moment it was out of sight (33).

Alice seems ready to reinterpret the caterpillar's apparent hallucination, make meaning of it in her own terms. Of course, the mushroom is round, and it really has no sides until someone names them.

It is somewhat like the Caucus Race, with no beginning or end, until someone opens it to language and human meaning. At this moment, Alice is not yet prepared to use her voice to fully shape and articulate the situation, but she uses her body (her right hand and then her left hand) to orient herself, to define a context (a left side and a right side). The gesture allows her to begin to create meaning and move ahead.

Half way through her adventure, Alice is more clearly gaining confidence. She leaves the woods where she has been wandering, and enters what appears to be a more civilized dimension of Wonderland. But her encounters remain strange and increase in violence. Hoping "to get into that beautiful garden" (35) where she began, she encounters instead a Pigeon who aggressively insists that Alice is a serpent, and then meets a Duchess who tosses her "baby violently up and down" and enjoys shouting, "chop off her head" (39). When she meets the grinning Cheshire Cat, though, she, for the first time, timidly gives it a name: "Cheshire-Puss" (41). She does not know if the cat will like its new name, but she hopes it will. When the cat widens its grin, confirming its pleasure, Alice, too, is pleased. Sharing a moment of reciprocal desire, both Alice and the cat have something in common.

The Cheshire Cat might be considered strange in terms of the ordinary world above ground, but he is also considered "mad" in Wonderland, as everyone in Wonderland claims to be, everyone, that is, except the ordinary dog who "growls when it's angry, and wags its tail when it's pleased" (42). Apparently the dog's behavior sets the norm in Wonderland, defines the familiar. The Cheshire Cat is "mad" once those linguistic terms are set. As the cat explains, "Now I growl when I'm pleased, and wag my tail when I'm angry. Therefore, I'm mad" (42). But this is a logic without narrative texture, solipsistic thinking without the personal knowledge acquired through the transforming quality of linguistic narrative transforming "real life" experience. Alice's response to the cat's nonsense is telling: "I call it purring, not growling" (42), suggesting her own growing ability to stabilize her identity through her own remaking of language.

The Cheshire Cat appears to be going nowhere, although it does have the uncanny ability to mysteriously appear and disappear. Its mystery leaves a wondrous after-effect. In fact, the cat is as much a dimension of Alice's growing consciousness as he is a material object in the world of Wonderland. His profound after-effect—"a grin without a cat" (43)—is the most curious thing Alice ever saw in all her life. It remains at the radical border of all language, but Alice now seems capable of giving it her own meaning.

The world of Wonderland appears as a dream world, a world of contingency and coincidence, especially when compared to the ordinary world above ground with its apparent order and structure. But to believe in that kind of distinction is to miss much of the meaning of Alice's journey, the meaning of most human quests for that matter. Human experience is lived as contingency; human destiny is the necessity of that contingency revealed through linguistic narrative, through the telling of the tale. Madness and nonsense occur when human beings stop movement (their quest for expanding self-knowledge), kill time (their temporal and mortal selves; their sense of past, present, and future), and abandon the richly meaningful dialectic between contingent experience and linguistic narrative (the metaphoric function). Wonderland is no more an illusion than life itself before the telling of the story. The Mad Tea Party helps Alice (and us) experience just this sort of insight.

When Alice meets the mad March Hare, the mercantile Mad Hatter, and the dormant Dormouse, they are all stuck at "six o'clock," the moment the Mad Hatter killed time. Around the Tea Party table, they talk in riddles, closed off nonsense. They move in endless circles (like the Caucus Race) without beginning or end. They are caught in the dull round of inconsequentiality, one taking the place of the next around the table. Their only hope is in story, but when the March Hare asks Alice for a story, she can only say, "I'm afraid I don't know one" (48). When the Dormouse offers his story, though, it does not serve their purpose either, based as it is on letters ("M") and word-play cut off from any reference to the felt experience of "real life."

That Alice rejects such stupidity is to her credit, moving on from the Tea Party before nonsense permanently sets in. As a result, she eventually finds herself once more in the long hall where she began her journey. There she notices "that one of the trees had a door leading right into the garden." "'Now I'll manage myself better this time,' she said to herself, and began by taking the little golden key, and unlocking the door that led into the garden." Passing through that tree, "she found herself at last in the beautiful garden, among the bright flower-beds and the cool fountains" (50).

The Queen's garden reminds us of Adam and Eve's experience in Eden after eating the apple. On the Queen's Croquet Ground, there is no common ground, and what appeared to be ideal and beautiful is experienced as corrupt and covered over by spectacle. The natural white roses have been painted red, the gardeners call themselves by numbers ("five" and "seven"), and, just as we experienced in the Garden of Eden, they blame each other: "'I couldn't help it,' said Five, in a sulky tone, 'Seven jogged my elbow'" (51).

Wonderland lacks common ground, flattened out like a pack of cards, spectacle rather than substance, a place teetering on the edge of nonsense (not Paradise). The roses have been transformed into spectacle, mere surfaces for the pleasure of the eye of one person only, the Queen herself. Her garden is pure contingency, ruled by absurd power. Fortunately, Alice remains curious—and heroic.

When the Queen confronts Alice: "What's your name, child?" Alice quickly replies: "My name is Alice" (53), with some deference to the Queen, but also a sure sign of her growing ability to identify herself and locate herself among others. That she adds, to herself: "Why they're only a pack of cards after all; I needn't be afraid of them!" (53), marks a significant turning point in her journey, especially when she next responds to the Queen's nonsense by shouting, "How should I know?" (53)—further surprising herself at her own courage and recognizing that there are appropriate limits to gaining mortal knowledge. "It's no business of mine" (53), she finally asserts, refusing to participate any longer in such flattened out and solipsistic nonsense. The power of the Queen, like the image of power itself, is an illusion; it has no genuine human meaning. Alice is now beginning to understand that.

Each time the Queen shouts, "Off with his head!" (56), we, as readers, increasingly sense the emptiness of the rhetoric, the meaningless sound of the language. To make sense of language is to give voice to it, open it to the actual experience, embody meaning by shaping contingency into necessity through the ongoing dialogue between "real life" experience and language, doing and knowing, sensuous bodily movement and the telling of that movement in linguistic narrative. Such a process allows Alice to connect with others, to recognize similarities between herself and others, not only to acknowledge the familiar in "the other," but also to acknowledge differences and to make judgments about herself in relation to others. We admire Alice because, despite her anxiety and danger, she never gives up on this process. There is courage and respectability in that. As Wendy Steiner makes clear, despite "all the nonsense interruptions, all the spatial discontinuities and logical leaps" that Alice experiences, she struggles through her journey, a knower who refuses to be undone (Steiner 131). She is a seeker beginning to shape the chaos and contingencies of "real life" for herself. Unlike all the other croquet players—except the King and Queen of misrule—Alice in Wonderland is never put into custody or under the sentence of execution. She is innocent, but she is learning to take charge of her own life, make it her wonderful dominion as a respectable person.

Late in her journey, Alice agrees to the Gryphon's request to hear some of her adventures: "Come; let's hear some of your adventures" (69). Alice is still far from finding a mature voice that could shape her adventure into a coherent narrative, give duration to her temporal and contingent experience of events, but she makes a start. "I could tell you my adventures beginning from this morning," Alice says. "It's no use going back to yesterday, because I was a different person then" (69).

But the Gryphon is impatient, and he wants her to go further back in time. So, Alice begins her story with the time she first saw the White Rabbit, gaining courage as she goes on, as long as she can. When she runs up against the part where she first began to breakdown, though, a vulnerable moment of confusion and loss of stability earlier in her journey, she breaks off her story. Unable to further shape her story, she subjects herself once again to the obedience of law and command.

In her last adventure underground, Alice experiences directly the work of the law, and we are reminded that the rigidity of the law creates its own confusion and absurd violence. The Knave of Hearts accused of stealing the Queen's tarts is on trial in the court of justice. But the issue seems less to do with crime and punishment, transgression and righteous judgment, then with the shaping of linguistic narrative, the gaining of personal knowledge through the creation of story. If we are looking for justice, we will not find it in the exercise of the law, but in the interaction between the law and the narration.

In the King's Court, Alice's body furiously expands, disrupting the jury box, but giving her further confidence in herself as the trial proceeds. When she sees the jurymen sprawled about, she is reminded about the recent accident she had had at home, upsetting her goldfish bowl. Imagining the two events in association, she has "a vague sort of idea" that the jurymen "must be collected at once and put back into the jury-box, or they would die" (80). Alice has still not located herself in the world as a mature adult, nor has she gained the confidence to tell a richly detailed story, but she is growing increasingly sensitive to her sensuous body and her mortality, and she is clearly expanding her empathy for others. By mapping her past story onto the present, she is beginning to deepen her understanding of her self and her own narrative capability. That developing knowledge will give her freedom and purpose contrary to the absurdity of the law of misrule. It will allow her to discover her destiny in the world.

The King's Court lacks any rules of evidence, so we might, at first, agree with Steiner when she says: "Without any rules of evidence, anything is relevant—or irrelevant—and the relation between truth and judgment is destroyed" (Steiner 135). But even sophisticated rules of evidence limit the truth by their own contracted logic. There is always more to the story than logic can accommodate, and the law will always try to keep secret the desire that fuels the truth of the human story. As the verse that serves as the most important piece of evidence at the trial indicates:

"For this must ever be
A secret kept from all the rest,
Between yourself and me." (88)

That tacit knowledge, the secret between you and me (reader and author as well), lingers like an after-effect, achieved not through the rules of evidence or the law, but through felt experience shaped into story, the truth of shared "real life," whether it happened or not. In the end, it is the story that wins out.

By the end of the trial, Alice, having grown back to her full size, not only can call "stuff and nonsense" (83) what it is, but, she can also name the cultural and political world for what it is—a bunch of phonies, surface images without deep and human substance. As she puts it, "you're nothing but a pack of cards!" (83).

Like everything else in the narration, that pack of cards, which causes Alice both fright and anger in her dream world, turns out to be connected in the world above ground "to some dead leaves that had fluttered down from the trees upon her face" (84), as she awakes from her dream in the lap of her sister. For Alice, still open to wonder and possibility, there's a great deal to reflect on and shape now above ground, but before she moves on, she tells her sister all her "strange adventures" (84), as well as she can.

Inspired by Alice's telling, the sister, too, begins to dream in her own way, reminding us that story inevitably evokes story, creates an internal context for further storytelling. Her sister has clearly experienced Alice's story, her own imagination "alive with the strange creatures of her little sister's dream" (85). The sensuous details of Alice's story—the rattle of the teacups, the shrill voice of the Queen, the sneezing of the pig-baby, and so on—create the wonder of the experience, the after-effect that gives her purpose and direction, hope for the future.

Importantly, Alice's sister also dreams that her "little sister," as "a grown woman," will continue to tell her story of adventure, passing her "strange tale" of Wonderland, to "other bright and eager children," feeling all "the simple sorrows" and "simple joys" of childhood and "happy summer days" (86). Alice's sister has experienced the story only as a summer story, though, a reminder of innocence projected into the future, at times with overtones of romantic nostalgia: "perhaps even with the romantic dream of Wonderland long ago" (86). Yet, to us, Alice's adventures not only embody "the simple and loving heart of her childhood," but intimations of those "riper years", the grown woman's world of sexuality and death. Her story, shaped by the narrator (not Alice), offers more than Alice's sister knows. We do not hear Alice's rendition of her adventures as she tells them to her sister, nor do we know much about Alice's sister's own experiences in relation to the shaping of her own daydreams. As mature readers, though, we recognize the multidimensional levels of this complex story, the significant interaction between contingent experience and linguistic narrative, the mysterious depth of the human journey from innocence to experience—the ongoing quest to discover who we are.

Throughout her adventurous journey, Alice has remained innocent and young, an admirable voice that does not seem to lose her purity no matter what adventure she experiences. She is, at times, priggish, even class conscious, but she maintains a sense of connection, a sense of being more than just one: "for this curious child was very fond of pretending to be two people" (6). In this regard, she is a linguistic being, always in dialogue with herself and others; she cares. She is perpetually curious—"curiouser and curiouser" (7)—but she never becomes so obsessive that the obsession gets control of her. Her curiosity, like the language shaping her story, has a keen playfulness to it; it is not clawing or controlling, but joyful in pursuit of discovery. Alice works for stability in a world of instability, but she does not strive to grasp and control what she does not know.

Once in Wonderland, Alice acts and reacts to commands, never really obeying, although she has an appropriate sense of respect and an uncanny ability to adapt to each encounter. In the process, she remains flexible and gains confidence despite her entry into strange and forbidden territory and despite adolescent angst stirred by sexual growth and maturing. Whether it's the White Rabbit, the Mad Hatter, the Cheshire Cat, the Caterpillar, or the Queen of Hearts, Alice always seems to acknowledge these odd creatures as parts of her own self (her doubles), familiar but strange as they all are. She never forgets her quest for that wonderful Garden—"the loveliest garden you ever saw" (4)—the garden that she would like to get to, if she only could, but which, once experienced, is not what she first glimpsed, inevitably disappointing as a place of nonsense, but nevertheless also a place to imagine and dream.

Alice's innocence and playfulness keep her curious, but they do not make her obsessive. Her "curiousness" is a mark of human joy, the "mystical band" (viii) referred to in the Preface Poem. That playfulness also contributes to her healthy sense of distance in relation to the madness and nonsense of Wonderland itself. Although she often finds herself alone in Wonderland, she never seems to lose her familiar connection with her social self, the intuitive knowledge that she is connected to others. As a result, although often sensing instability, she does not become a total stranger to herself. She is always in dialogue.

5

Heart of Darkness

Heart of Darkness takes us on a journey to "the farthest point of navigation" (5), the culminating point of Charlie Marlow's experience, the threshold that "leads into the heart of an immense darkness" (72), where language gives way to silence and we, as readers, are left to carry on. As a narrative, it doubles back on itself, as most modern narratives do, opening a gap between "real life" experience (what happened) and the linguistic unfolding of that experience (the telling), a gap that we, as readers, can enter, if we dare, allowing us to glimpse "a kind of light," somber, not very clear (5), at the "uttermost ends of the earth" (72), the very edge of ourselves. We want to follow Marlow then on this adventure, knowing full well (as readers in the twenty-first century how could we not know?) that this journey will take us to Kurtz at the Inner Station in the center of Africa (the Belgian Congo), to the horror within the heart of darkness, the moment that seems to sanction the narrative itself, demands its telling, the apparent truth of the telling. In this context, we assume at the start that Kurtz is the beginning and, we might suspect, the end of Marlow's narrative, the experience that cannot be fully articulated, although perhaps glimpsed through the narrative telling.

That Kurtz is some kind of double for Marlow we can also assume, just as we might agree that Marlow's telling of this adventure is a demand for us to pay attention to him, to listen to his account of himself. If Marlow desires to preserve Kurtz's name, even his reputation, it is through his linguistic narrative that Marlow will create his own name, perhaps even the man within the name. It is nevertheless the difference between Marlow and Kurtz, the living and the dead, that is at stake in *Heart of Darkness*.

As readers, we do not start with Marlow, though, but with the language of an unnamed frame narrator. That language helps us locate ourselves on the "Nellie," a cruising yawl anchored on the Thames, at sunset, waiting for the tide to turn, overlooking London, "the biggest and the greatest town on earth" (1). The other men on the yacht—the Director of Companies (captain and host), the lawyer, the accountant and Marlow—are all connected by "the bond of the sea" (1), although Marlow, unlike the others, is still a committed follower of the sea, seaman, and wanderer. He is sitting on the deck, as we begin, in the pose of a Buddha, apart from the others, resembling an idol, not for worship, we suspect, but meditation.

If there is a "mournful gloom" (1) in the atmosphere, there is a sense of meditative possibilities from the start, but in the language of the frame narrator also a jingoistic tone of pride in London and in the heroic adventures of the great English seamen (Drake, Franklin et al.) who previously pursued "the mystery of an unknown world" and provided inspiration "for men, commonwealth and empires" (2). On the "Nellie," we seem to be at the heart of civilized life, stable in our evolution, our progress, among men of considerable status and success. If the sun is setting on the empire, the sun will rise again with the light of the morning, when the tide turns. The other men on the yacht—the Director of Companies, the lawyer, the accountant—wait on the Thames for the civilized light of day to arrive.

Like us, Marlow has somehow heard the murmuring language of the unnamed narrator, its patriotic spirit, its sense of English triumph, Western light, imperial success, language tinged with the melancholy of twilight, but embracing Western Enlightenment, light without darkness. It is a language carrying the promise of a bright and noble ending, but without much consideration of origins. We will supposedly hear Marlow through this frame narrator, but Marlow is the one we want to follow directly, as he suddenly responds to that narrator's murmur, undercutting its smug tone of satisfaction: "And this also has been one of the dark places of the earth" (3). If Marlow is thinking about where he is now (on the Thames, on a yacht in London), he is also thinking about the past, about Roman conquest, about the beginning—"very old times" (3)—the original darkness of this place. He is thinking, we might assume, about Kurtz as well, the seed of his story, the germ of his narrative, the narrative that he is about to start.

On the "Nellie," we find ourselves in a place similar to that of the frame narrator, anticipating a story from Marlow, one that, as the unnamed narrator says, will express its meaning "not inside like a kernel but outside, enveloping the tale . . . as a glow brings out a haze, in the likeness of one of these misty halos that sometimes are made visible by the spectral illumination of moonshine" (3). If the story is "inconclusive" (typical of Marlow), not very clear, misty, weighted with haze, it might nevertheless "throw a kind of light" (5), indirectly, on what otherwise remains unknown to us, dark and unseen.

Marlow begins by telling his listeners (including us) that he was restless in London (eight years ago, we calculate), eager to return to the sea, looking for a ship: that restlessness, that desire to go out, to explore new territory, apparently connected to his passion, since he was a boy, for maps, unknown places, blank spaces, the mystery that invited him to discover what had not been named or made visible. Since his boyhood days, though, with their innocent dreams of adventure and illumination, many of those unknown places have been discovered and named, as if innocence has given way to experience. Marlow has not given up those dreams, but those innocent dreams seem to have been seduced by the very desire that those names have created. Have Marlow's dreams been contaminated as well?—we wonder.

When Marlow looked at a map, as he wandered in the streets of London, he saw, as he tells us, a "mighty big river . . . resembling an immense snake uncoiled . . . And as I looked at the map of it in a shop window, it fascinated me as a snake would a bird—a silly little bird" (5–6). He was restless and fascinated then, a little bird charmed by a snake: the visible sign of a river on a map in a London shop seducing him as if it were the devil. We can call that snake the Belgian Congo (although Marlow never names it), but we might wonder if the devil is within the name, or if, by contrast, the name has created the devil, a devil appearing in place of the innocent dream, the adventure of boyhood, the glamour of a clear and unsullied truth tainted now by the brand of mortal naming.

The map reminds Marlow of his boyhood dream, but the image of the snake on the map (Marlow's perception of the representation of the flowing river) reminds him of "a big concern, a company for trade on that river" (6). That "big concern" turns out to be a continental company known to his aunt, whose influence will get him appointed as a skipper of a steamboat on that river. As Marlow tells us, this is out of the ordinary for him: asking others for help in such adventures, especially a woman peddling influence through circuits that he does not otherwise know about it. If we suspect there is something corrupt about his appointment, though, about his tacit agreement to get to the Congo "by hook or by crook" (6), there is also something glorious in the idea, at least as his aunt might understand it, something that makes Marlow, at the start, "something like an emissary of light . . . a lower sort of apostle" (10). The trading company in "the sepulchral city" (6), Brussels, would not publicly disagree.

Listening on the "Nellie" to Marlow's narrative in the darkness, we wonder whether it will unfold as a story that illuminates the beauty of an idea, brings light (even as a misty halo) to the darkness, or as a story that enacts seduction ("the hook") and corruption ("the crook"), the crime of mortal life itself, the payment owed for the restlessness and the pursuit of what cannot be known. In any case, we desire to know, to pursue through Marlow's telling, through his voice in the dark, the journey that he has experienced, the journey that he is now shaping through his language, repeating for himself (and for us as well).

At the door of the waiting room of the Company's Office in Brussels, Marlow witnesses two women knitting, ominous premonitions of his fate, somnambulists, the stranger within (or without) the human self. On a table is another map, with "the colors of a rainbow" (7), including the yellow that marks out the place Marlow is headed, "dead in the center" (7) of Africa, where the river (like a snake) remains fascinating and deadly. For Marlow, it is an ominous and uncanny moment, as he seals the contract with the Company, a sense of conspiracy joined: "Moritui te salutant" (8). Even the doctor who examines him appears mad, a headhunter of sorts, reminding us that the supposed evolution of science and civilization might well include its own degeneration. If the trading company is considered by some to be the pinnacle of modern success, the premiere example of rational control and of the "idea" of civilization, then it might not be what it appears to be, or even what it thinks it is. So, too, with Marlow, who seems unstable in that office, not just restless but existentially anxious, uneasy, if not yet diseased, as if he is becoming someone other than himself, "an impostor" (10).

We journey with Marlow on a French steamer down the west coast of Africa, on the edge of the jungle, enigmatic, "mute with an air of whispering, a general sense of vague and oppressive wonder" (11): Marlow's experience then, like his language now, hazy and heavy, hinting at nightmare. There is a sense of farce as well, though, something absurd, the French firing into the bush: "Pop would go on of the six-inch guns; a small flame would dart and vanish, a little white smoke would disappear, a tiny projectile would give a feeble screech—and nothing happened. Nothing could happen" (11). As readers, we need to question what kind of story this is, what kind of journey Marlow is really on. What purpose, if any, does this journey have? Yet, through the pressure of the language itself, we cannot deny the experience of the wonder that Marlow apparently experienced at the time, that he is attempting to evoke through his telling now, shaping that experience for us listening (he hopes) in the humid night darkness.

It takes 30 days along the coast before Marlow arrives at the mouth of the river and then another 200 miles inland before he can reach the place where he supposedly will begin his work for the Company. Along the route, there are other ominous signs, reports of a hanging, a railway truck looking "as dead as the carcass of some animal," "objectless blasting" (12) for no apparent purpose, as if desire itself has run rampant and death is everywhere.

Near the Company's station, six black men chained together in a gang suddenly appear at a distance. They are called "criminals" (13), named as such by the same kind of men who put the names on the map of this territory, those who, like Marlow himself, are contractual partners in "the exalted trust . . . the great cause of these high and just proceedings" (13), the same cause that not only the Company claims for itself, but that Marlow's aunt seemed to embrace.

Marlow did not know then what he knows now on the "Nellie." Seeing the chain gang, he had "blundered into" (13) a situation at the edge of the Company's Outer Station, which was strange to him, if not undefined, one that, interestingly enough, he did not make any moral judgment about, one that he did not confront directly. He preferred to avoid it, withdraw from it, let it pass without comment at the time: "Instead of going up, I turned and descended to the left. My idea was to let that chain gang get out of sight before I climbed the hill" (13). He was hesitant then, restless, perhaps frightened to confront the situation head on. It is a rhythm that we will see again and again in his experience, returning to it, shaping it through his narrative.

On the "Nellie" now, he needs to defend himself for his action then, and, in the process, he also defends the men controlling that chain gang. "I am not particularly tender" (he insists), ready to attack when necessary, "without counting the exact cost" (13). He admires the Company agents, "strong, lusty, red-eyed devils that sway and drive men" (13). It is as if Marlow wants to prove that he is in accord with the masculine status of his listeners on the "Nellie." But he is also accounting for himself now, for what he didn't do at the time, what he felt but didn't say.

Almost as an after-thought, an adjustment in the flow of his narrative, Marlow now allows something else to slip out, something about the slaves on the chain gang: They, too, were men. "Men—men I tell you" (13). Only then can he proceed with his story on the "Nellie," claiming that he "foresaw" the pretense of the "weak-eyed devil" (13), the insidious nature of the Company's manager, a man he was yet to meet.

Marlow was apparently conflicted from the start of his journey into the jungle. He was not aware then of much that he is aware of now, but the rhythm of his linguistic telling both reveals and conceals the rhythm of the experience that he is telling us about. He is conscious of his listeners, offering an account of himself, shaping that telling with them in mind. He is offering a story in the darkness, sanctioned, we assume, by Kurtz, a man, like the Company manager, whom he has not yet met in terms of the journey that he is telling us about, but who certainly seems to haunt him now. It is the future, as much as the past, that we, as readers, are experiencing, not Marlow's experience when it happened but his telling now that stirs our desire, if we dare to care about it.

Emerging out of the "mournful stillness of the grove" (14), a grove of death, at the threshold of the Outer Station, Marlow next meets the Company's chief accountant, "a vision" with "starched collar" and "varnished boots." He is a "miracle" in contrast to "the picture of a massacre or a pestilence" (15) experienced in that mournful grove of death. The accountant appears as "a hairdresser's dummy" (15) to Marlow, a figure without substance, but he also appears as "a miracle." He can keep order within the muddle, be efficient in an outpost of inefficiency. From the lips of this figure of bureaucratic order, Marlow first hears "the name of the man who is so indissolubly connected with the memories of that time" (15): "In the interior, you will no doubt meet Mr. Kurtz," the remarkable agent who sends "as much ivory as all the others put together" (16), the accountant tells Marlow (that "you" reminding us that Marlow also tells us). When Marlow first hears this description of Kurtz, we might suspect that "Kurtz" is, at best, just a name for him, yet Marlow has now heard that name, a "remarkable" name linked with the desire fueled by the Company, a desire for "ivory" (another name endlessly circulating in the air).

Fifteen days later, Marlow arrives at the Central Station, the place where "the flabby devil" (17)—the manager foreseen but not visible before—is running the show. Marlow has already witnessed death and absurdity, the inhumane treatment of chain gangs, the degeneration and illness of Company agents seeking profit, but he has also made it to his first destination. He seems primarily concerned with himself. When he hears that the steamship he was to pilot is "at the bottom of the river," sunk, he is "thunderstruck" (18). Apparently in a hurry to take the boat upriver, the manager has torn "the bottom out of her on stones" (18). At the time, importantly, Marlow "did not see the real significance of the wreck" (18).

As listeners (or readers), we continue to follow Marlow's story in the night air, his experience unfolding through the heavy atmosphere of his language, shaped by a disembodied voice emerging out of the darkness. He is attempting to offer us something of his experience, the sensation of a journey that he is committed to tell us about. Stepping back for a moment, we understand that Marlow was a man of adventure when he went out, a seaman and a wanderer, restless without a sense of home, charmed since a boy by the search for the unknown and mysterious, tinged with the possibility of romance, even the haze and mist emanating from the moonglow emerging from the darkness. Yet he is also apparently someone who respects efficiency and order, the application of work, its sense of focus and commitment, its practical results within the vast contingencies of human existence. If Marlow sensed that he might be an "impostor" on this journey into "the center of the world" (10), though, that there was something ominous, even horrifying in what he was seeing and experiencing, he seemed primarily interested in the doing itself, not in the meaning and implications of what was happening, but in the journey itself.

Arriving at the Central Station, learning that his steamboat had sunk, Marlow seemed, at the time, less concerned with the horror he had witnessed than about the delay in his further movement upriver. He was unaware of the manager's own plotting and deception. For Marlow, that "flabby devil" was "a chattering idiot" (19), but we might wonder about Marlow's own innocence (if we can call it that), about his unawareness, his inability to understand what was happening, his own complicity in the experience that he was undergoing.

It is not unreasonable to suspect that Marlow, with no clear purpose or intention since leaving from Brussels on this journey into the depths of Africa, arriving at the Central Station, discovering his steamboat sunk, was temporarily undone. He says as much himself: "I asked myself what I was to do there, now my boat was lost" (18). It is only the work, the repair of the boat, the facticity of rivets (yet to be delivered), that apparently secures him on the ground, gives him something to hold onto, that allows him stability in the midst of the dream, the nightmare that threatens to possess him.

Like us, Marlow, at the Central Station, hears the word "ivory"—"You would think they were praying to it" (20)—whispered everywhere, resonating as if it were a fetish, or an idol, the name itself circulating in the thickness of the air, stirring desire and fascination for the commodity, the mystery supposedly in its name. Marlow now hears more about Kurtz from the lips of the manager and then from another agent waiting to make bricks, a suspected spy for the manager, who pumps Marlow about his connections back in Europe, "in the sepulchral city and so on" (21). "Tell me, pray, who is this Mr. Kurtz?" (22), Marlow wants to know, as if he seeks the man within the name. When pressed, the agent responds with a description of the visionary Kurtz, the apostle of "the idea." The agent uses language derived from the Company and language we have heard before from the Christian sentiment of Marlow's aunt: "He is an emissary of pity, and science, and progress, and evil knows what else," the agent claims—"a special being" (22). But if Kurtz is unique in this regard, he is also the object of jealousy, a threat to the ambitions of the brickmaker and the manager. Kurtz is destined to make his way up the ladder of the Company from "Chief of the Inner Station" to "assistant manager . . . two years more . . ." to "general manager" (22). Like Marlow, we desire to know who this man named Kurtz really is. Is he a man of "the idea" or a man of "ivory"? Or is he something else altogether?

The general manager, who has "no entrails" (19), and the brickmaker, who is a "paper-mache Mephistopheles" with nothing inside but "a little loose dirt" (23), cannot tell us much about Kurtz, the depth of the man. However, when the brickmaker insists that Marlow, like Kurtz, is part of "the new gang of virtue" (22) with influence and connections to Brussels, we might at first wonder why Marlow did not take exception to the accusation. Instead of disagreeing with the brickmaker, he lets the brickmaker jabber on. As readers, we might think that it is a chance moment, a passing moment of contingency for Marlow, or perhaps another moment that he just as soon avoid. He withdraws from it, just as he withdrew from the chain gang on the hill.

The moment endures through Marlow's telling, though, his language giving it purpose and duration, and we need to consider the moment more fully, its rhythm and ambiguity. The brickmaker jabbers on, while Marlow leans against the wreck of his steamer. He senses "the primeval mud of the forest" (23) in his nostrils as he listens, confounded, not by the idle chatter of the brickmaker but by "the thing that couldn't talk" (23). Confounded by that "thing," Marlow seems to begin to gain purpose and direction: "I could see a little ivory coming out from there, and I had heard that Mr. Kurtz was in there. I had heard enough about it, too . . . God knows" (23). With the jabbering of the brickmaker in the background, Marlow now seems to commit himself fully to the pursuit of Kurtz, the name that he has heard, the invisible singularity anticipated through that name, "the thing" within the primeval forest, like "an alien" on "a distant planet" (23). For Marlow, the experience seems palpable as if it is beginning to shape his destiny. We might consider it the start of his compulsion to tell his story now.

As readers, we cannot help but sense the complexity of the moment, its doubleness, Marlow's withdrawal from the brickmaker and his subsequent commitment to Kurtz, his not saying anything at the time and his telling about it now. If the moment gives Marlow a sense of purpose, it is also woven with a lie—or better a near lie. If Marlow has gained direction, committing himself to Kurtz, distinguishing himself from the manager and the brickmaker, he has betrayed something else in himself, or, at least, left something unfulfilled: "I would not have gone so far as to fight for Kurtz, but I went for him near enough to a lie" (23). It is an odd confession, oblique enough ("near enough to a lie") to raise suspicion. We might even wonder in what sense Marlow has actually lied, since, as the bricklayer implies, Marlow apparently does have support and influence with the Company in Brussels. The moment is suspicious, creates in Marlow an existential anxiety, an anxiety at the time of the encounter with the brickmaker and now at the time of his telling. On the "Nellie," he is clearly disturbed.

It is not surprising that Marlow now breaks from his narrative and addresses his listeners outside that telling, reminding us that he is concerned with the reception of his story, our judgment of him. He desires our trust in him.

"You know I hate, detest, and can't bear a lie—it appalls me. There is a taint of death, a flavor of mortality in lies—which is exactly what I hate and detest—what I want to forget. It makes me miserable and sick, like biting something rotten would do" (23).

Marlow is concerned here about other lies that he will tell (and that we will eventually hear about) as a consequence of his commitment to Kurtz (the lie to Kurtz's Intended, in particular). But more immediately he is referring to his withdrawing from the jabbering of the brickmaker, "letting the young fool there believe anything he liked as to my influence in Europe" (24). Turning away from such idle talk, Marlow has let the brickmaker believe what he wanted to believe about Kurtz and himself. In the process, Marlow has acquired purpose and direction for his quest, but he seems entangled, disturbed. It is as if his journey is contaminated, and so, too, his narrative.

Understandably, Marlow has stepped back from the flow of his story. If he has done this to stabilize the moment, he is also acknowledging his frustration, the impossibility of conveying what he desires to tell, the "incredible" experience that he has yet to tell, the singularity of his "real life" story, a story unfolding like a dream, a "near lie," sanctioned by the necessity of its ending: "No, it is impossible; it is impossible to convey the life-sensation of any given epoch of one's existence—that which makes its truth, its meaning—its subtle and penetrating essence. It is impossible. We live, as we dream—alone" (24).

In this context, Marlow's telling of his journey is a dream, promising what cannot be fulfilled. But yet Marlow, his voice disembodied in the darkness, still hopes to inspire us "by this narrative that seemed to shape itself without human lips in the heavy night air of the river" (24). He is our dream as we are his, following him through his desirous language as he now follows Kurtz into the center of Africa. At best, we are witnesses for each other, listening to the voice of the other as it shapes the narrative, the "near lie" that might yet allow us a glimpse of what?—perhaps "the taint of death," "the flavor of mortality" (23)—what Marlow (and we) would prefer to forget, or at least withdraw from.

No wonder Marlow desires now "a certain quantity of rivets" (25), something solid to hold on to. It is the hard work that he has expended on that "tinpot steamboat" (25), what he leans on, that keeps him grounded. It is that commitment to what is right before his eyes that seems to matter. For the moment, it is the "love" for that object in front of him, the work he has done on that otherwise ruined piece of tin that has made him "love her"(25). It is the work that has allowed him to give the gift of life back to her. It is the work of Kurtz as well that he now claims he will pursue: "how Kurtz, equipped with moral ideas . . . would set about his work" (27) in the depths of Africa.

Marlow is thinking about the work of the man, but he has only heard the name. When he overhears the station manager and his uncle (having arriving at the Central Station as the leader of the Eldorado Exploring Expedition) discussing the man, annoyed by the man's ambition and behavior, plotting against him (a plot that Marlow remains unaware of at the time), Marlow seems to see Kurtz for the first time. It is not just the name but a visible representation of the man that now emerges from his imagination: "It was a distinct glimpse; the dugout, four paddling savages, and the lone white man turning his back suddenly on the headquarters, on relief, on thoughts of home—perhaps; setting his face towards the depths of the wilderness, towards his empty and desolate station. I did not know the motive. Perhaps he was just simply a fine fellow who stuck to his own work for its own sake" (28). If there is something of the dreams of boyhood adventure in this imagined image of Kurtz and something of the noble dream of work itself, we might question Marlow's ongoing naïveté. We do not know Kurtz's motives, and neither does Marlow. Is it the boyhood dream that still calls to Marlow? Or the nobility of work itself? Or perhaps it is "the depths of the wilderness" (28)? The growing fascination with Kurtz motivates Marlow. The representation of the man in Marlow's feverish imagination has gotten a hold on him. It is now a dream image of the man created through the language emanating from the lips of all those others that Marlow has heard. This is the Kurtz that Marlow is now focused on, a dream through which Marlow finds direction and purpose, one that seems to fill that empty restlessness of his previous meandering. We follow Marlow, as Marlow follows Kurtz, moving up "that river . . . traveling back to the earliest beginnings of the world" (30), to the inevitable encounter with Kurtz, Marlow's double, the one who will sanction his telling.

Marlow is repeating the journey from the Central Station to the Inner Station, repeating the journey that Kurtz made, as he works to keep the steamboat (repaired with love) from sinking. Others on the boat (the manager, the pilgrims with staves, and the black workers) are in pursuit of "ivory," the name circulating in the air, stirring their desire for the commodity that has become their fascination. For Marlow, though, there is only one single purpose now. For him, the steamboat "crawled towards Kurtz—exclusively" (31). As he moves closer to the Inner Station that "exclusively" takes on added fever. It is no longer the image of Kurtz or the mere name of Kurtz, which Marlow has heard from others that he is interested in; he is pursuing the Kurtz who dwells in the depths of "the heart of darkness," that prehistoric unearthly earth, the time before the unfolding of time, the beginning before the beginning, which Marlow desires to encounter. It is this kind of understanding that Marlow now seems headed toward, an impossible understanding that his soaring language attempts to convey to his listeners on the "Nellie":

"The prehistoric man was cursing us, praying to us, welcoming us—who could tell? . . . We could not understand because we were too far, could not remember because we were travelling in the night of first ages, of those ages that are gone, leaving hardly a sign—and no memories . . . The earth seemed unearthly" (32).

On the "Nellie," those (if any) who are listening to Marlow are disturbed by what they are hearing. Whether it is the racism creeping into his heated language or the racism of the listeners when Marlow suggests "the kinship" (32) of all men (English or African), or whether it is the edge of Marlow's tone when he implies that his own "true stuff" (32) stands up well against the civilized and secure success of his comrades on land, his friends seem to believe that he is ranting. To them Marlow is beyond the boundaries of acceptable discourse, roaring, like the primeval forest itself, forsaken, unhinged. They appeal to him to restrain himself, to continue with the adventure that can be spoken. Marlow does just that.

About eight miles (three hours) from Kurtz's Inner Station, Marlow and the others on the steamboat now unexpectedly hear through the fog a "tumultuous and mournful uproar" (35), shrieking, as if their ears are filled with the mourning of nature at the birth of time itself. Temporarily anchored, the steamboat beneath their feet is the only stability they have. Repaired by Marlow with love (or its illusion), that steamboat is their best hope now—"the rest of the world . . . gone, disappeared; swept off without leaving a whisper or a shadow behind" (36).

We assume that the "clamour and savage discord" (35) emanating from the edge of the world (and filling Marlow's ears), that mournful shrieking, is connected to what resonated with Marlow earlier in his telling, when he was ranting, claiming that he was committed to Kurtz "exclusively," the Kurtz whom he envisioned dwelling at the beginning of time, the singular voice at the edge of the mortal world. It is as if the material world was disappearing then on the river, only the steamboat remaining, buoyed by love (or its illusion), and, yes, perhaps, there is a trace of Kurtz as well, glimpsed in that dying of the world, that undefined mystery, a secret germ within the linguistic telling.

On the steamboat, the whites (Company agents) respond to the voices from the wilderness with fear and then with their Winchesters in hand ready to fire on what they assume to be the unrestrained and inhumane savages; the blacks on the boat, hungry cannibals (they still belong to the beginning of time) appear, by contrast, to possess an innate restraint, an "inborn strength" to resist "the deviltry of lingering starvation" (38). It is not the progress of Western Enlightenment, evolution through time, that makes us human, Marlow implies, but the acknowledgment that what might appear inhuman may be otherwise. As it turns out, that strange clamor out of the silence of the jungle is neither aggression nor defense, neither assertion nor withdrawal, but the voice of "unrestrained grief" (39). It is an articulation against inevitable loss, a mournful call, we might anticipate, for a response grounded in an "infinite pity" (71).

Unrestrained grief can evoke the depths of pity, but that was not what Marlow thought about in the jungle. Focused on what happened then, not what he might understand now on the "Nellie," he next tells us, ". . . even extreme grief may ultimately vent itself in violence . . ." (39). About a mile and a half below Kurtz's station, in a narrow passage, the "savages," vulnerable as they are, stiffen and attack, the flow of grief turning into "sticks" then "arrows," finally "the shaft of a big spear" (42), its rigidity caught in the side of Marlow's helmsman.

In turn, the helmsman's death does evoke grief, a personal grief from Marlow as profound as the inexplicable wailing from the jungle itself: ". . . he died without uttering a sound, without moving a limb, without twitching a muscle" (42). Within that silence, the helmsman's final glance up at Marlow, his face looking at his, doubles back on Marlow, reflecting for us now Marlow's own grief, his own profound sense of pity and compassion for the man. Marlow will not forget that moment; it remains a strange whisper just beyond the threshold of mortal life.

On the river, "the mortal shock" (42) of the death of the helmsman stiffened Marlow, unhinging him temporarily from his purpose. That death seems to resonate with other deaths as well, and it is not surprising that Marlow also imagined then that Kurtz, too, must be dead: "I suppose Kurtz, too, is dead as well . . ." (42). Not thinking about the Kurtz that served the Company through his work, "the remarkable agent accumulating ivory" (what Kurtz was), but the singular Kurtz (who he was), Marlow was then thinking about "the gift of expression, the bewildering, the illuminating, the most exalting and the most contemptible, the pulsating stream of light, or the deceitful flow from the heart of an impenetrable darkness" (43).

Telling all this, Marlow sounds again like "the savages in the bush," howling sorrow, disrupted and forsaken, "cut to the quick" (43) with profound grief. The men on the "Nellie" have no pity for him, though, responding to his ranting as they have before, not with empathy but with warning, advising restraint to prevent such absurd explosions from happening again in the narrative. Marlow modulates his tone, although he remains clearly shaken by the reminder of the death of the helmsman and Kurtz. Unlike the others, Marlow does not seem well-anchored on the "Nellie." We might imagine that he could disappear. As readers, we are with him, not quite anchored ourselves.

On edge, Marlow now appears to hear another voice—or is it an image that he envisions (we are uncertain): "Voices, voices—even the girl herself—now—" (44). It is a disturbing voice (or image), one that Marlow wants to bracket as soon as it slips out, as if he doesn't want to displace the purpose of his telling, his journey for Kurtz, onto this unnamed girl. If he wants to forget that other voice, though, withdraw from its call, keep it away from us as well, it is, nevertheless, an indication that this "girl" is implicated in his desire to give an account of himself. It cannot be mere coincidence now that we hear, for the first time, Marlow repeat words spoken by Kurtz: "You should have heard the disinterred body of Kurtz saying 'My Intended'; you would have perceived directly then how completely she was out of it" (44).

It is as if he is evoking the ghost of Kurtz in order to bury "the girl." He will not tell us about the Intended, but return us to Kurtz, the one who experienced a "particular region of the first ages in utter solitude" (44), in the "utter silence" that makes "All the great difference" (45). It is the unique and singular Kurtz, the man who journeyed into "the great difference," that we need to pay attention to, not "the girl," but the Kurtz that Marlow encountered. At least, that is Marlow's claim right now.

If "the girl" has temporarily disturbed Marlow, shaking the assumed attention of his narrative, he now seems to insist on accounting for Kurtz, and Kurtz alone. Marlow has not yet arrived at the Inner Station; he has not yet offered us a full unfolding of the adventure that he has experienced. But he wants to account for Kurtz now, and so he offers a premature summing up of the man. Why? We might suspect that he is also accounting to himself for something else—perhaps "the girl" that he does not want to talk about. He will resurrect the ghost of Kurtz, but keep the girl buried.

Marlow tells us about the "original Kurtz"—"all Europe contributed to the making of Kurtz," he says, emphasizing Kurt's writing, especially his beautifully written report to the International Society for the Suppression of Savage Customs, a report written before Kurtz himself presided "at certain midnight dances, ending with unspeakable rites" (apparently "unspeakable rites" conducted in Kurtz's honor). Only in the postscript to that report does Kurtz seem to lose restraint: "Exterminate all the brutes!" (46).

Kurtz is clearly driven, a drive to be reckoned with. He has had a significant effect on those who have met him and, by reputation and name, those who have heard about him. Marlow is fascinated by this force. For some, Kurtz is an idol. Like "ivory," he is worshipped with "unspeakable rites" (46). Marlow cannot forget Kurtz, and he wants us to remember him as well. But he also wants us to witness the effect Kurtz has had on him. It is not that Kurtz's life was worth more than the others (the helmsman's, for example), but that he was not "common," he could charm and fascinate others, fill our ears—but with what?—perhaps the dream sensation, the sense of difference, the singularity at the edge of our own linguistic being.

Arriving at the border of the Inner Station, Marlow sees through his binoculars "a white man under a hat like a cart wheel" (48). He appears like "a harlequin" (48), reminding us again of the farce within the rhythmic telling, the improbable and bewildering dimension of this adventure within the haze and depth of the linguistic atmosphere. If "the harlequin" appears absurd, though, he has also been exposed to grave danger, to the drive of Kurtz endlessly talking. The harlequin has encountered Kurtz close-up, nursed Kurtz, become fascinated by him. Uncritical and loyal to Kurtz, he has given himself up to the destiny of Kurtz without question. If he is a clown, he is also a true believer. He claims that Kurtz has enlarged his mind (at least filled his ears), but we might suspect there was a hollowness in him from the start. Perhaps there was a lack in Kurtz as well, a hollowness at the core that set his unrestrained lust into motion, enabling the circuitry of irresistible fascination to emerge.

Through Marlow's binoculars, we, as readers, finally glimpse Kurtz himself, his body at a distance appearing as an apparition, "an animated image of death carved out of old ivory" (55). If the visual of Kurtz at a distance connects him with death and ivory, though, close-up Kurtz remains very human. Face-to-face on the steamboat, Kurtz greets Marlow with a surprisingly pleasant tone: "I am glad" (55), he says, apparently having anticipated Marlow's arrival and pleased that Marlow has come to be with him, someone he can trust, someone who arrives, unlike the manager, specially recommended. Then Kurtz's mistress appears, the embodiment of Kurtz's own fascination, adorned with the "fecund and mysterious life" (56) that seems to inhabit her, the "tenebrous and passionate soul" (56), inside and out, silent in "her inexplicable grief and savage sorrow" (56). She is a palpable vision, disappearing back into "the colossal body" (56) of the land itself, the original place of her beginning and her end.

On the steamboat, behind the curtain, we hear the voice of Kurtz again, speaking to the manager. He is clearly very ill, needs to be taken back, withdrawn from the wilderness. "Save me! Save the ivory you mean. Don't tell me. Save me! Why I've had to save you" (56), Kurtz shouts at the manager. For the first time Marlow realizes that the manager has been plotting to remove Kurtz. If Kurtz is "mad," the manager is vile, a "flabby devil" of deception. If Kurtz lacks restraint and judgment, the manager is a product of bureaucratic method. If Kurtz is a dream turned nightmare, a nightmare of "unspeakable secrets" (57), the manager is a nightmare of lies and deceptions, the vile sentence of profane judgment. Unsound as he is at the moment, Marlow inevitably turns not to the manager but to Kurtz for relief: Not to Kurtz's body, though, "as good as buried," but to the singular Kurtz, the one who has experienced "the unseen presence of victorious corruption" (57), the one who has, Marlow must believe, glimpsed who he is. Marlow is seeking what we all seek, what we all dread, the fascination of what we cannot know, what we step back from if we are to continue to live.

Marlow seems fascinated by Kurtz, but he does not idolize Kurtz. Unlike the harlequin, who has stuffed himself with Kurtz, Marlow's solitude in the wilderness is his, and his alone. If Marlow wants to know what Kurtz has experienced, he is nevertheless different than Kurtz. In a sense, it is the wilderness, not Kurtz, that Marlow has chosen: "I had turned to the wilderness, not to Mr. Kurtz . . ." (57). It is as if Marlow is mapping his journey into the wilderness onto the journey of Kurtz, just as we are mapping our journey into the wilderness onto Marlow's. This is what Marlow's linguistic telling is now enacting. It will bring us to the threshold of Kurtz's experience as Marlow has experienced it, but no further. Experiencing Kurtz through Marlow's desirous telling, we, as readers, like Marlow before us, will be allowed to step back.

It is true that Marlow has chosen this nightmare, the nightmare of Kurtz, but that is not the whole truth, either. We do not choose our nightmares anymore (or any less) than they choose us. Nor do we choose our destiny anymore than it chooses us. We might suspect that this is what Marlow is thinking now: "I did not betray Mr. Kurtz—it was ordered I should never betray him—it was written I should be loyal to the nightmare of my choice" (59). A strange disruption in the story, we need to wonder about it.

We have assumed so far that Marlow committed himself to Kurtz "exclusively" back in the Central Station, acknowledging the purpose and direction of his quest at that time. Is he now simply reaffirming that commitment, asking us, his listeners, to trust his commitment? Is he saying that the hand of destiny had so written, and he chose to remain loyal to it, paying whatever price that commitment demanded? If so, Marlow deserves our respect; his achievement is marked with its own singularity: Marlow becoming one with his destiny, a destiny that shapes him as he shapes it—a way of discovering who he is.

The statement is striking: "It was ordered I should never betray him . . . it was written—loyal to the nightmare of my choice" (59). The language and the rhythm echoes with Biblical overtones, allusions to Greek fate, resonating with a sense of high ideals and heroic possibilities, even if those possibilities will end at a great cost. Yet we wonder: precisely who has done this ordering, who has done this writing, where is it written? We cannot help but recall the two women guarding the door of the inner office of the Company in Brussels—those mysterious figures knitting the destiny of the Company's pilgrims following the fragile thread of their journey into the future—and Marlow's uneasiness signing that contract, his sense of something "ominous in the atmosphere" (8) even then, some conspiracy that he had been let into, had become complicit with: "Morituri te salutant" (8).

Marlow has mentioned a number of times that he will not reveal any "trade secrets"—the first time being when he was telling us about signing the contract in Brussels: "I believe I undertook amongst other things not to disclose any trade secrets. Well, I am not going to" (8)—and it is not unreasonable to suspect that he is now not only struggling with the meaning of his commitment to Kurtz but with his commitment to the Company. Is it possible that the contract he agreed to in Brussels, the written document signed with his name, the one that has led him to where he is now, that ordered him to find Kurtz, ordered him not to betray Kurtz as well? Is it written that he should remain loyal not only to Kurtz but to the Company? Does his statement here suggest that Marlow has again, now in his linguistic telling, "gone near enough to a lie" (23)? Is his destiny not only complicit with Kurtz's but with the Company's as well?

We only know Marlow through his linguistic telling, its rich and ambiguous texture, what it reveals and conceals, and we might suspect that his "nightmare of choice," his obsessive pursuit of Kurtz also includes his contractual obligation to the Company—certainly his promise not to reveal "trade secrets." In this context, we are not surprised when Marlow, finding Kurtz "crawling on all fours" (59) at the edge of the jungle, actually tells us: "the knitting woman with the cat obtruded herself upon my memory as a most improper person to be sitting at the other end of such an affair" (59–60). That "improper" image of a woman knitting apparently haunted Marlow in the jungle, and it seems to haunt him now on the "Nellie" as he continues to tell his story. It is as if the end is in the beginning, and that beginning seems, at least for the moment, located in the Company's office. Were both his journey and Kurtz's contaminated from the start? Is his narrative coming close to a "near lie" now?

Crawling at the edge of the wilderness, Kurtz is "lost . . . utterly lost" (60). He has "kicked himself loose of the earth" (61), degenerated, mad, both body and soul, sick to death. Yet Marlow responds to that vulnerability, to the final struggle of Kurtz, his ultimate reckoning. Acknowledging that Kurtz is lost, Marlow seems to respond to a call, Kurtz's humanity face-to-face. If Marlow is still fascinated by Kurtz, he now also feels an "intimacy" with Kurtz, a shared vulnerability, a need to comfort the man even with a near lie: "Your success in Europe is assured in any case" (61). If the telling has suggested that Marlow was somewhat like a son in pursuit of a father, Marlow now supports Kurtz, carrying him—"his bony arm clasped round my neck" (61). He is alone with Kurtz at the edge of the wilderness, partners in the party of "unsound methods" (63)—no methods really, beyond the common and everyday exchanges of conventional existence, beyond the boundaries of "noxious fools" (like the manager and his accomplice, the brickmaker), bureaucrats who "number" (63) both Marlow and Kurtz with the dead.

At the edge of the universe, Marlow listens to the voice of Kurtz, fulfilling the ethical demand to listen to the other before him: "the original Kurtz" and "the hollow sham," the ambiguous and complex mortal Kurtz, the one who experienced "the invisible wilderness," "the impenetrable darkness" (63) that Marlow cannot know, but perhaps glimpse, as we, too, glimpse it through the haze, the dream sensation of Marlow's linguistic telling. As readers, we recall that Marlow has been telling us his story, not Kurtz's, that he has been mapping his journey onto Kurtz's. If Kurtz's story inhabits Marlow, it is Marlow's story that inhabits us. It is not the name, nor the man in the name, that binds us all together, that calls to us through the telling to respond; it is rather the sense of intimacy, "the infinite pity" created by the profound sense of "utter loss," the undefined desire overflowing through the linguistic narrative that binds us, one to the other, demanding that we pay attention.

Lying on his death bed, the shutter in the pilot house closed to the "invisible wilderness" (63), Kurtz moves through the final moments of his life, the culmination of what he has been. "I am lying here in the dark waiting for death" (64), he tells Marlow standing before him. Marlow is intrigued by the horrifying changes on Kurtz's face. It is as if Kurtz's whole life flashes before him in the instant, arriving at "that supreme moment of complete knowledge" (64): a dream, as Marlow experiences it, caught in the wonder of his own dream sensation. "Did he live his life again in every detail of desire, temptation, and surrender during that supreme moment of complete knowledge?" (64), Marlow wonders, questioning us as much as he is questioning himself. His telling putting both him and us into question.

Then we hear those final words from Kurtz through Marlow's telling, words echoing now for well over a century, "a cry that was no more than a breath" (64)—and no less than a breath—an enigmatic whisper, a summing up: "The horror! The horror" (64).

"Mistah Kurtz—he dead" (64).

It is impossible to know what Kurtz meant just as it is impossible to know what Marlow experienced at that moment. We can only speak about its after-effects, the way the riddle repeats itself, Marlow's subsequent wrestling with it, the way it haunts him, the way it continues to haunt us: "The most you can hope from it is some knowledge of yourself—that comes too late—a crop of unextinguishable regrets" (65).

Kurtz is Marlow's "nightmare of choice," but Marlow is different than Kurtz. Unlike Kurtz, Marlow has not crossed over the edge: "True . . . he had stepped over the edge, while I had been permitted to draw back my hesitating foot. Perhaps in this is the whole difference" (65).

Haunted by his experience of Kurtz, and his contractual obligation to the Company, Marlow now finds himself "back in the sepulchral city" (65), resenting the ordinary and the unimaginative jabbering of the managers and other agents of daily existence. When a bureaucratic representative of the Company appears, insisting that Marlow hand over documents that Kurtz had given him, Marlow offers the agent Kurtz's report on the "Suppression of Savage Customs." He tears off the postscript— "Exterminate the brutes" (46), though, preserving Kurtz's reputation, and keeps Kurtz's private letters, justifying his action by claiming to the agent that such writing "did not bear upon the problems of commerce or administration" (66). If it is another "near lie," it seems, nevertheless, to satisfy Marlow's contractual obligation and, at the same time, to allow him to remain loyal to Kurtz.

But what about "the girl" whom Marlow has refused to tell us about? If Marlow knows why he finally goes to visit Kurtz's Intended, he will not tell us: "I don't know . . . I can't tell. But I went" (67). The thought of "the girl" makes him stammer, but he did go see her, and he needs to make it part of his account now. We recall that "the Intended" were the first words from the ghost of Kurtz that Marlow repeated earlier in his linguistic narrative: "You should have heard the disinterred body of Kurtz saying 'My Intended'" (44). That "girl" has haunted Marlow from the start of his account of his story, and he cannot now complete his story without her.

Marlow speculates that the Intended may be a primary cause of Kurtz's journey in the first place: "I had heard that her engagement with Kurtz had been disapproved by her people. He wasn't rich enough or something . . . He had given me some reason to infer that it was his impatience of comparative poverty that drove him out there" (70). Was it love that originally motivated Kurtz? A desire for "the girl" that got displaced into a desire for ivory? We can only guess. But the Intended lurks further back than the administrative start of Kurtz's journey, further back than his contract with the Company, and Marlow needs to evoke the Intended through his telling on the "Nellie" now. In this sense, she is the beginning that Marlow has saved for the end, the subject and predicate of Kurtz's unfulfilled desire. It is a desire that Marlow hopes to satisfy through his meeting with her and his telling about it now.

When Marlow crosses the threshold of the Intended's house, a vision of Kurtz haunts him, memories and imaginings from the wilderness, and he again hears "the whispered cry, The horror! The horror" (68). It is as if the death of Kurtz mingles with the sorrow of the Intended. "I saw her and him in the same instant of time—his death and her sorrow—I saw her sorrow in the very moment of his death," Marlow claims. "Do you understand?" (69), he then asks, straining, if not demanding, that we pay attention, be self-reflective, question ourselves. Within the intricacies and ambiguities of the rhythm of the linguistic narrative, it is as if Kurtz's death has evoked the Intended's sorrow but the Intended's sorrow has evoked Kurtz's death as well. They are joined together, and Marlow needs to address both of them.

Just as he was fascinated by Kurtz, Marlow is fascinated with Kurtz's Intended. He speaks about his shared intimacy with Kurtz, thinking (we imagine) about the "utter loss" of the man, their shared vulnerability, the sorrow and grief of others, too, even Kurtz's African mistress (the Intended's double), certainly the Intended herself, face-to-face with him.

"Intimacy grows quickly out there," Marlow tells her. "I knew him as well as it is possible for one man to know another" (69). The Intended's response seems egotistical, at first—"I knew him best" (69)—desiring confirmation of what she believes: Kurtz's eloquence, his life as an exemplum of goodness, of light, his need for her, her undying belief in him. "He needed me! Me!" But she is also in the throes of sorrow, desperate in her longing "for something—something-to-live with" (69), something to keep her on this side of the threshold of human existence, to keep her in this world. We sense that she, too, is hesitating at the limits of utter loss.

It is a difficult, if not impossible, moment that Marlow now finds himself in. Listening to the Intended, her illusions, her egotism, Marlow grows angry, but that anger subsides "before a feeling of infinite pity" (71). It is an unrestrained pity, transgressing the ordinary limits, overflowing the finite boundaries of proper behavior, the acceptable limits of conventional emotion. If it is not the wailing grief of an African Mistress in the wilderness, it is a subdued double for it, just as Kurtz's unrestrained behavior seems to double back now on Marlow driven by this "infinite pity" permeating the Intended's home. Has Marlow returned to Kurtz's first desire, we might ask, an unfulfilled desire for intimacy and caring? Can Marlow fulfill the promise that Kurtz intended?

Marlow could withdraw at this moment, do what he has done before. He could say nothing more to the Intended, make no further response. Responding to the sorrow and grief of the Intended, though, Marlow now shakily blurts out: "I heard his very last words" (71). Then he stops, frightened by what "infinite pity" is driving him toward. He has created a dilemma for himself. To stay loyal to Kurtz, he must say what Kurtz has said (and continues to whisper): "The horror! The horror" (71). But it is as if these words of utter loss cannot be spoken to the call of sorrow, to the face demanding "infinite pity." This, too, seems the difference between him and Kurtz now. Pulling himself together, Marlow offers the Intended what might be called a gift of promise, a possibility for the future, life not death: "The last word he pronounced was—your name" (71). It is a linguistic gift and an outright deception, not a "near lie," but an explicit lie, a fiction. It is a lie born from a shared vulnerability, though, the taint of mortal existence, spoken as if "real life" itself is a dream.

If Marlow has not done justice to Kurtz in his dialogue with the Intended, he has nevertheless kept her alive. Has he betrayed Kurtz in the process? Perhaps at the time that it happened, but not now. He has told Kurtz's story to those listening on the "Nellie" (and to us), acknowledging not only "the horror" of the remarkable Kurtz, the nightmare of Kurtz as Marlow experienced it, but he has also accounted for his lie to the

Intended, the dream that allows her a life. If that life is a comfortable illusion, even a hollow deception, it is not for us to judge, but to question. It is no less "real" than the "nightmare of choice" that Marlow has also told us about. Dream and nightmare make up our life, hesitating on the threshold of the experience that we cannot speak, the threshold of what we cannot know.

Marlow has offered an account of himself through his telling (a telling told through a frame-narrator we have all but forgotten). If we have met the ethical demand to listen to him, experiencing his experience as it unfolded through the rhythm of that linguistic telling, its revealing and concealing, its overflowing desire, its sense of utter loss, we might yet glimpse the glow through the haze of that telling, the truth of our life as it stretches to the horizon, the threshold that leads "into the heart of an immense darkness" (72), the unspeakable and unknown knowledge that we cannot know until it is too late. If we have taken that journey with Marlow, we need not yet step over that edge into the unspeakable, but draw our own hesitating foot back into the dreams and nightmares, the ambiguous and complex mortal world that we have experienced through the rich texture of language. In this, we might locate our own ongoing journey that defines us, each in our own way. "And perhaps in this is the whole difference" (65).

6

The Old Man and the Sea

In conventional terms, the narrator of *The Old Man and the Sea* would be considered "third-person," an omniscient observer telling a story that appears to have the shape of a classical parable. There is much truth in that conventional identification, but in the postmodern world, we cannot easily embrace such a notion without acknowledging its problematic assumptions, especially as those assumptions relate to the always thorny relationship between author and narrator and the slippery nature of linguistic narrative itself, especially its connection to human desire. We might assume, for example, as Ben Stoltzfus does, that the Old Man, Santiago, is a "veiled metaphor of Hemingway's own desire" (Stoltzfus 196), a reasonable assumption that suggests not that we need to investigate Hemingway's biography, but that we might legitimately experience the novel as if it is primarily Santiago's story: that is, his "real life" experience shaped by the telling of the narrative as it unfolds. We experience the narrative, in other words, as the narrator's desire to articulate for us, the readers, the meaning of Santiago's journey and his life.

To put it in different terms, we approach the narrative language as if it is a taut line. As readers, we are the fisherman wrestling with a huge fish, struggling with, and hoping to embrace, a noble and wondrous marlin. That taut style of the language creates an elegant simplicity that pulls us forward into the vital tension of the adventure. The narrative demands that we follow Santiago. Caught by the narrative, we cannot do otherwise. We will follow the line of this linguistic narrative, as it pulls us into the depth of ourselves.

From the start, we learn that Santiago has been fishing for 84 days in a small skiff "without taking a fish" (9). A boy (later named Manolin) had joined the Old Man for the first 40 days, but his parents had ordered him off the skiff because the Old Man was "salao"—"the worst form of unlucky" (9). Even the sail of Santiago's skiff looks "like the flag of permanent defeat" (9).

The boy is always "sad" when he sees the Old Man alone, coming in each day with his skiff "empty" (9). But we will be reminded later in the narrative that "a man can be destroyed but not defeated" (103). If Santiago seems defeated and "unlucky" to others, we, as readers, might wonder right from the start if we are seeing only the tip of the iceberg (as Hemingway would put it). Despite the "sad" situation, Santiago continues to go out each day. His endurance seems almost heroic. If he appears unlucky to others, his eyes are "cheerful and undefeated" (10).

The boy loves the old man. As the narrative indicates, he believes in the Old Man, reminding him that in previous times, the Old Man's endurance has prevailed: "But remember how you went eighty-seven days without fish and then we caught big ones every day for three weeks" (10). If the others don't have "much faith" (10), Santiago and Manolin apparently are believers in what cannot immediately be seen. Like us, they are fishermen, connected to each other by faith and good works, serving one another through shared experience and shared memory. "I remember everything from when we first went together," the boy tells the Old Man, rejuvenating "his hope and his confidence" (13), his humility and his "true pride" (14).

Santiago is an experienced and disciplined fisherman who knows well the craft and rituals of his devotion and destiny. As a fisherman in the Cuban village, he might seem similar to the others, but he is also different from them. "I am a strange old man" (14), he admits. It is that difference, that strangeness, his drive for singularity that we need to consider as the narrative begins to unfold.

The boy helps the Old Man when he can, and the Old Man helps the boy. They share work together and are aware of "the fictions" that they also share, the rituals between them that go deeper than the material goods that might or might not be seen: "There was no cast net and the boy remembered when they had sold it. But they went through this fiction every day" (16). Each day is a new day, bound together by this natural piety.

Belief and resolution—faith in the Yankees and Dimaggio, for example, rather than fear of others such as the Tigers, or the Indians, or the Reds, or the White Sox (17)—create confidence and inspire the determination to discover the individual self, the uniqueness of your destiny, what makes you who you are. It is now September "when the great fish come" (18), when champions are challenged and determined, when Santiago and Dimaggio, each in their own way, can make the difference. As the boy indicates to the Old Man: "There are many good fishermen and some great ones. But there is only you" (23). That "only you" is each of us, the readers, as well.

At first, we might find it ironic that a large part of what makes Santiago "strange" (18) is his deeply felt rootedness in the natural world. Scarred and beaten, his body will eventually be destroyed by the rhythm of mortality. Even now, his eyes are closed; there is "no life in his face" (19). But yet when he dreams of Africa (24), his senses come alive. He hears the surf roar. He sees the native boats riding through it. He smells the tar and oakum of the deck and the land breeze brought on at morning. He senses the lions playing along the beach.

Such embodied experience remains invisible to most others. Manolin envisions it, though, through his belief in Santiago, and, as readers, we know it, too, through the language that allows us a glimpse of the interiority of the Old Man as his journey begins to unfold through the narrative that we are hooked into. Like the Old Man, or like the boy gently awakened by the Old Man even before the sun rises, we, as readers, move with this invisible and strange knowledge through the darkness, anticipating the battle ahead in the harsh light of the new day. As the boy says, "It is what a man must do" (26). It will not be "the smell of the land" (25) but "the smell of the ocean" (28) that drives the fisherman (and us) on.

The relationship between the fisherman and "the smell of the ocean" (28) is similar to the relationship between the reader and the rhythm of this literary narrative, or, we might say, the relationship between Santiago and "la mar": what people call the sea in Spanish when they love her (29). When we journey with this strange and singular fisherman from the land to the sea, far out beyond where other boats dare to go, we, as readers, are attempting, then, to glimpse the inexplicable mystery of mortal life itself, the invisible rhythm of love and death exemplified by Santiago alone in the natural world. Like Santiago, we are in pursuit of that "you" which is no other, that "I," the teller of our own story, the secret of that dimension of mortal identity that can never be fully articulated and never fully known until the journey ends.

According to the narrative, "Every day is a new day" (32), and if you are, like Santiago, a believer it might be a lucky day, but you have no control over such possibility. You can be "exact" and disciplined, prepared and practiced in your craft, but you might still be unlucky, "salao" (9), the worst form of unlucky. When you journey "far out" (41)—or in deep—then you will inevitably encounter what you cannot prepare for, the unexpected and contingent experience that shapes you; and because you cannot shape it, it will destroy you. But it will not defeat you unless you allow it to.

"There is only you" (22), the boy has explained. As Santiago has explained to the boy, if you have faith, not fear, even if you are destroyed, you will not be defeated. Each in our own way, each with our own story, we, too, are in pursuit of this truth. In such pursuit, we are at risk, but the narrative demands that we hook on to it, struggle with it, as it unfolds, acknowledge its singularity. It is Santiago's journey, and it is ours as well. As we move out into the ocean with Santiago alone on his skiff without the boy, we acknowledge how significant it is to go out alone, to be responsible for yourself by yourself, without a companion to help, to talk with, to relieve loneliness or anxiety. It is necessary to make this quest alone in order to know who you are as an individual, what you are capable of in your singularity, your uniqueness in the natural world.

As readers, we experience the natural world as a diverse place of abundance, a place where we sense, as the Old Man does, a hallowed resonance, an indwelling. The turtle whose heart is very much like ours, the birds helping us to spot tuna for bait, they all seem familiar with, respectful of each other. They are connected by cosmic design, but each has its own wondrous and singular purpose. We experience this as Santiago does.

There is dignity in the quest for individuality and a necessity to make such a quest alone. But Santiago also desires a companion, often wishes that the boy was with him. He is a social being, unique and communal, mortal and linguistic, even in the midst of the ocean. He recalls clearly how he "talked at night" (39) on the ocean with the boy "when they were storm-bound by bad weather" (39), and now he says "his thoughts aloud many times" (39), talking out loud to himself, remembering that he is a complex human being in a natural world similar to but also different than the other creatures around him. He has left the land (and his village), but he must return to that community before his journey is complete.

As readers, we might now wonder what precisely Santiago is seeking in pursuit of "the big one" (40). No doubt he wants to fulfill his destiny as a fisherman, to live out to its mortal limits "that which I was born for" (40). He wants to know himself, his individual self, that which makes him "only you" (22) and no one else. If we are readers of Hemingway, we know this solitary journey is similar to that of others, the leopard, for example, now frozen, in pursuit of something unknown in the "high snow mountains" (40), a place like Kilimanjaro where the writer Harry goes but only in his final dream. But Santiago wants more than this, more than the frozen leopard forever unseen atop Kilimanjaro, more than the knowledge that Harry glimpses alone in fantasy just before he dies. Such moments remain unacknowledged by others in the mortal world. Santiago needs to hook a great marlin far out in the ocean, but he also needs to make the journey back to land, if possible. He wants to bring his dream back to the others in the village, if he can. He wants them to acknowledge what a man can do.

"Today is eighty-five days, and I should fish the day well" (41). It is the same day that the Yankees are playing in the pennant race. If the Yankees are led by Dimaggio at the ball field, Santiago will lead us. If Dimaggio refuses to yield to the pain emanating from his bone spurs this day, Santiago will not yield to his pain, either. Dimaggio is driven on by belief in himself and in his fisherman-like craft that others (especially the next generation) have come to witness. He works for himself and for others, and Santiago will try to do the same, although he will do it differently. It is the eighty-fifth day, the day that Santiago hooks the great marlin. It is a day of destiny.

When Santiago hooks the big fish on this day, the marlin tows the Old Man struggling alone in his skiff "far out" (41). The two of them are now connected to the taut line just as we, as readers, are connected to the taut language of the narrative pulling us in deep, improvising as we go, moved and moving with the experience of the struggle. With Santiago, we have not yet seen the big fish, but we know it is "unbelievably heavy," of "great weight" (43). Like Santiago, we wish we could see the fish, at least once, so that we, too, will know what we have against us.

We cannot see the fish, but we sense that the fish is "wonderful" and "strange" (48)—like Santiago himself—and that the Old Man wishes that the boy was with him, not only to help him, but also to experience this miracle unfolding, to witness what a fisherman can do, what a man can endure. As readers, we are "joined together" with the narrative, just as Santiago is "joined together" with the fish in battle and in sympathy, questing out "beyond all people in the world" (50).

We feel the vital tension now emerging through the taut line of the language, the sense that we are experiencing a classic struggle between life and death. Its singular and unique nature pulls at us "beyond all people in the world" (50). We understand that Santiago might die. Lovingly he has declared aloud: "Fish, I'll stay with you until I die" (50). But we might remind ourselves now that, although the Old Man's story is ours as well, we do not have to die, even if the Old Man does. When the narrative ends, we can return to "real life," mindful of what the Old Man has accomplished and endured.

The fish might kill the man. But the man, who loves and respects the fish, hopes he will kill the fish instead. His hands cramped and bleeding, he remains respectful and determined: "I wish I could feed the fish he thought. He is my brother. But I must kill him and keep strong to do it" (59).

As a fisherman, Santiago has caught two big fish before this encounter, fish weighing more than a thousand pounds. But he has never before caught a fish this big while he was alone. When the great marlin finally comes up above the surface of the ocean, though, we see that it is "the biggest fish that he had ever seen and bigger than he had ever heard of . . ." (63). It is a worthy opponent, a true test of his character, a significant marker of his chosen destiny.

Seeing the great fish, Santiago is determined once again to show "what a man can do and what a man endures" (66). He has told the boy that he is "a strange old man" (66), and he has proven it many times. But each time is a new time, a unique time, a strange time, and he must prove it again this time. It is his strangeness, his unique individuality, the singularity of his human identity that he seeks, just as we do.

The fish is "strange," and the Old Man is "strange." Joined together by the taut line, they both journey out to discover their own destiny. Each one has chosen this journey just as each one of us has chosen it. The fish has chosen "to stay in the deep water far out beyond all snares and traps and treacheries" (50). Santiago has chosen "to go there to find him beyond all people" (50). Hooked by the narrative, we, too, have chosen to stay in the deep water, to discover what we can beyond all others, to pull and be pulled by the strange undulations of the taut line of language that allows us to make Santiago's experience our own. If Santiago's story is our story, we are close to the threshold, the edge of the mortal world.

To rejuvenate his confidence, Santiago again evokes "the great Dimaggio who does all things perfectly even with the pain of the bone spur in his heel" (68). Dimaggio's grace, his endurance despite the pain and suffering, his resolution and determination to continue on, not only for himself but as an exemplum for others, serves as inspiration for Santiago now, just as Santiago's narrative offers inspiration for us. Yet, despite the strength that emerges with such confidence, the rejuvenated breath of life that comes from such inspiration, we acknowledge that there is much that we cannot control and much that cannot easily be known unless experienced. Santiago indicates as much. He does not really know if Dimaggio could stay with the fish, given his bone spurs:

> "But would the bone spur hurt him too much?
>
> 'I do not know', he said aloud. 'I never had a bone spur'." (68)

And Santiago now realizes as well that he has no control of the sharks, the natural predators that threaten significant loss. "If sharks come, God pity him and me" (68), Santiago declares, referring to the fish as well as himself, their mutual destruction.

Santiago wants to win, but he does not want to humiliate his brother, the worthy opponent tugging on his line. He cannot yield to the full embrace of his brother because he would, in effect, lose his individuality, his strange difference, become one with the fish, the same, drown in the ocean. Like Jacob wrestling with an angel, Santiago wrestles with the fish, embracing him, but not yielding to him, determined to discover his singularity, the difference that makes him the unique person that he alone is.

Hooked to the fish through the taut line, Santiago knows that the journey far out (or in deep), the journey that takes him to the extreme limits of the mortal self, to the boundary of life and death, as dangerous as it is, is not enough to gain the full flourishing of the self. He needs to reel in the marlin, and, if possible, preserve the integrity of the fish. For him, the threat of the uncontrollable sharks looms large and undetermined. He must return to the land from this far out border as well.

Within the rhythmic depth of the narrative, we are not surprised that Santiago now recalls "the time in the tavern at Casablanca when he had played the hand game with the great negro from Cienfuegos who was the strongest man on the docks" (69). The arm-wrestling battle had gone on one day and one night that time, and Santiago had at the end "unleashed his effort and forced the hand of the negro down and down until it rested on the wood" (70). Everyone had called him the champion, then, and the memory now furthers Santiago's confidence as he battles the fish. But the memory of this youthful match against "the great negro" also evokes in Santiago a silent meditation on human vulnerability and humiliation. As a result of Santiago's victory, "the great negro" had lost all confidence in himself, flattening him out, reducing him to something far less than a worthy opponent, far less than a man with dignity and purpose. "The great negro" had become much like Santiago's own left-hand, "a traitor" who could not do what he was called on to do (70). Vulnerable and humiliated, he could not be trusted. He was not only destroyed but defeated.

Santiago seems now not only concerned with beating the fish but with his motives for going out to the radical limit (beyond where any other person has gone). Is he engaged in an act of hubris, pride that will not only destroy his brother but also defeat him, rob him of his own dignity, humiliate him? Can Santiago gain knowledge of his unique individuality, his singularity as a fisherman, become a champion, and at the same time preserve the dignity of his opponent, the other whom he loves, his friend who helps make his singularity, his difference, possible? Santiago seems to be wrestling with such questions, and we are wrestling with them as well.

Santiago empathizes with the marlin, but he is not the marlin. He feels sorrow for the marlin, but he is determined to kill him. He can prepare for the sharks, but he cannot control their attack. He is a man, ambivalent and complex, battling inevitable mortal contradictions, in pursuit of his destiny. That destiny will inevitably destroy him, but he might yet remain undefeated.

The Old Man is a mortal human being, not a god, and he knows that his responsibility is to what a man can do within the limitations of his existential condition. There are mysteries in the world that he cannot understand and contingencies that he cannot control:

"'I do not understand these things', he thought. 'But it is good that we do not have to try to kill the sun or the moon or the stars. It is enough to live on the sea and kill our true brothers'" (75).

Not pride but resolution drives Santiago on as he moves toward the third day of his momentous struggle with the fish, the big one connected to him by the taut line. Santiago is not battling with the sun or the moon, but within the mortal limits of humility; he battles with his "true brother." He has no desire to tear down (or transform) the cosmic design that he deeply respects and feels lucky to be a part of. But he is determined not to die until he has earned that peace that comes only at the end of all battles.

Aroused by the sudden jerk of the line, Santiago now focuses his attention on what he has been waiting for, the fish jumping and pulling, as the taut line of the language also moves deeper into the undulation and rhythm of Santiago's own interiority. "If the boy was here, he would wet the coils of line, he thought. Yes. If the boy was here. If the boy were here" (83). The boy is not "here" to help Santiago, but he is "here" in the narrative as we, the readers, are "here," witnessing what Santiago is experiencing. It is as if the fish and the narrative both begin to circle back and forth, struggling to keep stability. With Santiago, we, too, now work with "the pressure of the line,' allowing it to come in just as it reaches "the point where it would break" (86).

As the marlin circles closer and closer to the skiff, Santiago, faint and dizzy, nearly becomes unhinged. He battles to keep his head clear. He shares in the suffering of the fish, again acknowledging its beauty and its dignity, but also reconfirming that this struggle between life and death cannot end in a draw: "That way nothing is accomplished" (92). One, and only one, can emerge as the champion. Then, plunging the harpoon into the marlin's heart, pursuing the meaning of love and death, the Old Man finally glimpses the vision that he has been seeking: the fish is "silvery and still and floated with the waves" (94). His brother is dead, but in that death he is an illuminated wonder. Santiago has arrived at the heart of the matter.

But Santiago must still do "the slave work" (95), the work of service for the others; he must return to the land, make the journey home. As he looks at his battered hands and feels his back against the stern of his small skiff, he knows "that this had truly happened" (98). He had thought "perhaps it was a dream" (98), but he acknowledges now that it is true. The great Dimaggio would be proud of him today. He has experienced the vision that he has been seeking; it is part of him now, but he must still contend with the sharks waiting for him.

"The shark was not an accident" (100). It might appear as an accident, a contingent event that just happens, but "a very big Mako shark" (100) has its own singular beauty and huge jaws, ugly and prepared to humiliate. The shark is part of the cosmic design, part of the rhythm of living creatures. Fast and cutting, the shark is the enemy of all other fish in the sea, determined to "do exactly what he wished" (101). Lacking all humility, the shark threatens total humiliation. It reminds us of death; it brings inevitable destruction. When it mutilates the body of the marlin, it is as though Santiago "himself were hit" (103). He is hit, but not defeated.

"But man is not made for defeat . . . A man can be destroyed but not defeated" (103). With the attack of the sharks, the meat of the marlin valued in the marketplace at a high price will inevitably be lost just as the body of the Old Man, exhausted and weary, will inevitable be lost as well. It is no wonder that Santiago now feels "the nail go through his hands and into the wood" (107). It is his crucifixion and his destiny.

Despite Santiago's ongoing determination to attack the sharks tearing now at the meat of the marlin, the sharks overwhelm the fish; the violence— ugly and chaotic—again evokes sorrow in Santiago: "'I shouldn't have gone out so far fish' he said. 'Neither for you nor for me. I'm sorry, fish'" (110). But it is not sorrow, but the determination to fight on that dominates the rhythm of the narrative as Santiago moves closer to home: "'Fight them' he said. 'I'll fight them until I die'" (115). Only "the pain of life" (116) separates Santiago from death now, but he will not yield until he has earned the final sleep of peace.

As readers, we move with Santiago toward the Havana shoreline. The fight with the sharks finished, the marlin stripped of everything but its skeleton bones, Santiago sails his skiff "to make his home port" (119). He is "past everything now" (119), and that sense of an ending to his "real life" experience is reflected in the subdued tone of the narrative language as well. It is as if he has achieved a lightness of being, a knowledge deeper than sorrow itself.

On land, the Old Man shoulders the mast and starts to climb up the hill, toward his bed in the small shack. Suddenly he sees "in the reflection from the street lights" (121), as if in another visionary dream, the immense skeleton of the marlin, an enchanted reflection, an after-effect of his accomplishment and his loss. Stumbling and falling with the mast on his path home, he finally lies in his bed, sleeping face down, "his arms out straight and the palms of his hands up" (122). If he reminds us of Jesus, we await the response to his profound sacrifice.

Like Santiago, the boy has also seen the skeleton lashed to the skiff, and, like us, he knows what Santiago has endured, what the Old Man has accomplished. Seeing the Old Man breathing in his sleep, the Old Man's hands, his scars and wounds, the boy starts to cry with sorrow and understanding. If Santiago is destroyed, he is not defeated.

Santiago's singular battle with the marlin has unfolded through the narrative for us as readers to risk and to understand. The tension of that struggle resolved, we have glimpsed with Santiago, as if in a visionary dream, the meaning of that journey reflected in the immense skeleton of the marlin, the truth of the achievement, the accomplishment and the loss. Manolin understands this, too.

The fish did not beat the fisherman, but the rapacious and devilish sharks did. Both Santiago and Manolin agree:

"They beat me, Manolin," he said. "They truly beat me."

"He didn't beat you, Not the fish."

"No, truly. It was afterwards." (124)

The tourists on the dock will never know any of this, though, because, looking at "the long backbone of the great fish" (126), they have no context, no narrative to understand the truth of what has happened. As readers, we are sadder and wiser than they are.

In the final movement of the narrative, the tension between Santiago and the marlin, the remembrance of that great struggle, opens into the rhythm of love, the bond between the Old Man and the boy, and that love is sealed by the spear of the marlin. Santiago wants Manolin to take the spear as an emblem of what a man can do, and Manolin wants that spear as a remembrance of this singular event and for inspiration for heroic events to come. Santiago has earned the sleep of peace, the dream of the lions, and Manolin, bound by love, is ready to go out and bring another marlin home. Mindful of Santiago's journey, we, too, are ready to return to our "real life."

7

Catcher in the Rye

The *Catcher in the Rye* is "a novelistic novel," a literary narrative whose gravity is in the singular, at times peculiar, voice of Holden Caulfield, a character who, as Salinger claimed, "can't be legitimately separated from his own first-person technique" (Salinger, 1957 letter). It is not incorrect to claim that Holden offers us, as readers, a transitional moment in his life, a movement from innocence to experience, a teenager's angst on the border from childhood to adulthood, a profound hesitation at the gate east of Eden where the mortal world of sexuality and death stretches endlessly before him. But to make such a claim is to miss the enigmatic pull of desire in Holden's voice, the call to us, as readers, to take up the ethical demand to respond to the "madman stuff" (1) in his narrative, the singularity of his experience, which cannot be known or represented by the typical conventions of rule-governed discourse, but can perhaps be glimpsed through the infectious language of his linguistic telling.

Salinger claims that Holden has adopted an "extremely discriminating attitude to his reader—listener" (Salinger, 1957 letter). Holden desires that we pay attention to him, that we listen carefully to what he says, not because he appears, at times, charming (as well as cynical and narcissistic), but because he cares about what he is saying (or writing), and, more importantly, he cares about us, as readers. It is not primarily the contingent events of his "real life" at 16 (the happenings that have depressed him), but the telling of those events when he is 17 that make those contingent moments into a meaningful experience, an experience that he dares to share with us if we, in turn, dare to enter into the depth of his language.

There is more at stake for Holden than we might at first think. He is suspicious of us, as readers, as soon as he begins his narrative, assuming, in part, that we will miss what he has to say because we are "phonies," readers preconditioned for rule-governed responses, "all that David Copperfield kind of crap" (1). We might lose interest too quickly, yell out "digression" (183), close the book, and let him disappear before we acknowledge his singularity, the "madman stuff" (1) that makes him (and us) who (not what) he is.

But if Holden is suspicious, he is willing to take the risk, to trust that we "really want to hear about it" (1), that we are similar to his brother D. B. who, despite D. B.'s supposed loss of integrity in Hollywood, comes over to visit him at the rest home "practically every weekend" (1). As brothers, we are with Holden in that rest home as he starts his story, a linguistic narrative with minimal concern about linear progression, but rather a looping narrative, moving back and forth, taking us on a journey into the depths of the mortal self as it attempts to locate that self through memory and desire, continually circling back on itself, a repetitive movement shaping experience through language.

"Where I want to start telling is the day I left Pencey Prep" (2), Holden at first claims. He is apparently not interested in autobiography, in the impossible telling of his own birth, in childhood origins leading to adult endings. Instead, as if randomly, he starts when he wants to, and where he wants to, a temporal moment ("a day") located in space ("Pencey Prep"), time and space linguistically embodied, meaningful precisely because he is leaving. It is the sense of "good-by," the absence of this time and space evoked by his telling, that starts his narrative and that first calls to us as readers, that demands that we open ourselves to his language, his desire aroused by this sense of leaving. If we turn away, he will disappear. We need to follow him.

Holden is standing way up on Thomsen Hill that day, Saturday, alone, observing at a distance Pencey and Saxon Hall bashing each other on the football field, while he hears the yelling from the grandstand below. He's returned early from New York where, as manager of the fencing team, he left all the foils and equipment on the subway, preventing the fencing meet between Pencey and McBurney School. "It wasn't all my fault," he claims. "I had to keep getting up to look at this map, so we'd know where to get off" (3). As readers, we might wonder at such misdirection. Did Holden actually not want the meet to happen? He seems out of rhythm, almost as if he is falling into a gap.

With Holden, we move from Thomsen Hill over to say "good-by" to "old Spencer," his history teacher who knows what we, as readers, don't explicitly know yet. Holden has apparently been hesitant to tell us about it. "I forgot to tell you about that," Holden tells us. "They kicked me out" (4). We might have sensed this already, but now we know it, as Holden knows it, a shared moment of trust through his telling that evokes another confession: "All of a sudden I thought of something that helped make me know I was getting the hell out" (4). That "something" turns out to be the time (now a memory) back in "around October" (4) when he was chucking a football just before dinner with his classmates Tichener and Campbell. It got darker and darker then (as Holden remembers it now), until they could hardly see the ball, but they didn't want to stop until they had to. For Holden, as for us, it was a temporal moment enveloped in the fading light, an almost invisible moment, but one that lingered then, and lingers now, shaped not by something seen but real enough, human connectivity in the midst of the growing darkness, an enduring moment to be remembered as "a good-by," a sense of leaving, now shaped through his linguistic telling.

We run with Holden to Spencer's house, stumbling on the ice, almost frozen, nearly falling down, out of breath before we arrive. When Holden crosses a road on the way, he feels as if he is disappearing: "I felt like I was disappearing" (5). He wants us to feel that as well: "It was that kind of a crazy afternoon, terrifically cold, and no sun out or anything, and you felt like you were disappearing every time you crossed a road" (5). That "you" is "we" (each of us as readers) connected to Holden through his voice, his narrative unfolding. He cannot see us anymore than we can see him except through his language, through his voice rising from his bed in the rest home, but he senses that we, too, might be frozen, or might disappear, and then he will, too.

Holden has come to say "good-by" to Spencer who has written a note asking him to stop by before vacation. "You didn't have to do all that. I'd come over to say good-by anyway" (7), Holden kindly tells Spencer when he enters his bedroom, a place smelling like Vicks Nose Drops, an atmosphere of sickness and decay, vulnerability and, for Holden, further discomfort and sadness. Sitting on the bed, Holden hears (as we do) Spencer, in pajamas and bathrobe, lecture about life: "Life is a game, boy. Life is a game that one plays according to the rules" (8). We might imagine that this is not the first time Holden has heard this kind of lecture, nor the last. For him, though, life is not a game unless you are "a hot shot," a phony who benefits from the kind of rule-governed behavior that closes the self from itself and from others, that brings comfort by blocking the individual from experiencing the integrity of his own uniqueness, the singularity of his own "good-by." For Holden life is "no game" (8). It is not determined by rules, but by a mystery, a secret that threatens disappearance.

It is not incorrect to assume that Holden is moving from innocence to experience, that he suffers from arrested development as a teenager attempting to transition from boyhood to adulthood, or that he fears the corruption of the mortal world increasingly burdened by a growing consumer consciousness after an explosive and traumatic world war. But it is not just a naïve innocence that he wants to protect, or even a confused sexual identity that he wishes to stabilize; more urgently, it is the enigmatic depth of human desire that he wants to keep open, that he wants us to respond to and to enact.

Holden is just beginning his story for us, but, as readers, we might start to wonder if he still seeks an answer to the "interesting riddle" of the Egyptians, the secret of the ingredients they used "when they wrapped up dead people so that their faces would not rot for innumerable centuries" (11). If so, we might suspect that it is not because Holden wants to stop time, freeze the temporal movement of mortal life. Instead, he wants to slow time down, give it depth and duration, prevent flesh from rotting with the shame of meaningless disintegration, protect it from the horror of the kind of disappearance that freezes the flight of memory and desire. He wants to sense the human connectivity of a loving good-by, give it ongoing purpose and direction. Holden desires time to know who he is within the mortal world.

In terms of his narrative, Holden is still shooting the bull with Spencer, but he now wants us to think about something else: the lagoon down near Central Park South: "I was wondering if it would be frozen over when I got home, and if it was, where did the ducks go. I was wondering where the ducks went when the lagoon got all icy and frozen over" (13). Fish can adapt to the environment beneath that ice, but the ducks can't. Neither can Holden (or his readers). If we care about him, we apparently need to stay with him in flight. We can't disappear, and we can't freeze him out. We can't simply say "good luck" (15) to him (as Spencer does) and send him on his way.

Following Holden, we return to his warm dorm room, heated and cosy. He puts on his "red hunting hat" (18), the one he bought in New York just after he lost the fencing foils. He turns the "very very long peak of the hat around to the back" (18). He is comfortable and secure for the moment, open to us in his solitude, as he reminisces about his reading, especially about the authors he most enjoys, the ones you wish were "a terrific friend of yours and you would call up on the phone whenever you felt like it" (18). Holden must hope that we feel the same way about him, that we want to call him up, share his desire for our desire of him.

Holden next turns to Robert Ackley, a student who rooms near him, and then Ward Stradlater, his roommate at Pencey. Like Holden, Ackley seems an outsider, if not an outcast, "a very peculiar guy," with "lousy teeth" and a "lot of pimples" (19). He is a slob, annoying, and, not surprisingly, Holden claims not to care for him. When Ackley arrives in the room, Holden pulls the peak of his hunting hat around to the front, and then over his eyes, as if he were shutting himself off from the sight of Ackley, freezing him out. It is as if Holden is protecting himself from the visible glare of Ackley's presence, the annoying sloppiness of the mortal flesh demanding to be seen, but Ackley's behavior evokes in Holden a playfulness beyond the visible. The apparent darkness allows Holden to imagine a connection, a sense of a meeting beyond what can be seen, a moment of shared human sentiment, depth. It is as if Ackley's presence is fading into the consciousness of memory and desire, a meeting shaped now by the novelty and depth of language itself.

With his red hunting hat over his eyes, Holden cannot see anything. "I think I'm going blind," he says in a very hoarse voice to Ackley. "Mother darling, everything's getting so dark in here . . . Mother darling, give me your hand. Why won't you give me your hand?" (21). Ackley apparently thinks Holden is going nuts, that he should grow up. But the maternal warmth of the moment, as Holden tells it, seems to relax Holden, as Holden opening himself to the moment pulls the peak of his hat back around again. If Ackley cannot grasp Holden, neither can Holden grasp Ackley. They are both out of place, missing each other in the visible world. Within the linguistic moment, though, Holden has located himself. He is relaxed (and so are we).

By contrast, Stradlater seems the opposite of Ackley, an athlete with broad shoulders, a big man on campus, the kind of friendly and familiar phony, according to Holden, who enjoys walking around the dorm naked, always looking at himself in the mirror, comfortable in his skin. Like Ackley, Stradlater is a slob; but unlike Ackley, he is "a secret slob" (27), a year book picture of a handsome guy, the image and the illusion of perfection. Stradlater appears to fit in, a winner in the game of life; by contrast, Ackley seems to have "no game" (8), no smooth exterior, no sense of how to coordinate the rhythm of the mortal body with the accepted rules of mainstream culture. Ackley is out of step. Stradlater has a perfect build for the current game, a magnetism that keeps him in step with the cultural rhythms, the images of a consumer culture.

Holden seems less interested in their attributes, though, their relation to the game of life and its rules, than he is in the haunting sense of an utter alterity, a gap, a profound existential loneliness that drives him on, a lack that threatens his (and their) very disappearance. Ackley and Stradlater are not as different as they might appear. They bore Holden, at times, annoy him, and reflect dimensions of his own imperfections and contradictions. If they appear to be phonies, each in their own way, they are also connected to him in this world, indicators of a social, and so human relationship that keeps him from becoming utterly undone.

But Holden nearly "drops dead" (31) when Stradlater tells him that he has a date with Jane Gallagher (whom Stradlater carelessly calls "Jean"). Holden knows Jane, cares about her, and we might at first assume that Holden is telling us about her now because he is concerned that Stradlater will corrupt her, take advantage of her, sexually stain her purity, and adulterate her innocence and integrity. That is part of the truth, but not the whole truth (as Holden is fond of saying). Holden is not primarily concerned with naïve innocence when he thinks about Jane (or anyone else). Jane is a dancer, Holden tells us, who moves to the rhythm of beauty (like Holden's sister Phoebe, as we later discover), vulnerable to an ominous stepfather who might have abused her. Holden once kissed her all over her face (except her mouth) and held hands with her in the movies, where sometimes she would even caress his neck (like adults might do). It is not so much naïveté as sensual integrity that Holden seems concerned with.

Holden tells Stradlater that Jane wouldn't move any of her kings when they played checkers together: "She just liked the way they looked when they were all in the back row" (32). We might again think that Jane didn't move her kings out of the back row because she was naïve and innocent, but, more likely, she did it as a purposeful act resisting aggression. She was not interested in winning or losing, in gaining a competitive edge, but loved the beauty of the moment when her "lousy childhood" (32) transformed into joyful desire, opened to an act of shared attention and love. According to Holden, Stradlater has no interest in such moments. He is a "sexual bastard" (32), a narcissist closed to the mystery of what is before him, a phony interested in power and control of the tangible and visible, but incapable, or at least unwilling, to acknowledge what cannot be manipulated: the intangible, the mystery of each unique (and vulnerable) temporal moment. For Holden, Stradlater threatens corruption not because he is a sexual being (we all are), but because his sexual aggression reduces sexuality, makes it part of consumer behavior, pretends that to know the other is to possess the other, to make the other your own.

It is not so much that Holden fears sexuality, or more generally the rhythm of human experience, but that he is desperate to find an alternative to "the sexy bastards" (32) (like Stradlater) and the noisy bastards (like Ackley) or even the lecturing bastards (like old Spencer) who seem to believe that you can grasp what you cannot grasp, the uniqueness and integrity of the individual self, the unique voice saying more than what is said. For Holden, it is the telling that is his gift to us, more than the tale itself. The isolated episodes of his "real life," governed as they often are by consumer culture and the recent world war, may haunt Holden, frustrate him, sadden and depress him, just as sexual difference and its aggressive counterpart do, but it is as if such matters need to be approached indirectly now; they need his attention, luminosity, a voice embodied in language that will evoke our desire and our caring, acknowledge our own openness and singularity. As Holden later indicates, Emily Dickinson, not Rupert Brooke, is the best war poet for precisely this reason.

When Stradlater asks Holden to write a composition for him, it is the first time we hear about his younger brother, Allie. "He's dead now," Holden abruptly tells us. "He got leukemia and died when we were up in Maine, on July 18, 1946" (38). Allie died three (or perhaps four) years ago at about the same age as his sister Phoebe is now. No doubt the trauma of Allie's death had, and continues to have, a profound effect on Holden. His grief and longing, his flashes of violence, his existential loneliness and acute anxiety about loss and disappearance, as well as his profound sense of caring and connectivity, all seem related to this trauma. If Allie's death has a stark and permanent date attached to it, inscribed as if on a tombstone (July 18, 1946)—the only precise date in Holden's narrative—the traumatic event is as destabilizing as time itself. Allie's death permeates Holden's life, each and every present moment of it. "He's dead now" (38), Holden has said, now and forever. Allie is the other that Holden senses now and always, the other that he cannot know but deeply cares about, the nonrepresentational mystery of human life that he cannot grasp but will never allow to disappear. If Holden is telling his story for us, he may very well be telling it, at the deepest level, for Allie as well, to give himself a purpose and direction and to keep Allie alive. It is an act of ethical courage, a promise, an act of love. Allie's death has sanctioned Holden's story.

When Stradlater asks Holden to write a composition for him, he expects the stereotypical kind of composition, descriptive and mediocre, commas in the wrong places, the standard college dorm room essay, nothing peculiar or out of the ordinary, no originality. Holden will not write the standard description about a room or a house, though, but an original composition about Allie's baseball mitt with "poems written all over the fingers and the pocket and everywhere" (38). He does not know why he does it when he does, but when he is telling us about it now, we sense that it is not simply his adolescent stubbornness, a way of resisting the ordinary, but a gift to Allie, a way of acknowledging the strangeness and wonder of mortality itself (a gift to us as well). It is accurate to say that Holden wants to preserve the memory of Allie, to save the innocence of his brother (as if it were falling off a cliff, disappearing), but that's not the whole truth. Through his linguistic narrative, Holden is shaping the "real life" events of his experience, wrestling with the pain of Allie's absence, embodying through language the extraordinary sense of loss that haunts him (and all of us), that sense of a profound and inevitable "good-by" that we all share.

It is not so much that Holden suffers from arrested development or a Peter Pan complex or that he is stuck in a nostalgic fantasy about catching innocence, saving children from the corruption of mortal experience, but that Holden is courageously questing for an alternative, seeking a way to engage in the complexities and contradictions of the mortal world without losing himself, his individuality, the strangeness that haunts him, all that "madman stuff" (1).

When Allie died, that strangeness erupted. Holden broke all the windows in his garage, and his hand still hurts from that rupture four years ago. Like death itself, that trauma destabilized Holden, shook him up, instigated endless worry, and propelled him from one prep school to the next. But, as we might now suspect, that was actually the beginning of his story, the rules yielding to transgression, the birth of the experience that he is now telling us about.

As readers, we cannot expect Stradlater to acknowledge this anymore than Holden can expect Stradlater to say anything about Jane when he returns from his date with her. Nor can we expect Stradlater to acknowledge the significance of Holden's composition about Allie, except to claim, "You don't do one damn thing the way you're supposed to" (41). We might be reminded, though, of what Holden expects from us: that we will continue to listen to him, acknowledge his story.

When Stradlater, after his date with Jane, refuses to respond to Holden's heart-felt concerns, Holden becomes unhinged, striking out at Stradlater, a momentary eruption when it happened, and a momentary rupture in the narrative now, a moment that Holden barely remembers as he tells us about it: "This next part I don't remember so hot . . . I tried to sock him. It probably hurt him a little . . . I did it with my right hand, and I can't make a good fist with that hand. On account of that injury I told you about" (43). Once again, Holden seems to be inviting the reader ("you" and "I") to acknowledge his story, where he (and it) is coming from, who he is becoming, as he shapes the linguistic space (and creates the linguistic gaps) for all of us now to share.

But Holden also claims that he is a pacifist. "I'm a pacifist, if you want to know the truth" (46), he tells us after Stradlater hits him, blooding his nose, in response to Holden's own violence. He is a pacifist, sometimes, but he is also a potential killer, a suicide bomber caught in the logic of retaliation, if not resentment. He would have killed Stradlater, he claims, if he could, but he didn't, of course, and he can't (or he won't). Much later in his narrative, though, he will tell us: "Anyway, I'm sort of glad they've got the atomic bomb invented. If there's ever another war, I'm going to sit right the hell on top of it. I'll volunteer for it. I swear to God I will" (141). We might wonder: what alternative does he really have?

It's not surprising that after his break with Stradlater, Holden again seeks out a connection with Ackley, who is looking somewhat like a ghost: "He looked sort of spooky in the dark" (46). Enveloped by that darkness, Holden briefly talks with Ackley, even reaches out his hand to him, only to be rebuffed once again: "He pulled it away from me" (46). Then, with the dorm dark and everyone asleep, Holden becomes increasingly lonely, unbearably so. Suddenly, he decides to leave "right that same night" (51). He cannot journey straight home, though; his parents don't expect him until Wednesday. With his luggage in hand, ready to travel, he leaves Pencey, shouting and sad, an unsettled "good-by," at best, as he heads into New York City.

Leaving school, Holden must have been sad and depressed on the train to the city, but in his telling of it, he seems energized, not suicidal, making up stories while he talks to the mother of his schoolmate Morrow, connecting with her as they sit side by side, creating fiction for her about her son and about the "tiny little tumor" (58) he supposedly has on the brain. It is as if it is the language itself, his voice acknowledged by another, that keeps Holden going, the linguistic exchange evoking human sentiment that keeps him from being completely undone: not the reliability of his representations but the desire of his telling serving as a placeholder, preventing him from falling, from disappearing.

Arriving at Penn Station, Holden immediately enters a phone booth, feeling "like giving somebody a buzz" (59). He first considers calling family: D. B., then Phoebe; next an old girlfriend Sally Hayes and his old student adviser Carl Luce, who used to give sex talks to his advisees in the dorm late at night. Typically, Holden ends up calling no one, though, but finally gets a cab, absentmindedly, but significantly, giving the driver his home address. Then suddenly (half way through Central Park) he realizes he can't go directly home, at least not yet: "I'm so damn absent-minded, I gave the driver my regular address, just out of habit and all . . . I mean I completely forgot I was going to shack up in a hotel for a couple of days and not go home till vacation started. I didn't think of it till we were halfway through the park" (60).

It is possible that "habit and all" (60) is the cause (or the effect) of absentmindedness, a forgetfulness that brings you home, the illusion of stability at a moment of instability. For Holden (as for us), it might even be a temporary stay from trauma, a rest from high anxiety. But Holden is not yet prepared to regularize such affairs, to go to his parental home or a rest home (we anticipate), preferring "to shack up in a hotel for a couple of days" (60), instead. Not exactly a vacation, it is a way of delaying the inevitable.

As Holden tells us now, what seemed to break through that absentmindedness in the taxi, wake him up, was the sudden thought again of the ducks in the lagoon frozen over in Central Park. It was a sudden eruption of thought that demanded a further response from Holden at the time, an articulation of a question that might appear to some as a digression but one that he seems compelled to tell us about now. "By any chance, do you happen to know where they go, the ducks, when it gets all frozen over? Do you happen to know, by any chance?" (60), Holden asks the cab driver. Holden would like to know, and he wants us as readers to think about it, too. He needs us to follow his flight.

Holden "shacks up" at the Edmont Hotel where he witnesses through his window a cross-dresser in an adjacent room and in another room "a man and a woman squirting water out of their mouths at each other" (62). If the disappearance of the ducks (and further back, the disappearance of Allie) haunt Holden, the arousal of sexual desire, despite its links to violence and perversion from Holden's perspective, now keeps Holden moving. In his mind, Holden might be a killer and "the biggest sex maniac you ever saw" (62), but he is also a pacifist and someone willing to admit, "Sex is something I just don't understand" (63). He is a complex and ambivalent human being.

In his hotel room, we should not be surprised when Holden next thinks about Jane. Aroused by sexual desire, he considers giving her a call. But, to get her to the phone, he thinks, not surprisingly, that he will have to make up a story about death: how "her aunt had just been killed in a car accident" (63). Such an eruption, shaking things up, might lead to further conversation. Holden is "not in the mood" (63), though, so he buries it.

Holden does buzz Faith Cavendish, "a burlesque stripper or something" (63), a working girl who shacks up at the Stanford Arms hotel. Faith appears willing to meet for "cocktails or something" (64) the next day, but not right now, and so, Holden pulls back, short-circuiting the future meeting that will never be, still hoping for an alternative. As readers, it is a rhythm that we are growing accustomed to.

We might still assume that Holden is a typically anxious teenager, filled with fantasies of killing and sexual mania, unable to cope with the established adult world, the limits of the mortal body, desire and its termination, eros and thanatos. But if this is so, we, as readers, might also wonder if the undercurrents of such anxiety are not also our own, and if such torment can possibly be shaped, or directed, into an alternative. Wearing a clean shirt in his hotel room, Holden now seems to turn to just that alternative possibility as he begins to think about connecting with his sister Phoebe: the promise of "shooting the crap with old Phoebe for a while" (67). Connecting with Phoebe is apparently his best hope.

Phoebe and Allie seem uncannily like each other. "You should see her," Holden tells us. She has red hair (like Allie's), and if you tell her something, "She knows exactly what the hell you're talking about" (67). She is about the same age now as Allie was when he died, very smart and literate, although "too affectionate sometimes" (68). To know her, we might imagine, is to know Allie, or at least to glimpse an otherwise impossible knowledge, an innocent sexuality. Phoebe is what Holden desires (for himself and for us): "Somebody you always felt like talking to on the phone" (68). She is and is not Allie. "She killed Allie, too. I mean he liked her, too," Holden tells us. "She still kills everybody—everybody with any sense, anyway" (68). Phoebe is a kind of Eve figure in the Garden of Eden before the fall, a contrary to (and a reminder of) Allie, a double for the eruption of death. She is the spirit of romance hinting at incest, spilling over into the inevitable tragedy of leaving.

In New York City, Holden next patronizes the Lavendar Club where he encounters three tourists from Seattle, 30-something celebrity watchers (from his perspective): Bernice, Marty, and Laverne. To him, they are conventional phonies, although Bernice is "a terrific dancer" (70), at her best, a phantom of delight, a girl whose body in motion becomes, for Holden dancing with her, the dance itself, the intangible rhythm beneath his hand, a meeting, yet not quite a meeting, of bodies on the dance floor.

The girls' eventual dismissal of Holden depresses him, but this sense of the rhythm of the body, this glimpse of what emanates from the mortal world but cannot be caught or possessed, gets him thinking about Jane Gallagher again. Leaving the Lavendar Lounge, "I got old Jane Gallagher on the brain again" (76), Holden now tells us. Jane is "the only one, outside my family, that I ever showed Allie's baseball mitt to." Unlike Stradlater, she was "interested in that kind of stuff" (77).

Jane kept her kings in the back row when they played checkers together, but she didn't lack movement; she was not an "icicle" (79). Holden and Jane held hands together in the darkness of the movie theater, and just as Holden does at times to Phoebe, Jane, at times, put her hand on the back of Holden's neck. Her stepfather—"that Cudahy bastard" (79)—seems to have shaken up her innocence, although such experiences seem to be a dimension of her singularity, a mystery that Holden (and the reader) will never fully know.

"Jane was different" (79), as Holden indicates, and it is that difference that makes the difference for Holden, that drives him "mad" and onward.

Unlike the fish who stay beneath the ice in the frozen lake in Central Park all winter, Holden, we now more readily see, is more like the ducks who, unable or unwilling to adapt to the icicle-like environment, leave, driven by a desire not to "get frozen right in one position for the whole winter" (82). Such leaving implies the hope of a meeting, a response to the call of flight, a way of making such leaving into meaningful memory, a temporal experience of duration. It is a way of avoiding stiffening or rigidity (or even boredom). Holden indicates just this when he tells us next about his short encounter at Ernie's Club with Lillian Simmons and her "navy officer" who "looked like he had a poker up his ass" (86).

"'Holden come join us,' Lillian said . . . 'I was just leaving,' I told her. 'I have to meet somebody'" (87).

When Holden finally returns to his hotel, the "somebody" he meets is Maurice, "the elevator guy" (90) who offers to send a girl up to his room: a prostitute named Sunny, who ironically turns out to be as young and as innocent as Holden himself. She is from Hollywood, though, a location already marked by Holden as a place of prostitution and corruption, and although at times she might sound naïvely innocent—"I don't want to get my dress all wrinkly. It's brand clean" (95)—she is really under contract to Maurice, focused on the business proposition, the corrupt ratio of time to money, a fallen state of temporal consciousness lacking human caring: "Ya got a watch on ya, hey?" (95), she asks Holden.

We might again imagine that Holden, as an anxiety-ridden teen, is not yet ready for this kind of situation, anxious about entering the world of sexuality, compulsively fearful of the adult world that will betray him, the corrupt world of the phonies who seem to dominate it. He'd like to talk to Sunny, make a genuine connection with her, but he is unwilling, perhaps unable, to fall into that unclean world of aggression, the bodily rhythm of stiffening and release. Yet this is not the whole truth, either. Holden has been premature in his own calculations, as he tells Sunny; yet, he is at least willing to pay for his mistake. He cares. His mistake seems as much about making a contract with "somebody" like Maurice as it is about anticipating a sexual encounter with "somebody" like Sunny, a mistake, in other words, about the nature of human exchange, of imposing willful desire on another, the thrust of power to gain control, the attempt to possess the other, to add to the self at the cost of the other. Such a mistake intensifies human sadness, as Holden suggests. It is a betrayal of the other and of the self.

Once Sunny leaves the hotel room, this sense of sadness drives Holden to start "talking, sort of out loud, to Allie" (98), and we note that the narrative looping, Holden's linguistic rhythm, his memory and desire have always brought us back to Allie. Allie's absence haunts the language, sanctions the story that Holden is telling. It is a story about his journey for an alternative to the corruption of the integrity of the self, an alternative to the stiffening of the flow of mortal existence, even an alternative to the betrayal of the embodied self in relation to its other. Holden is attempting to save his life (and ours).

Still thinking about Allie, Holden recalls the time that he told Allie to "Go home and get your bike and meet me in front of Bobby's house" (98). It was spoken as a promise (an ethical contract) to meet. But that one particular day, it happened that Holden didn't want to take Allie with him. He left him alone. It was an unnecessary mistake, a betrayal nevertheless, a regretful misdirection, something a phony might do, something that Holden will always regret now, as long as he lives.

Maurice, the pimpy elevator guy, and Sunny, who has become "a pretty spooky kid" (98), force their way back into Holden's room, demanding an additional five dollars to complete their contract. Holden has anticipated this demand, and when he resists further payment, Maurice intensifies the violence, knocking Holden to the floor and taking the money: "I thought I was dying. I really did. I thought I was drowning or something . . . I could hardly breathe" (103). Overpowered by such brute force, Holden can only fantasize about retaliation, balancing the ratio of revenge by pretending a gangster movie, plugging Maurice in his fantasy, followed by Jane bandaging up his guts. It is a violent fantasy, but if we remember that Holden is telling his story from his bed in the rest home to save his own life (and perhaps ours), we might also acknowledge that he was close to suicide at the time, dreaming about strapping himself to a live bomb, or perhaps thinking about someone (like his old classmate James Castle) who might just jump out a window. In any case, Holden is not a pacifist, we realize, but he does not really want to kill himself or anyone else. Certainly, he does not want to die.

It is inaccurate to assume, as some readers apparently have (Mark David Chapman and John Hinckley, for examples), that Holden is primarily interested in such apocalyptic endings, eruption for its own sake, violent explosions, or even the logic of retaliation that suggests through the horror of total darkness we can gain transformed illumination. If his flights of fantasy take him to such apocalyptic moments, his feet remain grounded. Holden does not seek a final ending, but an alternative, a counterculture, a location in the mortal world that would allow him to know who he is and where he is. He is not interested in compromise either, but in the possibility of discovering the meaning of the complex, mortal self. If we, as readers, cannot see Holden, we are still listening to his voice, embodied in his linguistic narrative, as he lies on his bed in the rest home.

After his encounter with Maurice, Holden gives Sally Hayes a buzz from his hotel room the next morning, arranges a date with her to go to the Sunday matinee, and then heads out for breakfast where he meets two nuns also on a journey, their suitcases by their side. Holden contributes ten dollars to their collection basket (perhaps attempting to balance out the ten dollar payment to Maurice), strikes up a conversation with them, curious, in particular, about how these nuns teaching English respond "to books with lovers and all in them" (111). These nuns are full-grown human beings, adults who apparently appear authentic to Holden (like Jane, or Phoebe, or Allie). Not phonies, they collect money to help others (not to attend fancy charity balls, as his mother does), and they enjoy reading and discussing literature. If Holden is not completely at ease with these adults, he is nevertheless engaged, curious, willing, and able to respond to them: "To tell you the truth, it was sort of embarrassing, in a way, to be talking about *Romeo and Juliet* with her. I mean that play gets pretty sexy in some parts, and she was a nun and all, but she asked me, so I discussed it with her for a while" (111).

After breakfast, Holden "walks over toward Broadway," looking for a "hard record to get" for Phoebe, "Little Shirley Beans" (114). It is not a cute innocent song about a little girl who has lost her two front teeth, sung by a white girl, but a song from 20 years ago, with counsel and resonance, a voice that has traveled from a different (and distant) place. "It was a very old, terrific record, this colored girl, Estelle Fletcher, made," Holden tells us. "She sings it very Dixieland and whorehouse, and it doesn't sound at all mushy" (114–115). For Holden, the song evokes a voice of singularity, a voice of sadness and loss, but also of an innocent sexuality, a promise, the call of desire, the blues. It resonates with his past and his future, his fear and his hope. Holden buys it as a gift for Phoebe, an act of love at a distance, at a cost of five dollars, the same payment originally agreed to with Maurice.

When Holden next notices a family—"a father, a mother, a little kid about six years old"—walking along the sidewalk (115), we might at first think it happens by chance, but in terms of the rhythm of his narrative—the looping, back and forth, which we are becoming accustomed to, as we listen to his voice—we acknowledge the necessity of the encounter. It is a "nice thing" (115), as Holden says. It makes him (and perhaps us) "feel better" (115), less anxious, even hopeful. The "little kid" is separated from his parents, "but right next to the curb," alone but not lonely, in solitude but yet connected with others. He is pretending to walk a straight line (as if anyone really could), singing and humming. "He was just singing for the hell of it" (115), repeating the words, "If a body catch a body coming through the rye" (115). The experience seems to stabilize Holden for the moment, but we might wonder if "the little kid" actually sang "catch a body" (rather than the original words of the song—"meet a body"), or, as likely, if Holden actually mishears the exact wording: the word "catch" then not only making Holden fantasize about becoming "the catcher," the protector, even the savior, of innocent children, but also (wrongly) suggesting that the mortal body can be grasped, that such impossible knowledge can be possessed.

It is Holden's fantasy for the moment, in any case, the contrary to other fantasies that he has had, all of them seeming to emerge from the depth of his own interiority (the mad bomber, the gangster killer), the intensity of desire at the very edge of his mortal self. If becoming the catcher in the rye cannot be achieved in the visible "real world," the fantasy nevertheless allows him some sense of hope for the moment. Like the death of Allie, it is a memory with duration. It has seeped into his identity, become part of who he is, joined the past to the present, anticipating the future.

Holden buys two tickets to the Broadway show *I Know My Love*, starring the Lunts, for his date with Sally Hayes and then, thinking about the past and the future, he thinks about Phoebe, as he walks through the park to the Natural History Museum. Without entering, he reminisces about his school visits there, especially the Indian room with its permanent exhibits of Eskimo fishing through the ice, birds flying south for the winter, a very spooky witch doctor, and a squaw with a naked bosom. They are exhibits that might remind him (and us) of his own concerns in a different register. For Holden, the museum has always been "a nice place," like the family he has just seen, "a dry and cozy place where nothing every changed" (120). But it is not a place stripped of mystery or intrigue. If it is a place where "nobody'd be different there," a place where "Everything stayed right where it was" (120)—like Jane's kings in the back row—it is also a place where "you would be different" (120) each and every time you experienced it (like a reader of Holden's story). It is a place, in other words, to meet the strangeness of yourself, until you leave it and return to the hustle and bustle, the contingent and chance happenings of "real life" city streets. Like linguistic narrative, it is a place filled with memory and desire, eros and thanatos, a place of duration that can keep you alive. If Phoebe had been there that Sunday afternoon, Holden would have gone into the museum to meet her. But she isn't there, and he doesn't go in. For the moment, he has a date with Sally Hayes.

Holden claims that when he first saw Sally approaching, he wanted "to marry her," felt like he was "in love with her," although he also quickly tells us that he doesn't really like her much, that "she is a pain in the ass" (124). Sally is very good looking and open "to horsing around" (124), which Holden seems to enjoy while in the taxi with her. He seems both attracted and not attracted to her, a variation on a rhythm we, as readers, have become accustomed to. We are not surprised by such ambivalence (and rhythmic complexity). Holden has responded to others in just this way, and to himself for that matter, moving back and forth, both in his "real life" experience and in his linguistic telling of that experience, a rhythm we acknowledge in ourselves as well.

At the Broadway show, the Lunts (the featured actors) appear to Holden much the way Ernie did at the piano bar the night before. Although they are talented, they have made themselves into celebrities—"showing-off" (126), as Holden puts it—more interested in the visible mirroring of themselves than the act itself, being seen rather than sensing the depth of the other (that which cannot be represented).

After the play, Holden and Sally go ice-skating at Radio City, Holden clearly drawn to the "little blue butt-twitcher of a dress" Sally puts on, enjoying "how cute her little ass looked" (129). But it is not sexual conquest, or even visual sensation, in general, that Holden seems primarily interested in, but something more inexplicable, what he claims to love about Sally, what he cannot possess, or perhaps even know, what he cannot define, not the what but the who of Sally.

To Sally, Holden's conversation now turns crazy. It seems chaotic, barely understandable, too loud, a rambling digression. "I don't know what you're even talking about" (131), Sally tells Holden. Like the nuns when Holden focused on the death of Tybalt rather than the central characters, Romeo and Juliet, Sally wants Holden now to change the subject. But, as readers, we sense his turmoil and distress, his call to Sally (and us) to pay attention. Is Allie driving his conversation here, evoking all that "madman stuff" (1)?

Taking Sally's hand, Holden offers his dream: Drive up to Massachusetts or Vermont, stay in a cabin, later get married or something. If it's a fantasy, it's an alternative, a possibility including the promise of marriage itself. (It is one that Salinger himself seems to have adopted in variation.) To Sally, at the time, it is an immature rambling, though, and nothing more. "The whole thing is so fantastic, it isn't even . . ." (132), she claims, as if unable to define it. "It isn't fantastic. I'd get a job" (132), Holden responds, cutting her off. For Sally, there will be time for such things later. After college and marriage, "oodles of marvelous places to go to" (133). But for Holden, who pleads with Sally now to "open your ears" (and deeply listen to his language), after college "It'll be entirely different" (133) than what Sally claims. They'd be doing what everyone else would be doing, living (or dying) a postponed life. For Holden, Sally just doesn't understand. Her fantasy offers no possibilities. It is merely an escape from the existential moment. It is the same as everyone else's. It lacks the alternative, the difference. "You don't see what I mean at all" (133), Holden can only say.

Holden hopes that we understand what he is saying, even if Sally doesn't. No doubt Sally sounds to Holden like one of those phonies, practical and rule-governed by cultural norms, not able to open herself to his craziness. Holden does not desire banality, the consumer set of clichés, the phoniness that Sally seems (to Holden at least) to represent. For him, Sally has become all too familiar. If she is correct in her assessment of Holden, that she cannot understand what he means, Holden probably does not know what he means, either. But how could he? Who could possess such impossible knowledge?

We are following Holden's story as he is telling it to us, and he has now arrived at a moment when he is on edge, at the boundary of his own language, close to the breaking point. But he did not fall silent with Sally then (nor does he fall silent now). Instead, he reduces Sally to tears: "You give me a royal pain in the ass, if you want to know the truth" (133), using language "no boy ever said" (134) to her before in her entire life. It is an act of verbal aggression, reflecting his own violent fantasies. When he attempts to apologize for it, he does not meet with any success. As readers, though, we acknowledge it, nevertheless, another moment in the ongoing complexity of his madman journey, his "real life" experience being shaped through his telling now for us.

Leaving the skating rink, Holden calls Jane without response, attends the Christmas Show at Radio City Music Hall, and then meets up with Carl Luce, his old student advisor from Whooton School. Holden seems, at first, to be looking for some advice about sex from Luce, but what he is most concerned about is that Luce, like Sally (and Allie, of course), might just "get up and leave" (145). Holden cannot bear another "good-by" right now, so he shuts up when Luce warns him to. But Luce doesn't sound much different than Sally, despite all their apparent differences. "Listen," he says to Holden, "Let's just get one thing straight. I refuse to answer any typical Caulfield questions tonight. When in hell are you going to grow up?" (146).

When Luce begins to talk about Eastern philosophy, though, the difference between the West and the East—the idea that in the East they "happen to regard sex as both a physical and a spiritual experience" (146)—Holden grows genuinely excited. It is as if, for a moment, he has discovered another possible alternative, an opening consistent with his own belief and desire. He wants to discuss it with Luce. But Luce shuts

Holden down again, stiffens, freezing him out. Luce won't risk anything too personal. He is not willing, or not able, to offer Holden anything about his vulnerable self. "Your mind is immature" (147), Luce insists, as if he is defending himself from Holden's questions (and his own).

Luce suggests that Holden go see his father, a psychoanalyst: "He'll simply talk to you, and you'd talk to him" (148). Whether it's Holden or Luce who really needs a psychoanalyst remains unclear (perhaps they both do). Then Luce, "another pain in the ass" (149), according to Holden, leaves.

Holden is wounded, and that wound is not healing. It's dripping blood, an intimate fissure that no one is acknowledging, and he is drunk, screaming. He is almost unhinged, a madman, shivering, his body in pain. It's been about 24 hours since he left Pencey, but he doesn't want to see his parents until Wednesday, although he is drifting toward home. His only hope seems to be Phoebe, as he moves, in the dark, heading back to Central Park.

"Then something terrible happened just as I got in the park. I dropped old Phoebe's record. It broke into about fifty pieces" (154).

It just happens.

But he gathers the pieces together, puts the shards in his coat pocket, as if saving the remnants for future exchange and ongoing possibility. He can't throw those fragments away anymore than he can throw his life away. He doesn't want to die, although he apparently almost did then.

Drifting toward the lagoon in the pitch dark, everything "getting darker and darker, spookier and spookier" (154), Holden's life appears to be becoming increasingly ghost-like. The lagoon is "partly frozen and partly not frozen" (154). The ducks have taken flight, left, and Holden is almost dead, ready to be dumped in a river (he thinks), ready to leave forever.

If it were not for his imagined attachment to Allie, for his desire for Phoebe, for his memory of his parents, while he sits alone in the darkness of the park, he would have died then. But those memories fuel desire, and he gets "the hell out of the park, goes "home" (156), thinking, in particular, about how Phoebe would feel if he did die (and about the way he does feel about Allie's death, we assume).

Holden has to sneak into the family's apartment "like a crook" (158), undetected, but, as usual, transgressive. Once inside, though, he makes it clear that, like the museum, this is a genuine location for him, a familiar place but a singular one as well, a place like nowhere else "but you always know you're home" (158). Holden doesn't precisely "know what the hell it is" (158) that makes such places what they are, but he senses it, experiences it, and, through his language, he wants to embody it so we can experience this strange familiarity as well.

Holden arrives home about the same time he left Pencey the night before, the rhythm of leaving deepening his rhythm of return now. He moves with stealth across his apartment toward Phoebe's room. If he is a typical teenager, he also seems "mad," like a Poe narrator, haunted, taking an impossible amount of time to enter the room of the other, one he intends to meet (if not to kill): "Finally, after about an hour, I got to old Phoebe's room" (158). Missing her there, he finally discovers her instead in D. B.'s room; she is sleeping, though, her mouth "way open" (159)—like Jane's often is. After reading her personal notebook, sharing her intimacy while she sleeps, Holden wakes her up.

Phoebe is affectionate (sometimes too affectionate, according to Holden); she is excited to see Holden (as he is to see her). They talk about their brother D. B., movies, the school play coming up in which Phoebe is cast as Benedict Arnold, the traitor and betrayer. Then, Phoebe accepts the gift of fragments that Holden offers her, putting the broken "little Shirley Beans" record in her bedside drawer for safekeeping. It all seems typical, familiar, brothers and sisters chatting. But when Phoebe hears that Holden has been kicked out of school again, there is a moment of unanticipated violence. Phoebe erupts (like a madman), smacking Holden with her fist (much as Holden had done earlier to Stradlater). "Daddy'll kill you" (165), she yells, hiding her head under a pillow, hiding from the sight of Holden, obsessed by the thought of another family trauma. "She was ostracizing the hell out of me," Holden responds. "Just like the fencing team at Pencey when I left all the goddam foils on the subway" (166).

Although Phoebe is anxious about the prospect of their father killing Holden (admittedly an exaggerated claim), Holden does not appear anxious about such a threat. "Nobody's gonna kill me" (165), he first responds. Then, "The worst he'll do, he'll give me hell again, and then he'll send me to that goddam military school. That's all he'll do to me" (166).

If Holden remains without secure footing, he is apparently not shaken by the law of the father. He is determined to transgress that law (corporate and militaristic as it is) in order to discover an alternative possibility, a dwelling place (imagined if not real), for his singular self, for his innocent (perhaps spiritual) inviolability. It is not death or violence that he seeks (or fears), but a way of living within the world. "I'll probably be in Colorado on this ranch" (166), he now tells Phoebe, expanding on his earlier Thoreau-like dream of a cabin in the woods, a dream which Sally had rejected.

Holden now gives Phoebe a brief account of his experience at Pencey, a gift of telling: "Take my word for it" (167). It is an act that Phoebe generously responds to by listening, an ethical attentiveness that helps create just the kind of place that Holden is searching for, a linguistic space for dwelling with the other: "She always listens when you tell her something. The funny part is she knows, half the time, what the hell you're talking about. She really does" (167). What more could Holden (or anyone else) ask for?

We might recognize now, if we didn't before, that, for Holden, it is not what is happening, the contingency of the existential moment, but the telling of those moments, shaped by linguistic narrative, listened to by the other, that allows joy to rise from depression and despair. It is not so much the possession of knowledge as information, or the attributes of geographic terrain, but love itself, the gift of linguistic exchange, the intangible human connection glimpsed through the depth of language itself, which Holden seeks. It is that which he is trying to convey.

When Phoebe claims that Holden doesn't "like anything that's happening" (169), Holden insists that he does, but we might suspect that it is not what is happening, but what has duration, what endures that he really means. When she asks him to name something he likes, at first he can only name James Castle and Allie (two unique people whose singularity endure for him through memory and conviction), and then Phoebe herself. Pressed further by Phoebe, he finally moves to "the edge of some crazy cliff" (173), as close to his own singularity as he can get. It is as if he has again reached the limits of his own mortal possibilities, again in danger of being unhinged.

Holden now evokes for Phoebe his fantasy of becoming "the catcher in the rye" (173) coming out from somewhere (like a madman) to catch the "little kids" (173) before they go over the edge. He has reached the boundary of his own linguistic telling, the limits of his human identity as such. After that, all that he can do with Phoebe is dance in silence, seeking the rhythm of the unnamed body itself. In the dark, beyond the visible, Holden and Phoebe exchange gifts, the giving (like the telling) creating a "good-by" to be remembered.

Leaving Phoebe, Holden next seeks out his former English teacher, Antolini, a friend of the families who, with his wealthy wife, lives near the Caulfields. Holden seems to have a rare respect for Antolini, in part because he was the one person at Elkton Hills who cared for James Castle, the only one willing to go near him when he jumped from his window, to cover his body when he was lying dead—a corpse on the hard ground. Holden tells Antolini, as he told Phoebe, about his frustration at Pencey, the phonies who irritated him, the attempt to suppress uniqueness, to define eruptions of individuality as "digressions" (183). But Holden has clearly grown weary, his body seems on the verge of collapse. Since leaving Pencey, he has gotten little sleep, has had trouble breathing, and now he has a "terrific headache" and a "stomach-ache" (183). He is drifting.

Antolini is "hot to have a conversation" (187), though, to offer advice to Holden, and, as we have seen, Holden may be annoying, at times, but he is polite and generous. If old Spencer, his history teacher back at Pencey, had a final lesson for Holden, Antolini, fueled with alcohol, appears to have something more to offer Holden, a degree of empathy and a kind of wisdom to dispense. He demands that Holden listen. He has something important to tell him, so important, he claims, that he will not only tell it to him now but also write it down so Holden can review it later.

Antolini's advice, based on the writing of the psychoanalyst Wilhelm Stekel, seems to offer a certain wisdom, a sense of humility and shared knowledge, a sense of history and poetry as a "reciprocal arrangement" (189), a sense of ethics on the journey to know thyself and its location in the mortal world. We might even imagine that it offers Holden another alternative possibility, a way forward, an opportunity to save the remnants of his apparently fragmented life, a way to stop him from falling off the edge of the cliff, the precipice that he seems so close to. "I have a feeling that you're riding for some kind of a terrible, terrible fall" (186), Antolini tells Holden.

But it is not what is said (the descriptions and information, the lessons and the themes) that moves Holden, although he appreciates Antolini's concern: "Thanks a lot sir. You and Mrs. Antolini really saved my life tonight" (191). It is something else.

Holden was dead tired, at the edge of the world, that night. As he falls asleep, thinking about his conversation with Antolini, it is as if the Antolinis had become the catcher in the rye for him. But that fantasy lasted only for a moment. As readers, each in our own way, we might wonder not about what Antolini has said but about who he is, not about Antolini's rendering of Stekel the psychoanalyst, but about Holden's sense of Antolini, not just the generosity and caring, but the hot talking, the drinking, the disruption that finally disturbed Holden, the happening that shook him from the necessity of sleep, from the solitude at the limit of mortal life.

"Then something happened. I don't even like to talk about it. I woke up all of a sudden. I don't know what time it was or anything, but I woke up" (191).

That something that happened was Antolini crouching next to the couch, stroking Holden's head in the dark. We cannot know anymore than Holden knows whether Antolini intended admiration (as Antolini suggests) or is a "damn pervert" (as Holden, at least initially, believes). It is an unresolved complexity, an enigma in the context of the narrative. It might remind us, though, that Antolini is as strange as Holden himself.

That disruptive something that happened seems, for Holden, to be the threat that is always there, the threat to the mortal self, the trauma that we all experience but cannot possess, the thing that we cannot know. At first, it might remind us of the touch of Phoebe's hand in a moment of meeting, or Holden's hand gesturing to Ackley in the dark, or even Jane's hand on the back of Holden's neck in a dark movie theater. At this moment, though, it is "some guy's hand" petting Holden's head, an eruption disturbing him from the solitude of sleep, reminding Holden, we imagine, of Allie's disappearance, the haunting other that perverts "real life" (at least the promise of life as Holden would like life to be). It is the betrayal of life as much as the caring for it, resonating with the menace of Jane's stepfather, the bullying to death of James Castle, the "perverty" stuff that apparently has "happened" to Holden "about twenty times" since he "was a kid" (193). Holden can only get up and leave.

With Holden, we return to the streets of New York, up Fifth Avenue, when "all of a sudden, something very spooky starts happening." He is in free fall: "Every time I came to the end of a block and stepped off the goddam curb, I had this feeling that I'd never get to the other side of the street. I thought I'd just go down, down, down, and nobody's ever see me again" (197).

Antolini had warned Holden that he was riding for a horrible fall, like a man falling but not "permitted to feel or hear himself hit bottom" (187). But Holden knows that there is really no bottom to hit, just as he knows that there is really no catcher in the rye who can save us. Only the ghost of ourselves—the spooky and strange other that we cannot completely know (but whose desire we desire), the acknowledgment of the lack that we cannot possess (but perhaps can glimpse in its very absence)—can help get us to the other side of the street, keep us alive. It is Allie who will now save Holden, get him across the street, prevent him from disappearing.

Allie is not exactly Holden's catcher in the rye, but he is now a revenant whom Holden asks for help: "Allie, don't let me disappear. Allie, don't let me disappear. Allie, don't let me disappear. Please, Allie" (198). Holden repeats that chant over and over again, and then Allie seems to grant his request, Holden thanking him in return for the generous gift. It is a gift similar to the gift that Holden is giving to us, the linguistic narrative that, he hopes, we are responding to.

Lying on his bed in the rest home, Holden next begins to bring the story he is telling us to a temporary ending, reminding us that he was, after leaving Antolini, still pursuing alternative possibilities, not dreaming about becoming the catcher in the rye, but living in "a little cabin somewhere" (198), a place out West, a sunny place, hidden and singular—like D. B.'s secret goldfish (1), a place where he might even get married and have children who would read a lot of books and write. First, though, he needed to return to Phoebe: "All I wanted to do first was say good-by to old Phoebe" (199).

In pursuit of Phoebe, Holden attempts to cleanse the world of what cannot be cleansed, the "fuck you" graffiti (201) on the walls of schools (and tombstones). But now he realizes the impossibility of what he seeks, although he is apparently still in wonder at the "secret chemical" that the Egyptians used to prevent for thousands of years their faces from rotting even in the tomb. "Nobody knows how to do it except the Egyptians. Even modern science" (203), he reminds us.

When he first spots Phoebe at a distance, she is wearing his crazy red hunting hat: "You could see that hat about ten miles away" (205). She is also dragging his big old suitcase with her. Weighted down, she wants to fly west with him, pleading with Holden to take her with him. Holden responds abruptly, though. "Shut up," he shouts. He is on the edge of passing out, close to hitting her. "She started to cry" (206).

If Holden is freezing her out, we might imagine that he is protecting himself, acting like a typical adult, insisting that she stay home and go to school, sounding somewhat like the father who would kill his child unless he (or she) obeyed the rule-based behavior. But, as likely, he is concerned that Phoebe is acting too much like him, not being herself. If she went away with Holden, she wouldn't be able to play the role of Benedict Arnold in the school play. Holden cares about Phoebe just as he cares about Allie (and us), and he wants Phoebe (and the others he cares about) to take special care of themselves, to acknowledge the difference that each of us shares, the distance between us, each in our own way.

When Holden and Phoebe arrive at the carrousel, with its timeless songs and its eternally repetitive movement, Holden buys a ticket for Phoebe to ride. He sits on a bench at a distance to watch Phoebe (and the others) try to grab the gold ring, risking a fall. Holden is not there to catch Phoebe now, nor does he say anything or do anything that will disturb her: "The thing with kids is, if they want to grab for the gold ring, you have to let them do it, and not say anything" (211). If they fall, they fall. Phoebe, like all of us, deserves that solitude, that silence, that opportunity, and that sense of trust. At such moments we might experience the risk of love, what power does not know, what the phonies, according to Holden, rarely, if ever, imagine. Holden has arrived at that knowledge.

Soaked by the rain, wearing his red hunting hat, Holden watches Phoebe "going around and around, in her blue coat and all." He is "so damn happy" for the moment. He wishes that we, as readers, "could've been there" (213). If we have taken the risk, we are with him there, as he heads home with Phoebe.

Holden's narrative ends where it began as a voice calling to us from his bed in the California rest home, his unique voice now fading back into the silence, a voice that we, as readers, will miss just as he misses everybody that he has told us about: Stradlater and Ackley, and even Maurice. He does not know what he will do next, anymore than we know what we will do next as his story ends. Yet, it is difficult, perhaps impossible, not "to feel some kind of a good-by" (4), to wish him a fond farewell.

8

One Flew over the Cuckoo's Nest

Ken Kesey's novel *One Flew over the Cuckoo's Nest* challenges us from several different directions, not the least being the mixed heritage of Chief Bromden, the narrator, "the Vanishing American" (67), "the half-breed Indian" (5). Bromden's journey is a quest for origins, a beginning more than an end, but those origins are buried so deep within the landscape of contemporary America—much like his village home cemented over by "that big million-dollar hydroelectric dam" (311) imposed by the Government—that we might wonder how such a journey now, so belated, can possibly meet with success.

As a red man, the Chief has not only been betrayed by the white world, but by the trauma inflicted when he was given his family name, Bromden, a white woman's name that fixed him, breaking the connection with his Native American beginnings, his tribe, the imagined name that he might have envisioned for himself. It is as if the red man has all but vanished (as his father has), made invisible by the rigid rules and regulations of the Combine and by the privileging of white names (like his mother's), abstractions that block him from his Indian identity, the rhythm of his body connected to his ancestral home and tribal community, now apparently buried deep along the Columbia River in the Dalles.

In this context, the Chief's challenge is to discover his legacy as a Native American, a Vanishing American, in search of the place of the father, the original territory of the Native American, invisible now except through the visionary imagination. The Chief and his people seem overrun by the abstract power of arbitrary names and the dehumanizing technology of a bureaucratic culture that threaten their very existence.

As readers, we need to believe in the Chief in the same way that we need to believe in the visionary imagination. The Chief is the other, at best, on the margins of an arbitrary and established discourse that sees but does not believe, that attempts to make invisible what it does not want to see. Unlike this well-oiled bureaucratic machinery, though, we cannot dismiss the Chief's linguistic telling. We cannot define the Chief as a psychopath or as a schizophrenic as if he is a crazed Indian (what many critics have done). We need to believe in him, in his apparent "ranting and raving" (8), his telling of his story. If we believe it, we will acknowledge it as "the truth even if it didn't happen" (8). It is his singular way of offering us an account of who he is, his way of shaping "real life" into visionary possibility. We need to pay attention to him for his sake and for ours.

We will not follow him in every detail of his story, but acknowledge from the start that his journey is particularly treacherous for two intertwined and personal reasons: (1) the invisibility of the legacy that he seeks, the buried authority of his existence, the broken story of his father and (2) the distance he feels from his own sensuous body, the birth of his own feelings and emotions seemingly cut off and abstracted by the name he has been assigned, the name of his white mother (Bromden). We need to ask how Chief Bromden can possibly gain back his identity, who he is. How can he rediscover his origins, when his experience in his own immediate family and in the dominant culture seem to have denied all beginnings, privileging instead the rules and regulations that refuse to acknowledge such knowing. For most of his life, the Chief has been operating under the name of his mother and all that that name represents, a type of castration that has cut him off from his own body and from his Native American experience.

As a Native American, the Chief needs to reconnect with his father, take up again the story that his father left broken, and, by extension, he must reconnect with the land of his upbringing, the rhythm of the natural world that he experienced when he hunted with his father in the early morning fog and the rhymes and rhythms of his grandmother, the poetic sensibility that brings vision about. It is a tall challenge even for a big man.

When the Chief starts his narrative, it is difficult to locate him either in space or in time, and it is difficult to know whom (other than us) he might be talking with. "They're out there" (3), he says, hoping that we will connect with him (rather than side with "them"). The Chief is playing deaf and dumb, even though he can speak; he is the silent other to them, to those who are part of the fixed, established order (The Combine), but he wants us to believe in him, to acknowledge the voice that conveys the silence of his own existence. He will start with a "cagey" (3) narrative for this reason: "to fool them" (3), but not to fool us. It is a trait that he has acquired from "being half Indian," and that has helped him survive: "If my being half Indian ever helped me in any way in this dirty life, it helped me being cagey, helped me all these years" (3). But it is not this caginess, not mere strategies for survival, but a way of knowing that he really desires. Through his voice, he will enact vision for us, a way of knowing who he is.

When Big Nurse first appears, she is carrying her "woven wicker bag" (4) made by Indians but used by her to carry the tools that she manipulates to maintain her dehumanized control over the ward. Like the Chief's mother, Big Nurse uses and controls the Indian, but is not of the Indian. Yet, the Chief quickly also remarks on "those big, womanly breasts" (5) hidden beneath her starched and rigid exterior, suggesting a mistake in her manufactured image, implying that she, too, is something other than a bureaucratic automaton, that she, too, is imperfect and vulnerable, human, if we could only believe it. Those breasts eventually, and inevitably, will need to be exposed. If Big Nurse appears as a representation of "a near perfect work" (6), her "skin like flesh-colored enamel" (5), she is a reminder of that kind of manufactured desire that has created bureaucratic power and control, the kind of power that stripped his father of his original name and that buried the origins of the tribe and its identity deep in the red clay of the earth. But beneath Big Nurse's starched white uniform, "those big, womanly breasts" (5) also remind the Chief of the carnal body of his origins and the territory of his authentic identity that he now needs to revisit, remember or, better, reimagine.

For the Chief, it is his father that serves as the way back to himself, to memories of his early childhood, the bonding with his father on the land, their hunting trips in the early morning fog in the Dalles. At first, it is only nostalgia for the past that seems to evoke these memories, though, memories that he uses to protect himself, memories that do not connect with his deepest desire, do not open to the present, and do not yet spill over into the transforming power of his imagined telling: "I try to think back and remember things about the village and the big Columbia River, think about ah one time Papa and me were hunting birds in a stand of cedar trees near The Dalles . . . But like always when I try to place my thoughts in the past, and hide there, the fear close at hand seeps in through the memory" (6). It is a way for him to hide for a while from the present (as if he were in a fog), from the anger of the "black boys," from Big Nurse. But it does not allow him to overcome the fear that separates him from himself, that blocks him from the flow of his own imagination. Silent in his nostalgia, he has only become "Chief Broom," an object of Big Nurse's threats of extinction, the last remnant of the Native American, a trace of himself.

With such silence and disconnection, Chief Broom is easily held down, violently fixed: "They hold me down while she jams wicker bag and all into my mouth and shoves it down with a mop handle" (7). It is his telling, though, the way "now it's gonna roar out of me like floodwaters" (8), that he wants us to listen to, that he wants to be sure we experience and acknowledge. "But, please," he pleads with us, "It's still hard for me to have a clear mind thinking on it" (8). Yet, as he insists, "it's the truth even if it didn't happen" (8).

Suddenly and disruptively, Randle Patrick McMurphy (RPM, revolutions-per-minute) appears in the ward, reminding the Chief of the voice of his father, the articulation of his desire, the way his father used to talk : "He talks a little the way Papa used to, voice loud and full of hell . . ." (11). It is not that McMurphy looks like the father—"he doesn't look like Papa" (11), nor that he takes on the surrogate role of the father for Bromden (assumptions often made by critics), but rather that McMurphy is and is not like Bromden's father. His laugh is "real," contagious and spontaneous. McMurphy is real, not manufactured. His story is the story that the Chief will map his story onto, locate himself through. In this sense, McMurphy's overflowing desire, like his contagious laugh, will infect Bromden, as it "spreads in rings bigger and bigger till it's lapping against the walls all over the ward" (11).

McMurphy is more of a double for the Chief than he is a surrogate father figure. He is the playful body that the Chief needs to return to, the touch and the feel of human flesh, an authentic voice hinting at origins, the beginning of mortal identity at the threshold of language itself. When McMurphy arrives on the ward, not surprisingly he asks Bromden directly: "What's your story, Big Chief? You look like Sittin Bull on a sitdown strike" (22). It is as if he knows from the start that Bromden is resisting, protesting, and that the Chief needs to find his story, to tell it. "What's your name, Chief?" (22), McMurphy then asks, as if he is preparing the Chief to name himself, imagine the name, and envision the impossible possibility: not what the Combine has made of him, but who he is.

It is not that McMurphy wants Bromden to tell McMurphy's story for himself or for us, but to tell his own story, his singular story, the one he is responsible for, the one he believes in, the one he imagines, the true story of himself. He wants the Chief to create an imagined name, a vision beyond the fixed names he has been defined by, the Brooms and Bromdens that have ruled his mortal existence, all but buried that existence.

McMurphy invents strategies (from games to gambling to fishing trips) to inspire the Chief to reconnect with the potency of his sensuous body (at six feet seven or eight). He offers his hand to the Chief to get the blood flowing, to make the initial connection, a transfusion of shared human desire: "That palm made a scuffing sound against my hand. I remember the fingers were thick and strong closing over mine, and my hand commenced to feel peculiar and went to swelling up out there on my stick of my arm, like he was transmitting his own blood into it. It rang with blood and power" (23–24). It is this kind of movement and flow that allows the Chief to begin to mingle memory with desire, to open himself beyond the nostalgic fog, to begin to move back and forth from the past to the present, from the present to the past, to begin to create the depth of his own story, in other words, from what he imagines is in front of him now.

Despite the bureaucratic efficiency and obsessive tidiness of Big Nurse, the Chief, from the start, is attempting to call up the myth of himself, let memory and desire flow from the past to the present, give direction to his future. Inspired, in part, by McMurphy, it is as if he begins to locate himself within the depth of himself. "I was an electrician's assistant in training camp before the Army shipped me to German and I had some electronics in my year in college is how I learned about the way these things can be rigged" (27), he tell us, giving meaning through his own telling for the machinery and electric circuits that he believes Big Nurse controls. Slowly it seems that he is driven by an erotic sense of language as well. His memories of "spindles reeling" (38) and "shuttles jumping around and bobbins wringing the air with string" (38), when he used to work in a factory, stir desire and help him to believe now that "the ward is a factory for the Combine" (38). We will not be surprised when he later tells McMurphy, "My Papa was a full Chief and his name was Tee Ah Millatoona. That means The-Pine-That-Stands-Tallest-on-the-Mountain, and we didn't live on a mountain. He was real big when I was a kid" (207). It is the imagined name, not the assigned name of "Bromden" that he seeks, a communal name, mythic yet singular. "My mother got twice his size" (207), the Chief claims, but when he says that, he is already well on his way to locate himself through his imaginative account of his singularity.

Big Nurse—"that smiling flour faced old mother" (46)—defines and represents the ruling order, the Combine that threatens the Native American, the established order that robs the body and voice of its sensuous flow. But when McMurphy appeared in the ward, he was someone who seemed comfortable in his own skin, able, capable of functioning along the lines of control established by Big Nurse, on the boundary of her system of language. On that boundary, McMurphy found gaps in that system, imaginatively transforming the rules, twisting them from his own position.

It takes a while, but through such a rhythm the Chief begins to find a voice that carries with it both memory of his past and desire to move ahead, a way of opening what is before him and exploring the depth of his buried past: ". . . I'm after dust mice under his bed when I get a smell of something that makes me realize for the first time since I been in the hospital that this big dorm full of beds . . . has always been sticky with a thousand other smells . . . Pablum and eyewash, of musty shorts and socks musty even they are fresh . . . and sometimes the smell of singed hair—but never before now, before he came in, the man smell of dust and dirt from the open fields, and sweat, and work" (97–98). It is the smell and the taste of the body, the sense of touch, the dust and dirt of our shared mortality, the red clay of the natural earth that vibrates back and forth through the consciousness of the Chief, as his linguistic narrative now unfolds, distinct from the abstract and rigid law, his own distinct voice calls to us like the dust and dirt of the open fields of his childhood.

The Chief is playing deaf and dumb, but the voice of his telling is the contrary of that pretence of silence. It is the voice of plenitude and joy, a celebration of the fullness of the body, a voice that does not so much pound to a climax, nor drive to a determined point, but offers the richness of intimate experience, the risk and gamble of the complexity of mortal life (the dust and the dirt of it). It can be infectious, like McMurphy's laughter, both voice and laughter unique and communal at the same time. In terms of the 1960s, we might understand it best as a voice of polymorphous eroticism, a voice to be discovered at the margins of Big Nurse's own rigid discourse, a voice of the body and of the Chief's own past, the voice of the counterculture itself. It flows in disruptive opposition to the "big log book" (14) with its language of shame and in opposition to the "little brass tablet tacked to a piece of maple wood" (17) fixed to the wall with its rigid language of compliance and control. It is a growing presence that puts pressure on the ruling discourse, which has done what it can to silence it, to make the visionary presence vanish.

This is not to suggest that any of this is easy for the Chief. His experience is not the same as his telling of that experience. He is traumatized, often lost, or nearly lost, not simply hiding in the fog, but nearly undone. At times, he seems ready to give up: "The trouble was I'd been finding that door my own self because I got scared of being lost so long and went to hollering so they could track me . . . I had figured that anything was better'n being lost for good, even the Shock Shop. Now, I don't know. Being lost isn't so bad" (126). It is the struggle through that kind of loss, close to an utter loss, which has made him a believer now, and it is the repetitive rhythm of his struggle, shaped by his linguistic telling, that helps move him forward through that loss. The name of his mother "Bromden" making him small, Harding's wife making Harding feel impotent, Billy Bibbit's mother shaming him to death, Big Nurse lobotomizing (mentally castrating) her patients—they are all part of such repetition, but it is repetition fueled by desire, embodied not by the language of tragedy but by the lapping and roaring of imperfect lives, the laughter that surpasses understanding. It is not simply a repetition compulsion fixing him, but an acknowledgment of differences within apparent similarities, a way of movement, a hesitating foot stepping forward.

It is too simple to say that the Chief returns to himself only through his encounter with McMurphy. McMurphy has touched him, opened new possibilities for him; McMurphy's laughter and talk connect him back to his early memories of his father and the land. But such experiences also intensify the journey itself, make it more difficult to retreat into the simplicity of things, the rhythm of fear and hope becoming more complex for the Chief as his vision deepens, as the past presses on the present. When the Chief sees "old Colonel Masterson," we are reminded of just this, that it is not that the Chief is a victim of some psychopathic illness (let Big Nurse label it what she wants), but that he is slowly becoming a "seer," dying from what he has been made into, working to regain who he is. "I see him so clear I see his whole life" (128), the Chief tells us when he comes face-to-face with Masterson. "His voice as deep and slow and patient, and I see the words come out dark and heavy over his brittle lips when he reads" (129). It is "tell-a-vision," as the Chief experiences it. If the Colonel has been dismissed as an incurable Chronic speaking nonsense, the Chief sees it otherwise. If Colonel Masterson seems to be muttering nonsense, the Chief is discovering a way to "the truth" (even if others don't believe it). It is the way of his linguistic telling: "You're making sense, old man, a sense of your own. You're not crazy the way they think, Yes . . . I see" (129). It is what the Chief wants us to believe, his own singularity, the experience enacted through his linguistic rhythm, what he is beginning to discover. Unlike Big Nurse with her bureaucratic belief in perfection and totality, her simplistic attempt to clean life from the taint and dirt of mortality, the Chief must embrace a sense of ongoing and endless movement, the infinite flow of mortal human life.

If the Chief appears fearful, even lost, at times, he is nevertheless in pursuit of himself. McMurphy remains his best hope. McMurphy is "what he is, that's it" (153). He is extraordinary, the singularity of a self that the Chief is in pursuit of. When the Chief looks at his face in a mirror, though, he still cannot recognize himself: "That aint me, that ain't my face. I wasn't even really me . . . I was just being the way I looked, the way people wanted" (153). He doesn't want to be what McMurphy is, but discover who he himself is, the singularity of the mortal self, a self responsible for keeping the presence of his tribe, the imagined name, Tee Ah Millatoona, alive.

McMurphy encourages the playfulness of the polymorphous erotic body. Like a counterculture hero, the other resisting the established order of the dominant culture, McMurphy expresses, through winks and behavior, through talk and story, the natural playfulness of his own self: "Yes sir, that's what I came to this establishment for, to bring you birds fun an' entertainment around the gamin' table" (12). If he takes "a short retirement" (193) when he learns that most of the patients in the ward are "volunteers," not " committed" (182–183) as he is, he returns quickly from that momentary retreat to play out his own destiny. Unlike Big Nurse who wants to clip the wings of those "birds" (12), it is as if McMurphy wants to help them to envision flight. He suggests a fishing trip beyond the border of the ward and the Combine, out into unknown territory, a lark (the name of the boat that will take this crew fishing), a flight beyond the Cuckoo's Nest. "And the more he talked about fishing for Chinook salmon" (197), the more the Chief (the biggest bird of all, the one who will eventually fly over the Cuckoo's Nest) wants to go.

If McMurphy is the immediate inspiration for the Chief, though, it is the visionary presence of the Chief's tribe, in particular his father and the land, his childhood and his own memories that the Chief is really struggling to imagine (for himself and for us). It is an act of resistance, a way of countering his own vanishing (and that of his tribe). He is working to locate himself (and us) through an innate sense that believing in yourself can prevent you from vanishing, prevent final burial. Through his telling, he is bringing a trace of his presence back into existence, resisting the vanishing that the Combine has insisted on. It is as if the Chief is mapping his story onto McMurphy's so he can envision himself and remember how to tell it to others. In the process, what begins to vanish is not his identity, but the Combine itself.

"I was seeing lots of things different. I figured the fog machine had broken down in the walls when they turned it up too high for that meeting on Friday. . . . and one night I was even able to see out the window" (154). What the Chief sees out the window is not just a dog on its own journey, but a reminder of "the exact same thing when I was off on a hunt with Papa and the uncles and I lay rolled in blankets Grandma had woven . . ." (155). It is not only what is immediately beyond the window, but his expansive past and his future that he is able to envision as he moves on.

The night before the fishing trip, the Chief, lying in his bed, thinks back to when he was ten years old "still living in the village on the Columbia" (198). It is a detailed and extensive remembrance, striking in comparison to the other memories the Chief has told us about so far. It is the story of the government officials coming to the village, not listening to him, not talking to his father, waiting for his mother to take control, make the tribe understand "the advantages of having a hydroelectric dam and a lake instead of a cluster of shacks beside a falls" (202). Anticipating McMurphy's fishing trip, the Chief has moved much deeper into himself, opening himself to the movement from present to past, from past to present in a significant moment. "I was kind of amazed" (203), he tells us. Not only by the contents of the story, but that he remembered it now—". . . amazed that I'd remembered that. It was the first time in what seemed to me centuries that I'd been able to remember much about my childhood. It fascinated me to discover I could still do it. I lay in bed awake, remembering other happenings . . ." (203).

It is also the first night that the Chief starts talking again, apparently finding language through his remembrance of events long ago mingled with the immediacy of McMurphy's singing and their shared sense of laughter over the gum beneath the Chief's bed. When McMurphy gives the Chief some Juicy Fruit, a genuine gift no doubt, the Chief, not realizing what he is doing, tells him: "Thank you" (205). Those grateful words, the first that the Chief has spoken in years, open to conversation and an exchange of stories. Then, as if inspired by the expanding exchange of language, the Chief tells McMurphy about the tribe, his father, his mother. It is as if his telling, like McMurphy's laughter, "spreads in rings bigger and bigger till it's lapping against the walls" (11).

In turn, McMurphy meets the ethical demand placed on him, listening to the Chief as the Chief expands his story still further, connecting his family history with the Combine itself. If the Chief is "talking crazy" (210), as McMurphy says, he is nevertheless making sense (as McMurphy also acknowledges). He is learning to be who he is, and to envision who he is for others as well.

When the crew returns from the fishing trip, they bring "the sea home" (241) with them, all that is different from the land possessed by the Combine. They have risked the unknown and collectively return with a vision larger than the rigid boundaries of the Combine, the rules and regulations of Big Nurse. The Chief brings new memories of the depth of his own self with him as well, memories connected to the natural land and the poetry associated with that land: "I was feeling better than I'd remembered feeling since I was a kid, when everything was good and the land was still singing kids' poetry to me" (243).

The fishing trip further expands the Chief's vision, gives him renewed confidence, allows him to more fully understand that his vision (and his body) is bigger than Big Nurse's, that he does not have to live out the name he was born into, but can create a name for himself, an imagined name. But when that expansive vision is carried back into Big Nurse's rigid boundaries, there is bound to be conflict, violence, even death. Big Nurse responds as expected. A price must be paid. But, in turn, the Chief also responds, not with revenge, though, but with resistance, coupled with his sense of commitment to others (to "us" rather than "them"). Compassion drives the Chief now. Battling for the others in the showers, the Chief eventually finds himself, with McMurphy, up on Disturbed.

Amidst the "lightning flashes . . . colors striking" (272) from the Electro-Shock treatments administered by Big Nurse, the Chief resists, the rhythm of memory and desire moving him backward and forward again. Hearing the chant of his grandma in the midst of those electric currents—"Ting, Tingle, tingle tremble toes . . . one flew east, one flew west, one flew over the cuckoo's nest" (272)—the Chief recognizes himself more distinctly now, not only in the past but in the future, as a young boy with his grandma, playing with the rhythms and rhymes of the world and as a Native American in the future, that "goose flying over the cuckoo's nest" (273), like a Canadian honker. His destiny seems to emerge now with increased clarity, his connections to his tribe leading him toward the future and back to the past: the time his Papa and Uncle Running-and-Jumping Wolf, together with him, resisted the white authorities by digging up his grandma's corpse after a white burial, hanging it in a tree, giving it the dignity and authority of tribal rites and communal story. After that EST experience on Disturbed, finding the gaps in those electric charges, the Chief seems to move still closer to knowing who he is: "I had them beat . . . It was the last treatment they gave me" (275–276).

Drawing on the ludic and poetic memories of the past—his grandma's life and death, her vulnerability and her vision—and headed into the future, the Chief now participates in the Dionysian celebration of McMurphy's inevitable end. The Chief's vision has grown as McMurphy's life has been exhausted, and it is McMurphy's final gift to the Chief (and the others on the ward) to invigorate once again the erotic playfulness of the mortal body, the laughter of the communal human spirit. It is a reminder of the impossible possibility, what can happen if you believe. As the Chief puts it at the end of the party: "Drunk and running and laughing and carrying on with women square in the center of the Combine's most powerful stronghold! I thought back on the night, on what we'd been doing, and it was near impossible to believe. I had to keep reminding myself that it had truly happened, that we had made it happen" (292).

For the Chief, McMurphy, with his red hair, has become "ol' Red McMurphy" (276), not his personal savior, but a member of the tribe, the tribe of human doing, resisting the inhumane mechanisms of the Combine. One of us, rather than one of them. Inhumanity persists, though, and when Billy Bibbit is shamed by it—"The Nurse's tongue clucked in her bony throat. 'Oh, Billy Billy Billy—I'm so ashamed for you'" (300)—McMurphy can only respond by attempting to expose that shameful inhumanity one last time. Unlike the Chief's father, who had finally succumbed to it, losing his story to the fixed name of Bromden, McMurphy plays out his story, his destiny, who he is, for the others. Face-to-face with Big Nurse, her inhumanity, McMurphy's "red fingers" penetrate "the white flesh of her throat" (305), ripping down her white starched uniform, her breasts, for a moment, revealed: "the two nippled circles started from her chest and swelled out and out, bigger than anybody had ever imagined, warm and pink in the light" (305). If it is only a vision for a moment, it is nevertheless a glimpse of the vulnerable and the human, the mortal and sensual body, the beginning of intimacy leading to the inevitable end.

After the attack, Big Nurse orders a lobotomy for McMurphy, who is then brought back to the ward, "wheeled in this Gurney with a chart at the bottom that said in heavy black letters, "McMurphy, Randle P. Postoperative" (307). But it is only the abstraction of the name that Big Nurse controls. As the Chief knows, it is the singularity of the red man now, not the abstract name, nor the vegetative body, but the vision discovered through memory and desire, that will continue on.

When McMurphy, now in a vegetable state, is returned to the ward after his lobotomy, ordered by Big Nurse, the Chief's "shadow" falls "across the body, seeming to cleave it in half between the hips and the shoulders, leaving only a blank space" (309). It is as if the Chief is now ready not only to encounter his double, but to fill that "blank space" with his own doing, his responsibility to himself and to others, the patients in the ward and his tribe, his own story and destiny. It is his belief, his vision, that he is pursuing. Vulnerable, he is hopeful, able to take the risk. He is obliged and determined to put an end to the McMurphy who is no longer there.

As McMurphy vanishes, the Chief continues to gain strength: "The big, hard body had a tough grip on life. It fought a long time against having it taken away, nailing and thrashing around so much I finally had to lie full length on top of it and scissor the kicking legs with mine while I mashed the pillow into the face. I lay there on top of the body for what seemed days, until the thrashing stopped. Until it was still a while and had shuddered once and was still again" (309). In a poignant blending of homoerotic love and death, risking intimacy, the Chief seems to have regained his confidence, the rhythm of a vision embodied in his own mortal self, in his experience rendered through his linguistic telling.

The Chief can now lift Big Nurse's control panel and throw it through the window, the glass splashing "out in the moon, like a bright cold water baptizing the sleeping earth" (310). That earth is the natural land of his home, a place baptized by the flow of vision that he has enabled, as he breaks free: "I felt like I was flying" (310). If, like a Canadian honker, he is destined for Canada, he is headed first for the Columbia Gorge to see "if there's any of the guys (he) used to know back in the village" (311). The overflow of hope and desire drives him on, the impossible possibility that "some of the tribe have took to building their old ramshackle wood scaffolding all over that big million-dollar hydroelectric dam" (311). Envisioning the resilience of human vulnerability in the face of the inhumanity of the Combine's technological power, he will glimpse the flow of human desire along the way, the vision of his tribe "spearing salmon in the spillway" (311), a vision of the uncontrollable overflow emanating from what the Combine cannot know, what they cannot control.

If the Chief has found a voice that allows him to articulate his experience, though, we, as readers, need to remember that Big Nurse and the Combine are still out there. As the Chief has said: "It's still hard for me to have a clear mind thinking on it. But it's the truth even if it didn't happen" (8). That "truth" is the burning fear and manic roaring of consciousness that makes up the Chief's telling, what we have experienced as his vision. If we can hear the voice, we also know that the inhumanity of Big Nurse can return, as the repressed always does. The Chief has" been away for a long time" (311), as the last words of his story say, but still "They're out there" (3), as his first words indicated. If his telling offers a beginning, it is difficult nevertheless to locate that telling in any particular place. As readers, we have listened to "the truth" of that telling. It is the vision of the other, a linguistic being whose presence will continue to put pressure on the fixed and rigid structures that surround him. It is a linguistic telling that demands our attention. The Chief has offered us his truth, and it is his singularity that we must acknowledge. It is his story that makes our story possible.

9

Fight Club

Fight Club is marked with instability, with the slippage of language, with the postmodern condition of the collapse of boundaries, and with intimations that we begin where we end. What we need to bracket from the start, though, is any sense that we are watching a film on a screen, although it is Fincher's film version of this linguistic narrative that made the novel into a cult classic. The unnamed narrator is not Ed Norton, nor is Tyler Durden really Brad Pitt. It is only the language that we, as readers, experience, the language that creates an intersubjective space for us to enter. We are in dialogue with the literary narrative from the start, helping to create it from the beginning to the end: ". . . the first step to eternal life is you have to die" (11), we are told in the opening sentence. If that "you" is the unnamed narrator, that "you" is also us. The gun pressing against "the back of my throat" (11) may be Tyler's, but that throat is also ours. We seem to be at the edge of murder or suicide at the start of this narrative, and we'd like to know how we arrived here and where we are headed. Yet, as readers, we might also speculate that there is no real danger. As Tyler says, "We really won't die" (11).

As the story begins, it appears as if we are near the end of something. The unnamed narrator is on top of the Parker-Morris Building, a building ready to topple over the edge and "slam down on the national museum which is Tyler's real target" (12). But who is this Tyler Durden? The narrator seems obsessed with him (having mentioned his name four times in the opening three sentences). "People are always asking, did I know Tyler Durden" (12), the narrator tells us. He must have known Tyler. Tyler got him a job as a banquet waiter, and Tyler is now pressing a gun in his mouth and talking to the narrator. Yet, we never really know anyone, do we? Even ourselves. There is something strange here, from the start.

Perhaps the unnamed narrator is not really telling the story. Maybe Tyler is the narrator? The narrator claims, "I've been here from the beginning" (15) and that he remembers everything. But Tyler has also been there from the beginning. (In fact, "Tyler" is the first word spoken in this enigmatic and puzzling narrative.)

Like Jekyll and Hyde, or Chief Bromden and McMurphy, or Frankenstein and the Monster, the unnamed narrator and Tyler seem connected, doubles. But, as the narrator indicates, this story has also come into being because of Marla Singer: "I know all of this: the gun, the anarchy, the explosion is really about Marla Singer" (14). There is apparently a love triangle here: "I want Tyler. Tyler wants Marla. Marla wants me" (14). Perhaps this narrative, as impossible as it seems, is really Marla's?

On the advice of his doctor, the narrator starts attending support groups to relieve his insomnia, to get closer to something more real than his IKEA consumer life as a recall specialist. At first, it doesn't seem to work. When he imagines his pain through the guided meditation provided by Chloe—"a skeleton dipped in yellow wax" (20), the narrator still feels estranged from himself and his own experiences, "a copy of a copy of a copy" (21). At Remaining Men Together, though, a support group for testicular cancer, the narrator encounters Big Bob who temporarily releases him from the symptoms of his insomnia. Crying into Big Bob's body, the narrator finds a moment of comfort and warmth in Bob's womblike embrace, making him feel "lost inside oblivion, dark and silent and complete" (22). But then, reborn out of that womblike state, the narrator sees mirrored on Bob's shirt a wet mask of how he looks crying.

Is this the first sign of a rebirth of sorts for the narrator, the beginning of a revived self-consciousness, or is it further recognition that life is simply "a copy of a copy?" (21). In either case, we are reminded that moving from such womblike origins out into the world is always fraught with mortal contradictions, although such movement is necessary for human growth and development. If leaving the womb offers freedom, it is not a boundless freedom. In fact, as the narrator indicates, the immediate sense of this momentary feeling of release (or rebirth) is that it is a freedom without hope. "Losing all hope was freedom" (22), the narrator now claims.

If he has nothing left to lose, then he must have hit bottom, the narrator now assumes. Crying with others in the support group, he has, supposedly, become "the little warm center that the life of the world crowded around" (22). He can now sleep better than a baby. But isn't that "warm center" very much like Chloe's guided meditation, an escape from the pain of the body? Is it a way out or a way in? If the narrator is fooling himself, it is nevertheless the narrator's "real life," as he is telling it to us, that we, as readers, are now experiencing.

The narrator claims that he remembers everything (which seems unlikely). But perhaps he does remember now that we all live with a gun to our head (or in our mouth), an existential condition similar to sensing that the body is a host to cancer or blood parasites (even if we have not been diagnosed as such). Crying with Bob might have emptied out the narrator when it happened, providing him with a momentary sense of cathartic cleanliness, but, at the time, the narrator must have been far from knowing himself (or knowing that he had a gun in his mouth). He was faking his life as if it were a type of guided meditation—like the one Chloe offers—taking him to 'the garden of serenity" (20), not back to his mortal body, but away from it. He might not have understood all this then, but we know it now because the narrative tells us as much.

When Marla appears at the support group and starts watching him, the narrator can no longer cry. Why not? For the same reason, we might imagine, that Adam was befuddled when he realized that Eve was watching him after they ate the apple in the Garden of Eden. "With her watching, I'm a liar," the narrator says, quickly adding: "She's a fake. She's the liar" (23). Seeing Marla watching him exposes the narrator to himself, but unlike Adam, the narrator does not acknowledge the similarities and differences between the man and the woman. He insists on their sameness. "In this moment, Marla's lie reflects my lie, and all that I can see are lies" (23), the narrator claims. He remains flattened out in a desperate world of consumer culture, the IKEA world where "even death and dying rank right down there with plastic flowers and video as a non-event" (23). At the time, the narrator could not make distinctions; he had no sense of difference.

If Tyler Durden is an alter ego of the nameless narrator (who never reveals his real name to us), Marla Singer must also be a dimension of this narrator, a part of him as disturbing as Tyler must be. But, when they first encountered each other, both he and Marla were tourists in a consumer culture. Nodes in the consumer network, they were fundamentally disembodied, far from hitting bottom, floating in the world without authentic engagement or differentiation. Their "real lives" were fakes, contingencies, illusions; only the narrative-telling can make those lives meaningful now.

As readers, we follow the unnamed narrator traveling from airport to airport as a recall campaign coordinator. Although he seems to be mobile, he is not on the ground moving, but disembodied, floating in the air. He creates ratios for cost analysis, applying formulas to "keep the secret intact" (30). The unnamed narrator seems to be a consumer abstraction himself. He does not appear to be in pursuit of any significant secret: the mystery of human existence, his own complex and contradictory mortal identity. Rather he seems an object possessed by the consumer culture. He works to avoid risk for the company and himself, to prevent the exposure of imperfections, to keep the secrets of the company and himself hidden. He is like the audience in a movie theater, unaware of the projectionist (like Tyler) who conceals the gaps between reels, not allowing the audience to acknowledge the gap. The audience views simply the smooth flow of the film's story. They never seem to notice the cigarette burns that appear between reels. It is only the narrator's telling that reveals those cigarette burns for us.

In his IKEA world, the narrator remains numb to, or perhaps resistant to, any sense of difference. He knows where the skeletons are, but holds that secret in reserve, using it not to explore the possibilities of his life, but for job security. He seems especially numb to any sense of sexual difference—in particular, the sexual difference between Marla and himself. Even at the testicular cancer group (a strange place for Marla to appear), the narrator and Marla seem much the same, both "fakers," without distinction. From this perspective, Tyler is apparently the only one that can make the difference: ". . . there's the flash of an erection. Tyler does this" (30).

But who is Tyler? The narrator claims that he first met him on a nude beach. Whether the narrator was dreaming or awake, whether he met Tyler by accident or necessity, is unclear. Tyler pulled driftwood logs out of the surf up the beach then, setting them upright in the sand. Then he drew a line in the sand "to gauge the shadow cast by each log" (32). For "one perfect moment" (apparently all that anyone can hope for), the shadow became "a perfect hand," and Tyler sat within its palm. As the narrator says: "Tyler had sat in the palm of a perfection he'd created himself" (32). According to Tyler Durden, "one minute was enough . . . a person had to work hard for it, but a minute of perfection was worth the effort" (32).

Whatever else we might make of this "minute of perfection" with its shadowy hand and its emphasis on human agency and satisfaction (as momentary as it might have been when it happened), it now propels the narrative forward (and backward). Tyler makes the effort possible (in the same sense that he makes an erection possible). But if we assume that Tyler is the narrator's power animal, we are quickly brought up short. Marla, the faker, quickly reappears in the story, and the narrator tells us that she is the one who is really his "power animal" (36). At the time, though, he still could not open himself to Marla—his "charkas stay closed" (37). Like Marla, he still had "no real sense of life" (38). He could not make much of an effort.

At the time that this all happened, the narrator appeared flattened out in his IKEA world of endless contingency, closed off from himself and from Marla, but the linguistic narrative is now opening itself within itself as it moves forward; it is in dialogue with us as readers. If the unnamed narrator was, like Marla, closed-off in the disembodied IKEA world of consumer perfection, the narrator now, like Tyler, is making an effort. It is as if the narrator through his telling of the story is becoming increasingly aware of the cigarette burns (the gap) between reels, and so is beginning to position himself in the midst of the language he is creating. He is awakening to the meaning of the "real life" that he had led. As readers, we have that opportunity as well. The narrator's language, looping forward and backward, allows us to awaken to the difference between the illusion and the reality, the fake and the real thing, the contingent events of "real life" and the necessity of those events shaped by the linguistic telling (as blurry as that difference might be).

We next hear that the narrator's apartment blows up. Then, the narrator calls Tyler on Paper Street (a place to create a story). When they meet at a bar, Tyler wants the unnamed narrator to hit him: "I want you to hit me as hard as you can" (46). This is the beginning of Fight Club. As readers, we do not yet know who, if anyone, blew up the narrator's apartment, whether it was an accident or not, and we wonder, at first, whether the narrator is even capable of hitting another person and whether the black eye and swollen face he claims he has are due to Tyler hitting him back or to a later encounter at Fight Club. Whether we know or not, though, the narrator supposedly knows. (He claimed as much at the start of the story.) But perhaps it is better to say that the linguistic narrative knows. It tells us more than the narrator's contingent experiences initially told him. It reminds us of the gap between "real life" experience (when it happened) and the telling of that experience now. We remain puzzled, though, baffled in the midst of the story.

If the unnamed narrator hits Tyler, Tyler hits the unnamed narrator. If Tyler puts a gun in the unnamed narrator's mouth, the unnamed narrator puts a gun in Tyler's mouth. Either way, the narrative continues to move forward and backward, moving us with its doubleness, its apparent randomness, and its sense of necessity. This is not the experience of Fight Club when it happens, but it is the meaning of Fight Club experienced through the narrative. The narrative creates a boundary and a difference: "Who guys are in fight club is not who they are in the real world" (49).

"What happens at fight club doesn't happen in words" (51), but Fight Club needs language just as "real life" needs linguistic narrative. "The first rule about fight club is you don't talk about fight club" (51), but Fight Club needs people to talk about it if it is to survive and flourish. Fortunately people do talk about it, all the time. The law creates its own transgression, and it is a good thing it does. The experience of Fight Club brings people into a shared space, and it also hints at a sense of difference, both inside that space and outside it. But it is the linguistic telling that makes meaning from that experience. "Who I am in fight club is not someone my boss knows" (51), the narrator tells us.

As the narrative continues to unfold, the unnamed narrator now returns to the initial fight scene between Tyler and himself, the beginning of Fight Club. They hit each other, and the narrator experiences a surge of confidence and control: "I felt finally I could get my hands on everything in the world that didn't work" (53). Fight Club just happens, but that happening can happen again. If what happens doesn't happen in words, though, language can make what happens matter. If the unnamed narrator does not seem to immediately know this, we, as readers, know it. If the unnamed narrator didn't quite understand this at the time, we do as he tells it to us. He might not even understand it right now. But Tyler does. As the narrator claims, "Sometimes Tyler speaks for me" (52).

We recall that earlier in the narrative, the unnamed narrator claimed that at the time it happened the relationship between him, Tyler and Marla was clear: "I want Tyler. Tyler wants Marla. Marla wants me" (14). According to him, this wasn't "about love as in caring. This was about property as in ownership" (14). He was still thinking then with an IKEA consciousness. His identity was his possessions, a commodity stuck in the ratios of consumer abstraction. After a month on Paper Street, though, living at the edge of consumer culture and participating in Fight Club, the relationship between Tyler and the narrator apparently deepens, developing complications as it should, opening itself to similarities and differences, mortal complexities and tensions, secrets that cannot simply be kept in reserve for the sake of comfort and security. We discover that Marla, too, lives on the edge, desperate and desirous, seemingly located at the sleaze bag Regent Hotel, although her ghost-like presence also appears on Paper Street, intensifying the haunting undertone of the narrative.

On Paper Street, the narrator begins to wonder "if Tyler and Marla are the same person" (65). As readers, we might at first assume that they are the same person, except for their sexual difference: "Except for their humping every night in Marla's room" (65)—that is, the other room where the narrator is not. According to the narrator, Tyler and Marla behave just like his parents used to behave (invisible to each other), at least until his father went off and left the family. Without a father-figure, the narrator must have felt abandoned, a profound sense of absence apparently filled, at the time, by the consumer culture that he now seems to be moving away from. Like the narrator, Marla also feels a similar sense of absence, leaving her stuck and confused as well. If her "humping" (65) with Tyler is her attempt to fill that absence, though, it is not much of a commitment: "she's confused and afraid to commit to the wrong thing so she won't commit to anything" (61). For the moment that lack of commitment might be to her advantage.

It is as if the narrator is and is not Tyler. Is it possible that Marla is and is not the narrator as well? The narrative telling evokes these questions more insistently now, embodying the complexity and depth of what otherwise might be flattened out moments, contingent happenings. As Tyler indicates: We need to pay attention. "Because everything up to now is a story, and everything after now is a story" (75). That present moment of "now" might be the greatest moment of our life, a disruptive event opening to a new beginning, but that moment is meaningless without the story that gives it its dwelling and depth. That moment is pregnant with possibilities because of the story. Without story, that moment threatens to end in abortion.

It becomes increasingly clear that the narrative generates questions not answers, uncertain possibilities not consumer confidence. It is similar, in other words, to the painful kiss that Tyler imprints on the back of the narrator's hand, a kiss that supposedly seals a promise burnt with lye into the mortal flesh. Like us, the narrator needs a scar to be mindful of the beginning and the end of mortal identity. That kiss, painful as it is, becomes a kind of birthmark, a reminder of the promise of mortal life lived with others, the bond of friends and family, but, inscribed in the flesh, it is also a reminder of our singularity, our strangeness, a glimpse of death alone. If Tyler's kiss is a promise, it also carries with it its own betrayal.

The narrator and Tyler soon become "guerrilla terrorists of the service industry" (81), disrupting banquet parties and consumer confidence. But they also establish their own business, manufacturing soap on Paper Street. According to Tyler, the best soap uses human fat as a primary ingredient, a process of transformation connected to the ancient and heroic tradition of human sacrifice. Without sacrifice, we would have nothing. This is true, we might think, but not the whole truth. Tyler is not wrong, but it is a question of perspective. When he is talking about sacrifice, is Tyler exploring love as in caring or is he lecturing about possessions as in ownership? Or can anyone any longer tell the difference? The Paper Street Soap Company gives Tyler, for the first time, real money to play with. We might question what Tyler sacrifices in the process.

Marla's mother also practices sacrifice, sending Marla her own body fat. It is self-sacrifice, a gift made to Marla's "collagen trust fund" (91) for the purpose of smoothing out Marla's wrinkles, puffing up her lips, and boosting her self-esteem. Is this about consumer goods or love? How certain can we be about motives anyway? For no apparent reason, Tyler sends Marla's mother a 15-pound box of chocolates. We might conclude that Tyler wants more human fat in order to make more money for himself. But perhaps Tyler was thinking about his own absent mother when he sent those chocolates. Or perhaps the unnamed narrator actually sent those chocolates? Or maybe Marla did?

When Marla discovers that they are using her mother's fat at the Paper Street Soap Factory, Marla is understandably outraged. Screaming, she accuses the narrator: "You boiled my mother!" (93) But who would possibly boil the body of a mother? Cannibals and Nazis, and agents of the consumer culture—anyone who has forgotten their origins in the mortal body. The narrator needs Marla if he is going to reconnect with the origins of his body, rediscover his mortal self.

Having traveled some distance with the narrator, we wonder now what kind of story this is. At the start, the narrator claimed he knew everything, and we might assume that he has at least been giving us clues to the secret that he knows. But is that secret connected to the mystery of mortal life, or simply a distraction to keep us interested in what will turn out to be another consumer fraud? The narrator has indicated that what he is telling us might only be "a copy of copy of a copy" (21). Now he says it again: "The hole in my cheek, the blue black swelling around my eyes, and the swollen red scar of Tyler's kiss on the back of my hand, a copy of a copy of a copy" (97). Is he simply unreliable and, at best, confused? Or is he genuinely hesitant to tell us all that has happened (or that he believes has happened)? As he says, "There are a lot of things we don't want to know about the people we love" (106). He is tentative and uncertain, but that may very well be a virtue, a sign of human love and caring.

Both the narrator and Marla have a birthmark, and, like the narrator, "Marla has the scar from Tyler's kiss on the back of her hand" (106). If we are ethically responsible readers, we care about the narrator and Marla because we, too, have a birthmark and a scar; we, too, will die. Such knowledge not only makes us tentative, but it also makes us more than an object of disembodied consumer consciousness. Maybe we can distinguish between the mystery of mortal life and the illusions of consumer fraud. As Tyler explained to the narrator long ago, "Someday you will die, and until you know that you are useless to me" (76). As readers, we remember that from the beginning we have had a gun in our mouth—and so has the narrator.

If people think you are dying, the narrator now tells us, they give you their full attention. They listen to you rather than just waiting for their turn to speak: "And when the two of you talk, you are building something, and afterward, you are both different than before" (107). We need to be in dialogue with the narrative telling. This is the way support groups work as well, the way Fight Club works (sort of), and the way linguistic narrative works—providing we as readers dare to commit ourselves to it. It is the human exchange within a shared space, risky business, that opens us to the other, and that makes the difference. We need to trust it as a promise, but also to acknowledge that that promise might betray us in the end. If the promise is important (and it is), then the knowledge of its betrayal is also important. Such knowledge stirs desire in us, brings us back to others and then forward to the contingencies of "real life." It connects us to our commonalities as mortal human beings and offers a glimpse of our singularity. It keeps us questioning, questing, and moving with a healthy skepticism. This is what this story invites us to experience.

As the narrative expands and develops, Fight Club evolves into Project Mayhem. To put it that way, though, is somewhat like saying that the law precedes its transgression, or that a promise precedes its betrayal, or that eros precedes thanatos, or that biology precedes biography. It is better to suggest that as the narrative continues it begins to articulate more fully the historical and religious impulses already embodied within it. Project Mayhem is and is not a consequence of the experience of Fight Club. Project Mayhem happens. Within the rhythm of the narrative language, though, it happens next. Project Mayhem does and does not evolve from Fight Club. Unlike death, it is and it is not inevitable.

As readers we first notice Project Mayhem when the narrator reports that "It's in the newspaper today" (118). It is front page news accompanied with a photo. Unlike the primarily private and psychological experience of Fight Club—happening underground and hidden from the mainstream consumer culture—Project Mayhem is more readily experienced as a public event, a carnivalesque mirror image of the disembodied consumer culture. It is a bureaucracy of anarchy, organized chaos, committees with homework assignments. To us, Project Mayhem may look similar to Frankenstein's Monster, the Devil standing upright speaking, Fascism with its promise of unbounded freedom. It is similar to the medical waste dump generating resentments that can then be used for revolutionary effect. Like the consumer culture, it promises a return to the Garden of Eden or to Heaven, and it can turn into an addiction as quickly as shopping can. Project Mayhem is connected to Tyler, and it could be connected to us, especially if we as readers do not pay close attention and continue to question. "You don't ask questions is the first rule in Project

Mayhem" (122), the narrator tells us. Project Mayhem is based on blind faith, complete and total trust.

Earlier the narrator was personally concerned about hitting bottom, and he now wants the "the whole world to hit bottom" (123). We are no longer focused primarily on the individual body but the collective body (the world body): "We wanted to blast the world free of history" (124). With Project Mayhem, we are apparently on the verge of apocalypse, hoping for the end of time and the beginning of something else. We have entered a world of uniformed black shirts, guns and murder, total and complete trust for Tyler without question. If the consumer culture's goal is the disembodiment of the human (and so the destruction of the individual temporal body), then we might believe that the goal of Project Mayhem is "the complete and right-away destruction of civilization" (125), followed by the resurrection of the world body (as Tyler claims). But if we believe that, then we have not been paying attention. Project Mayhem is the dark underside of the IKEA culture, its displaced libido, its abjection. It is blind to its own limitations and imperfections. Like the consumer culture, its goal is absolute and complete denial of the contradictions and complexities of the mortal self, denial of the unique and imperfect snowflakes. It makes us all "part of the same compost heap" (134).

Interestingly, as Project Mayhem develops, Marla, despite her confusion, appears as the one individual disturbing its smooth surface. She is outrightly resistant to the space monkeys—"Get screwed" (133), she tells them—and she remains particularly attuned to the rhythms of the natural world. She names the plants when she walks with the narrator through the garden at Paper Street, and she is the one who challenges the narrator with important questions: "What are you going to do?" (136). In terms of the narrative, as Marla moves closer to the narrator (or perhaps it is better to say, as the narrator moves closer to his awareness of her), Tyler becomes more problematic and distant.

With the spread of Project Mayhem into public consciousness, Tyler becomes a celebrity and a legend, front page news, a public image, and as his name becomes increasingly familiar to the public, his identity as a separate individual seems to fade. The unnamed narrator may not have noticed this at the time it was happening, but we know it as he tells it to us through the narrative. In fact, despite his uncertainties, the narrator now seems increasingly capable of distinguishing between his own narrative and the accidents and contingencies of his past "real life." He is growing in confidence as a narrator of his own life story, and he is increasingly aware of the way that he can create a sense of temporal duration for the apparent accidents of life. When the Cadillac mechanic, for example, crashes the car he was driving while on assignment for Project Mayhem, the narrator offers us this:

> Too late, the truck swerves but the rear of our Corniche fishtails against one end of the truck's front bumper. Not that I know this at the time, what I know is the lights. . .and I'm thrown against the birthday cake and the mechanic behind the steering wheel. (145)

That accident is made into "one perfect second" (146) by the narrator, linguistically shaped into meaning. It is a chance happening rendered as destiny, a memory of his birth and a reminder of his death: how small he is (and we all are) in the vast starry universe. As if created by a shadowy hand, it echoes the narrator's first meeting with Tyler. It is a near perfect moment that we can dwell in, a glimpse at the stars, where we are going, where we have been.

If that revelation is apparent to us, though, it is not immediately apparent to the unnamed narrator, at least not before he renders the narrative for us. At the moment of the accident, he still believed that he had no story to tell: "I am nothing in the world compared to Tyler" (146). But he is telling us this now, confessing and shaping his story, differentiating his experience then from the telling of that experience now: "My tiny life. My little shit job. My Swedish furniture. I, never, no, never told anyone this, but before I met Tyler, I was planning to buy a dog and name it 'Entourage'" (146). If Tyler was gaining control over the narrator at the time, the narrator is offering us an account of his life now, telling us who he is and who we are. He is and is not Tyler.

In the context of the story being told, the narrator now goes out on another homework assignment for Project Mayhem and confronts Raymond Hessel. Under the rules set up by Tyler, he has a gun ready to shoot Hessel. If he has a gun, though, he also feels pity and compassion. Seeing Hessel crying (as Hessel thinks about his own family), the narrator hesitates. With a gun at Hessel's head, he compels Hessel to confront death. But he does not sentence him to death. Instead, he asks Hessel a question: "How did you want to spend your life?" (146)—evoking in Hessel a life story (rather than death), the possibility of a "tomorrow" (146) that will be the most beautiful day of Hessel's life. It is not Project Mayhem but linguistic narrative that allows such hope to become possible.

Separated from Tyler, the narrator intensifies his search for Tyler. If he still seems obsessed by Tyler, he is also sharpening the sense of difference between himself and his obsession. Strangers still identify him as Tyler, though, and Marla does not acknowledge the difference, either. She still thinks the narrator is Tyler, the person who saved her life the night she accidently attempted suicide at the Regent Hotel. On the phone, the narrator asks her what his name is: her reply, "Tyler Durden" (160), the one who appears to use her for sex at night and avoid her during the day. To break free of his obsession, the narrator needs Marla to keep him awake and to acknowledge the difference between him and Tyler.

The unnamed narrator is not Tyler anymore than Jekyll is Hyde or Frankenstein is the Monster or Chief Bromden is McMurphy. The narrator follows Tyler, and Tyler follows him. We follow the narrative, and the narrative follows us. If the first rule of Fight Club is not to talk about Fight Club, it is that talk that has made Fight Club—as well as Tyler and Project Mayhem—meaningful. It is as if Marla has become the deep desire haunting the language of the narrative. She is "the power animal" (36) that can make that meaning happen.

We are "the middle children of history" (166), and that is our existential condition as mortal human beings. As middle children of history, we cannot completely know our beginning or our end. We can help shape history, but history also shapes us. We have a gun pointed at our head from the beginning, but we have also emerged from a mother's body from the beginning. What we render meaningful in the temporal moment between our beginning and our end—in the middle of the history, which started before we were born and will continue long after we are dead—is what is important. We need to stay awake and know who we are.

"Long story short," Tyler tells the narrator, "when you're awake, you have the control, and you can call yourself anything you want, but the second you fall asleep, I take over, and you become Tyler Durden" (167). The challenge for the narrator now is to make sure he does not fall asleep, stays awake, and makes sure that Tyler does not gain complete and total control. To accomplish that, however, he needs to acknowledge that he desires the desire of Marla, and he needs to know that Marla knows the difference between him and Tyler.

What action does the narrator need to take to achieve this kind of relationship with Marla? He must break the promise he has made to Tyler: that he will not talk to Marla about Tyler. At Denny's restaurant, Marla and the narrator meet, sitting at a window booth, face-to-face, talking. The waiter insists that the narrator is Tyler, but the narrator tells Marla he is not, showing her his driver's license (with his real name on it) and claiming that at least his parents know who he is. When Marla asks, "So why are you Tyler Durden to some people but not to everybody?" (172), he responds by telling her the story that we, as readers, already know, repeating the story about Tyler that he has already told us. Reflecting on that story, the narrator acknowledges to Marla that he felt "trapped," at the time: "I was too complete. I was too perfect" (173).

The repetition of the story, as he now tells it in abbreviated form to Marla, helps stabilize the narrator, allows him to recognize himself, his mortal imperfections, opening a shared space for Marla and him. In turn, Marla responds: "Everybody has their little quirks" (173), acknowledging the familiar and the strange in the narrator. The narrator needs Marla to keep him awake and to acknowledge him, just as Marla needed someone to keep her awake and so save her life the night she called from her hotel room. What they both desire is the desire of the other.

As readers, we now see that the narrative is emerging as a romance, a love story of sorts, but we also remember that embedded in every promise is a betrayal. If we are reading a romance, we are not merely experiencing guided meditation, a drug store romance with a happily-ever-after ending. The promise of this narrative will lead us back into the complexities and contradictions of our "real life," what we cannot fully name, a reminder of our incompleteness. We are more than our names: "Only in death will we have our own names since only in death we are no longer part of the effort" (178). We need to make that effort as long as we desire to live. (Ask Big Bob aka "Robert Paulson.")

As the story moves toward its conclusion, the narrator reminds us that we kill the thing we love, and love the thing we kill. Despite his ongoing frenzy and desperate confusion amidst the contingencies of life, he seems to be moving with the narrative itself developing an increased awareness of the inevitable rhythm of promise and betrayal, and a sense of ethical responsibility: "My boss is dead. My home is gone. My job is gone. And I'm responsible for it all" (193). To acknowledge such responsibility suggests that he does care. But what can he do about Tyler? And what about Marla?

The narrator cannot get rid of Tyler without killing himself, but by telling about Tyler, he can take care of him. He needs to acknowledge Marla as well: that he cares about her. "There's Marla, and she's in the middle of everything and doesn't know it . . . Somebody has to tell her" (193). Marla still doesn't know the difference between Tyler and the narrator, though. Before Marla can acknowledge that important difference, the narrator will "have to take care of Tyler" (197).

The narrative circles back on itself once again, back toward its beginning. In its looping movement, it starts to empty itself out, demanding that we, as readers, recognize both the boundary between literary fiction and "real life" and the porous nature of that boundary, a boundary always blurred and ready to be transgressed. As it speeds up,

Marla and the narrator meet again, where they first met, as if in a dream flickering quickly from past to present to future. "It happens that fast" (196), the narrator claims.

"Why should I believe any of this" (197), Marla wonders, as she listens to the narrator. As readers, we want her to believe it because we know it's true even if it didn't happen. It's not a drug store romance or even an "Agatha Christie" (196) mystery fantasy that the narrator has been telling us. He cares enough about us not to offer that kind of superficial love and death formula, the kind that masks the pain of mortal life and gives us the ease of speedy consumption. He likes us too much for that, just as he likes Marla, as he now admits. He needs to take care of her and Tyler. "What happens doesn't happen in words" (199), the narrator reminds us again, but what happens takes on meaning through the linguistic narrative that continues until we return to "real life" with the narrative in mind. Project Mayhem and Fight Club continue until we die, the narrator knows, but so does the will to live. We need to make the effort. "My will to live amazes me" (202), the narrator can now say.

Finally, the narrative circles back to where it began. "We're down to the last eight minutes" (203) with Tyler holding a gun in the narrator's mouth. "Three minutes. . . . And now I'm just one man holding a gun in my mouth" (204). We're on top of the tallest building in the world, the Parker Morris building. But we see something we did not see before. . . . "and it's Marla coming toward us across the roof" (204) with the cast of characters from all the support groups ready to help, ready to sacrifice themselves for us and the narrator. There's no explosion, no apocalyptic end, but, importantly, Marla is there, shouting that she likes the narrator, not Tyler but the narrator, and that she knows the difference between them. "I know the difference" (205), she exclaims. It is another "perfect moment" (132) within time, a fleeting epiphany within the narrative. It should sustain us when we return to the happenings of "real life."

The unnamed narrator still needs to take care of one more thing before the narrative ends: the gun that has been lingering since the beginning. The gun doesn't have to go off (pace with Chekhov), but, as narrator, he needs to "pull the trigger." And he does. "And I pull the trigger" (205), he tells us.

We might anticipate that that sentence triggers the end of the narrative, a death sentence ending the narrator's life. That would make the narrative an impossible one, though (unless the narrator is telling it from heaven). But we know now that the narrative is and is not an impossible one. So it continues, apparently not in heaven but in a mental institution where the narrator, understandably, is hesitant to immediately return to "real life," although he will not forget what he now knows, what he has rendered in his telling of what happened (and continues to happen).

The narrator (always unnamed) lives on as do Tyler and Marla, as do Fight Club and Project Mayhem, as does the consumer culture. Unnamed, the narrator (like us) remains an incomplete human being, not perfect or total, but infinitely questing, a person who has become part of the effort. As readers, we are like those others at the end of the narrative, ready to move forward into the real world, whispering to the narrator: "We look forward to getting you back" (208).

10

The Sense of an Ending

Julian Barnes's *The Sense of an Ending* offers a doubleness in its narrative that intrigues us as readers. It is as if while we are following the experiences of Tony Webster, an ordinary man telling an ordinary story, the version he likes to tell himself, another story is emerging, an extraordinary story, the one he needs to tell us now. It is not as if he is confessing but assessing himself, hoping that we will think well of him as he converses with us.

At first, we might believe that Tony's story is average, ordinary, even mundane, not worth our time, not "novel-worthy" (16), unless, we, as readers, are, as he claims he is, drawn to the click-clock rhythm of the second-hand that protects us from the mystery, the secret of time itself. But, as we will see, his narrative works against itself, the apparent ordinariness of a mundane life yielding to the depth of memory and desire. It is not so much what Tony says but his saying, the way the past dissolves into the present, opens to the future, which puts us, as readers, into question.

As Tony tells us at the beginning: "We live in time—it holds us and moulds us—I've never felt I understood it very well" (3). For Tony (and for us), to live in time is to live within his story, to be on a quest, to be put into question. To read his story is to follow his journey, to risk, as Tony warns us, the acknowledgment that "the longer we live, the less we understand" (143). Or to put it in the mathematical terms that Tony seems to favor: "Life isn't just addition and subtraction. There's also the accumulation of loss, of failure" (113).

As readers setting out with Tony, we know neither ourselves nor others; like Tony's, our impressions are our dreams, and we dream as we live, alone. Yet, Tony wants us to listen to him, to engage in conversation with him. We agree that it is our obligation to do so, open ourselves to ourselves and to him, read the account of the other offered to us, as we attempt to know what we cannot know, the impossibility of the secret that we seek. If we cannot grasp that secret, we might glimpse it, even learn to care about it, care about Tony and ourselves.

Tony Webster is counting on us from the start, on his and our shared sense of desire to tell each other our stories. *The Sense of an Ending* demands to be read with this in mind: that we, as mortal human beings, innately sense an ending from the start, that the end is in the beginning, and that, as a result, we need to tell our stories and listen to others, even if that story is only a fiction, a fake well done. What we need to assume is that what is average and ordinary is also surprising and extraordinary, what is familiar is also strange. As we read Tony's story, it is the gap between his "real life" and his story that opens to us, the complexity of mortal existence, its banality, and its wonder. We need to follow Tony's telling as if we are following ourselves, examining what we might be, who we are.

Tony Webster, ordinary as he seems, now an aged voice with faded memory, starts his story with an apparently mundane list "in no particular order" (3). It is a list of fragmented moments from his past. Yet it is a list hinting already of the flow of rivers, of time, of desire, eros, inside and outside the mortal self. Only the last memory on his list—"bathwater long gone cold behind a locked door" (3)—suggests the sense of an ending, death itself, thanatos, a moment never directly witnessed by Tony. It is a remarkable list to get us going, sending Tony back in time, to his childhood days at school.

"School is where it all began" (4), Tony tells us, the best fake he can offer at the start, although it is the arrival of the new boy, Adrian Finn, which actually sets Tony's narrative in motion: "There were three of us, and he now made the fourth" (4). As readers, we do not hear the voices of his three friends (Colin, Alex, and Tony) in history class that first day as they discuss Henry the Eighth's reign, but we are there, listening to Marshall, the "cautious know-nothing" (5)—according to the three—who assesses the period as one of "great unrest" (5). It is an assessment dismissed at the time by Tony who judges it as "idiotic" (5), ordinary at best, but ironically it is an assessment that Tony himself will adopt much later as the final words of his own narrative: "There is great unrest" (163).

After Marshall, Adrian offers his response to their history teacher's question about Henry the Eighth: "But there is one line of thought according to which all you can truly say of any historical event—even the outbreak of the First World War, for example—is that 'something happened'" (5). For a schoolboy, such response seems extraordinary, not "idiotic," certainly not ordinary. If Adrian is right—that all we can say is that "something happened"—then their teacher, Old Joe Hunt is "out of a job" (6), and so are writers and artists, historians and literary critics, anyone interested in giving time a sense of duration, a sense of purpose and direction, a sense of an ending. Ironically, Adrian evokes "great unrest." If Marshall appears ordinary, Adrian, by contrast, appears unique. He seems novel-worthy.

As Tony tells it, in these early schooldays, he is, along with his friends Alex and Colin, also ordinary. They are all products of "the genteel social Darwinism of the English middle classes" (8), bright enough, but not deep thinkers. By contrast, Adrian is different, singular, the "Serbian gunman" (12) who starts the "ball rolling" (12), who comes from a broken family, who, unlike the others, believes "that principles should guide actions" (10), who understands that "I can't know what it is that I don't know" (12). Adrian is serious, while the others are just "taking the piss" (13). At least, that's the way Tony saw it then, the way he narrates it for us now, at the beginning of the story. Adrian's life is "novel-worthy" (16), unlike the others, unlike Tony himself.

When their schoolmate Robson hangs himself, rumored to have gotten his girlfriend pregnant, this "happening," too, seems almost "novel-worthy," eros and thanatos, its conflicts, its mystery demanding a story. But we don't get that story from Tony, only an anecdote, an impression, and then another judgment dismissing the event: Robson's "action had been unphilosophical, self-indulgent and inartistic: in other words, wrong" (15). It's Tony's judgment, though, one that seems to tell us as much about Tony, at least as an adolescent, as about Robson himself.

We suspect that the narrative—its judgmental tendencies, its gestures toward mathematical logic (addition and subtraction in the case of Robson), its philosophic abstractions—is already working against itself as we are experiencing it. It is as if Tony is attempting to impose order on the sensuous flow of time, Marshall's "great unrest," the contingent events of "real life" that just happen. Is Tony offering a false paradigm, a flight from time that would serve as a fixative, a way of avoiding the great unrest, the inevitable end of his own life experience? We sense that there is much more to the story than he has said; it is as if he is offering us the version of the story that he likes to tell himself. As readers, we need to work on it, acknowledge that there is more to it than has been told, something much deeper in the telling than Tony is yet willing to reveal.

If "history is the lies of the victors" (18) and "the self-delusion of the defeated" (18), or, as Finn puts it, "the certainty produced at the point where the imperfections of memory meet the inadequacies of documentation" (18), we might suspect now that Tony's telling will reveal a story other than the one he intends. Its sense of fading memory, its rhythmic hesitancies, demand that we, each in our own way, listen to it, no matter what. We are ethically responsible as the only witnesses to the account Tony is offering. But even if he wants us to accept it as settled and conventional, we sense that he is compelled to tell it to us, and in the movement of that language, its looping filled with desire, it might become "not a fixative but a solvent" (67). What seems average and familiar might be stranger than Tony wants to reveal, or perhaps stranger than Tony knows. We are justified in wondering if there is a secret to be discovered.

Following Tony, we journey with him and his friends through predictable territory. "Adrian, to nobody's surprise" (20) wins a scholarship to Cambridge; Tony reads history at Bristol; Colin goes to Sussex; and Alex into his father's business. Tony gets a girlfriend, Veronica Mary Elizabeth Ford, not "very different from other girls of the time" (24). It's the 1960s, "but only for some people, only in certain parts of the country" (25). Not unexpectedly, Tony settles "into a contented routine of working" (27), spending his free time with Veronica, and back in his room "wanking explosively to fantasies of her splayed beneath me or arched above me" (27). For Tony, the relationship with Veronica is one of "trade-offs," "infra-sex" but not "full sex" (24), dating as a social convention, never asking her intimate questions, a sort of bargaining for "a wrangle for a ring" (24)—as the poet Larkin put it back in Tony' early schooldays. Even the watch, which Tony used to wear on the inside of his wrist—"an affection," but one "that made time feel like a personal, even a secret thing" (6)—is now turned around, putting "time on the outside as normal, grown-up people did" (27). Tony is becoming a conventional and cautious adult, in other words, the tick and the tock, the click and the clack, governing that kind of adulthood, the mechanical and mature logic of time marching in linear fashion, progressing according to the rules of the genteel social Darwinism of the English middle class.

It is not the linear progression of Tony's experiences, though, but his impressions of those experiences now, his telling of those experiences as they unfold for us, as readers, that we are drawn to, that we experience. So, when Tony next reports about his invitation to meet Veronica's family in the suburbs of Kent, we should not be surprised by the growing tension in the narrative itself. Tony seems again to be accounting for rather ordinary behavior: meeting the family, not risking much of anything, maintaining a stability in his life. But, in terms of the story itself, we might note something else, a strangeness seeping into the rhythm of his telling as if those experiences, over 40 years ago, may have been ordinary at the time, but through his half-memories, his impression of them now, they are open to question, causing great unrest.

As he tells us about this family visit, it is as if Tony is suddenly telling us a crime story in need of detection. He indicates that the large suitcase he brought with him that weekend made him look like "a potential burglar" (28), but if he has committed a crime, he appears unaware of what that crime might be. Nothing seems fixed or self-evident, and we might begin to wonder how reliable any of what he has been saying actually is.

At a routine breakfast in the morning with Mrs Ford (Veronica's mother), the ordinary seems slanted, increasingly strange: Mrs Ford breaking one of the yolks of the eggs she is frying, throwing the hot frying pan into the wet sink, steam rising at the impact as she laughs (31). She is apparently enjoying the erotic mayhem. If it seemed ordinary at the time, the language seems to make it memorable now, sensuous and overflowing, as if something significant happened, or was dreamt.

As readers, we again sense a story beneath the story, unanswered questions opening within the linguistic narrative, making space for us to enter, creating questions that Tony is barely aware of. How routine was that breakfast 40 years ago? Why did Mrs Ford warn Tony: "Don't let Veronica get away with too much?" (31). Why does Tony tell us that she gave him "another egg. . . . despite my not asking for it or wanting it?" (31). Why did Mrs Ford seem to smile at Tony when he was leaving the next day, as if the two of them shared a secret? And why did she signal her goodbye "with a sort of horizontal gesture at waist level" (33), which even Tony notes is anything but normal?

It is difficult, impossible, for us, as readers, to know what has actually happened at the Ford's: Whether the family is ordinary or extraordinary, familiar or strange, or both; whether Tony ("the potential burglar") has transgressed in some way or been victimized, tricked somehow; whether he is unaware of a mystery that lurks just beneath the suburban surface or whether the meeting with his girlfriend's family was simply ordinary. We cannot be certain, only sense that there is unease in his telling. The only factual memory that he is sure of is that he was constipated the whole time. He seems relieved now, recalling that when he returned home from the visit," I had a bloody good long shit" (33). If it is a joke, a distraction from unease, the memory of bodily relief returns him and his narrative to some kind of stability.

Regaining that stability, Tony next tells us that he introduced Veronica to his old gang—Colin, Alex, and Adrian—a week or so after his visit to the Fords. They took photos together, acted like tourists, average and normal young people growing into adulthood. It was an easy time then, we might imagine. But Tony wonders now if Veronica was calculating even then, "went in for tricks" (35). We assume that it is not something he considered at the time, but his linguistic telling now stirs such questions, not the grey surface of his "real life" then, but the flow of his impressions and half-memories now stirring his desire (and ours) to want to know. Despite itself, his linguistic telling, his grappling with the past, raises questions that lurk beneath the surface of his ordinary life.

When Veronica suggests that their relationship is "stagnating" (37), that Tony is "a coward" (37), that he does not respond to questions that she asks him, we might understand her frustration. But Tony wants to live a "peaceable" life (38), as he says to her, a way of avoiding unrest, a defense against the unsettling rhythm of intimacy and engagement. When he tells Veronica this, it seems as if it is the beginning of the end of their relationship, although we might already suspect that such beginnings and ends are, at best, good fakes, attempts to seal off, to fix, what cannot be controlled, the sensuous flow of time, memory, and desire now turning that time back on itself.

Within the looping rhythm of Tony's linguistic telling, the apparent loss of Veronica, the break-up of their relationship, average as it might have been when first experienced, now evokes in Tony another memory, different than the others so far, a memory distinct from the ordinary ones of a mundane life. As Tony indicates, this one is "single" and "distinct" (38), and it is somehow related to the loss of Veronica. For Tony, it is an unsettling moment, mysterious, otherworldly.

It was the night that Tony went with Veronica to witness the Severn Bore at Minsterworth. The rhythm of the river then, like the rhythm of his narrative now, suddenly swelling and reversing. It was, as he remembers it, a mysterious phenomenon, a peripeteia of sorts, nature and time strangely switching directions, revealing a singularity, for an instant, obeying only itself. Tony insists that he was alone on the bank when it happened, by himself, experiencing a moment that seemed connected with sublime terror, one that left Tony shaken, in touch with his strangeness. Through his telling about it, we might imagine that he had glimpsed the awful mystery of himself, his destiny then.

But the event, overflowing with sublime possibilities through his telling, appears to have had little, if any, effect on Tony at the time. We might even wonder if it ever happened, at least the way he is telling it to us now. Later Veronica will remind him (and us) that they were both at the Severn Bore that night: "Yes, we did go to Minsterworth together. There was a moon that night" (140). Was it sublime terror that he experienced that night, or mundane loneliness? Or was it the glow of romance, avoided and denied? Was it the overpowering flow of the river that he experienced or the enchantment of moonglow that Tony is telling us about now? Was it a missed meeting with his deeper self or a missed meeting with Veronica? Or both? It is likely that Tony prefers to distance himself from all of these questions. As Veronica put it, perhaps he is "a coward," but his story raises these questions anyway. Most likely, he still cannot commit to much of anything, although he is telling more than he is willing to admit.

Tony is not offering us a linear progression of what happened. His telling is driven by memory and desire. The memory of his break-up with Veronica has evoked the memory of the Severn Bore experience, and now that "single, distinct event" (38) evokes another memory of Veronica, not surprising within the looping rhythm of the narrative itself. What is surprising, though, is what he remembers next: "After we broke up, she slept with me" (39).

As he makes this abrupt shift in his narrative, Tony is self-consciously aware of us as readers. If his tone is conversational, it remains defensive, as if he is concerned about our judgment of him: "Yes, I know. I expect you're thinking: The poor sap, how did he not see that coming?" (39). Given what he has told us so far, though, we might be as surprised as he is by this new development in his story—at least, until he repeats for us what he thinks we must be repeating to ourselves: "Yes, you can say it again: You poor sap. And did you think her a virgin when she was rolling a condom on your cock?" (40).

Did Tony think that before she slept with him, Veronica was a virgin? He claims he did: "In a strange way, you know I did" (40). Indeed. But perhaps after they broke up, Veronica was trying to seduce him, win him back. Or perhaps she was seeking pay back. Or both. In terms of their relationship, it seems to have made little difference at the time (at least to Tony). After "full sex," they immediately stopped talking to each other, and Tony again felt great relief. "No one had got pregnant, no one had got killed" (42), he says, as if summing-up the one-night encounter, thinking, we imagine, about poor Robson from his schooldays, the "great unrest" that Tony always seems to want to avoid.

Working on Tony's main story, we have now moved through about one-quarter of this account of a life, an apparently ordinary and average life, an account that seems more conceptual than affective, distant and defensive rather than intense and intimate in its telling, conversational, focused on the familiar rather than the strange. Yet, in the depth of his linguistic rendering of these memories, these impressions and anecdotes, there seems to lurk other stories, other possibilities, an overpowering flow (like the Severn Bore) that threatens the boundaries of Tony's "peaceableness" and his somewhat solipsistic sense of self. If he is tentative and anxious, at times, he remains noncommital; he wants relief and quiet, a safe place, a space to avoid "great unease." He may know more than he has said, but he is also saying more than any of us knows.

We might wish, as Veronica does, that he would say what he thinks, what he feels, what he means. But he prefers to believe what it suits him to believe (as Veronica also claims).

To put it in different terms, Tony prefers rational logic as a way of fixing truth, but logic cannot account for what happens, for the shock wave, the sudden shift in the flow of the river or the contingencies of mortal existence itself. Like the law that insists on judgment (the voice of the barrister in Tony's own mind), logic is a flight from the inevitable disorganization of time. "Logic, yes, where is logic?" Tony now asks. "Where is it, for instance, in the next moment of my story?" (43).

That "next moment" brings Tony (and us) back to Adrian, "the fourth," the new arrival who actually started Tony's story moving at the beginning of his account, Adrian, the supposed master of logic, the extraordinary one, the Serbian gunman. Tony is clearly conscious of us now, as he tells about this "next moment," hesitating to reveal what happened next: "You can probably guess that I'm putting off telling you the next bit" (44). That "next bit" is another surprise: a letter from Adrian to Tony asking him for permission to go out with Veronica and indicating that Veronica had encouraged him to write it. Tony has not kept the letter, so there is, in essence, no documentation. As Tony stresses, he is only offering his "reading now of what happened then. Or rather, my memory now of my reading then of what was happening at the time" (45). Or, we might add, our reading of Tony's telling now of his experience then, what he was thinking was happening at the time.

When Tony finally offers a proper response to Adrian's letter, he seems to be working again to mitigate his own pain at the time, trying to find a peaceableness, relief. In the letter he sends, he advises Adrian to be prudent, to protect himself from Veronica's seductions, especially because, as he emphasizes, "Veronica had suffered damage a long way back" (46). We might imagine that Tony is remembering another poem that he read in Phil Dixon's English class, "Love Again" by Larkin, whose own-self-doubt and inability to love, the poet traced back to "Something to do with violence/ A long way back, and wrong rewards/ And arrogant eternity." Tony has no real evidence that Veronica is damaged, as he admits, although he now claims sensing something odd about his visit to the Fords that weekend. As readers, though, we might begin to suspect that it is not Veronica but Tony who is "damaged." Or as his mother-in-law once put it: "I reckon we're all abused" (47).

It is not unreasonable to sense some kind of primal loss in Tony's telling here, one that Tony cannot know, that he cannot articulate, that he cannot discover through half-memories and impressions, through unavailable documentation or explicit testimony, but one we might infer from Tony's current mental state. He has told us as much: ". . . you can infer past actions from current mental states," at least in terms of the private life (48).

We are also reminded again of how self-conscious Tony is in his telling, how concerned he is about our judgment of him, how defensive he is. He continually anticipates what we are thinking: "You might even ask me to apply my 'theory' to myself and explain what damage I had suffered a long way back and what its consequences might be; for instance how it might affect my reliability and truthfulness" (49). Exactly, we might reply. We have been wondering about your reliability and, yes, whether that damage is really Veronica's or yours. But Tony is already prepared for such response. He quickly counters, "I'm not sure I could answer this, to be honest" (49). It is as if he has heard us.

We are in conversation with Tony, and it is this conversation that Tony desires, as he accounts for himself. We cannot know him anymore than he knows himself, but that seems to be part of his point in telling us about his life. If he is an unreliable narrator, though, can we trust him? Is he attempting to offer an honest account of himself, or is he purposely deceiving us? We know that Tony is not telling us his whole story, but this story (the one he is telling us) seems to be the significant one for him, the one that makes the difference. "Annie was part of my story, but not of this story" (50) he says, for example. This story, the one that makes a difference, must have chosen him as much as he has chosen it, a story that includes Veronica and her family, and, yes, Adrian, "the fourth," who started the story moving at its beginning. It is Tony's perspective and his journey, his destiny that he wants to share with us. We are obligated to follow him.

We have not been told what happened to Veronica and Adrian after Tony's reply to their letter, but we imagine they are still in a relationship together, while Tony is briefly traveling through America. We are again surprised by what happens next, though. There seems to be no logic to it. Like Robson, Adrian kills himself; but unlike Robson, Adrian has "left a full account of his reasons" (52), personal testimony and public argument in the form of a letter explaining his decision to cut his wrists in a bath of hot water. In Tony's judgment at the time, it was an act of moral duty, committed in order to renounce the gift of life that Adrian had not asked for, a logical decision superior to "the unworthy passivity of merely letting life happen to you" (54). Adrian was heroic, novel-worthy. He was not banal or ordinary.

Adrian appears to have responded to the only true philosophic question of the twentieth century (according to Camus)—that is, given the absurdity of human existence, why continue such meaninglessness, why shouldn't you choose to kill yourself? He acted on principle, his own personal logic. Adrian appears to be unique, extraordinary, as Tony indicates. But, "The law, and society, and religion all said it was impossible to be sane, healthy, and kill yourself" (54). For them, suicide could only be judged as irrational. If for Adrian it was "philosophically self-evident" (52), the only rational response to an irrational world, the mainstream world has made a judgment as well.

As we experience the rhythmic sway of Tony's telling, it appears to work against either side of this judgment. We might agree that in both cases the supposed logic of judgment attempts to put a halt to the inevitable flow of life happening. It is as if we, as readers, cannot accept from either side such "self-evident" judgment about the complexity of mortal human life unless we prefer a fixative to seal off the truth that we seek, the secret that we cannot fully know, that calls us on, filled with doubt as we may be. In terms of the rhythm of Tony's linguistic narrative, we might now better sense that it is not primarily the conceptual logic but the affective flow of the narrative shaping memory, driven by desire, that Tony is wrestling with, that he desires for us to experience.

With Colin and Alex, Tony speculates about "why" Adrian would do such a thing; the "how" is clear, not in doubt, but the "why" (56) seems, as always, problematic, evoking great unease. According to Alex, Adrian was "Cheerful. Happy" (55) when they last met, had told Alex that he was in love with Veronica, was headed down to her family home in Chiselhurst to see her. If Tony's assumption of Adrian's logic allows him to consider Adrian's suicide "exemplary" (53), even courageous, it also seems, as Alex puts it, "a fucking terrible waste" (54). If Tony can slot it into time, judge it as "exemplary," conceptualize it, and so dismiss it, it seems nevertheless to linger as an unhinged "happening," a nexus of eros and thanatos, an unresolved moment that Tony prefers to bury in the routine and peaceable. He claims to understand it, but we have our doubts. It is the flow of his linguistic narrative, not his judgment, that we need to consider.

It is no wonder that in just over two printed pages, Tony next reviews his life as an arts administrator, his marriage to Margaret, their divorce, his role as father to Susie (and as a grandfather), and his retirement (59–61). It is a normal adult life, one that we might have anticipated, ordinary and average, yielding thin memories of 40 years as a survivor, "neither victorious nor defeated" (68). It ends the first part of Tony's narrative. We might wonder what else he could possibly tell us. It is as if he is summing up, completing the account of his life. He has survived to tell the tale, but the record seems thin, like the life itself, not unremarkable, but moving with easy assumptions, a grey flow excited, at best, only at the surface, peaceable. "Every day is Sunday" (68)—not a bad epitaph, Tony claims.

When the second section of Tony's narrative begins, we might speculate that, as he suggests, he was just "not odd enough" (60): That he was content with a familiar life, lacking imagination, conventional, unable, if not unwilling, to confront the stranger in himself or to engage the odd and mysterious in others. Or, to put it another way, he is like most of us—unable, or unwilling to see clearly what "happens underneath our noses" (66). That seems the counsel for us, his readers: Do not be like Tony.

But Tony is obviously not ready to end his story, and we might be reminded that Tony has spent most of the first part of his story focused on Adrian and Veronica. It has been 40 years since that "humiliating weekend" (70)—as Tony now calls it—the weekend with Veronica and her family in Chiselhurst, a weekend that he claims he has not thought about for a long time, at least not until he receives a solicitor's letter. The letter, marked "In the matter of the estate of Mrs. Sarah Ford (deceased)" (69), serves as a reminder that "memory is what we thought we'd forgotten" (69). In the context of Tony's tightly drawn narrative, though, we have certainly not forgotten the Fords. In fact, by contrast to most of Tony's life, that weekend seems anything but forgotten.

The solicitor's letter informs Tony that he has been left a bequest of "five hundred pounds and two documents" (69), puzzling Tony (and us). One of the documents turns out to be a letter from Mrs Ford, apologizing for the way the family treated Tony that weekend, announcing that she is leaving him a "little money" (72) and a "memento of long ago" (72). In a postscript, she concludes that the last months of Adrian's life were happy.

As readers, we know (or think we know) that Tony does not like puzzles, mysteries (real or imagined) that remain unresolved, the untidiness that threatens "a state of peaceableness" (75), the messiness of the undercurrents of mortal life. Yet, Mrs Ford's letter appears to have arrived to stir up that kind of mystery, as if it has been sent from the grave, evoking the buried memories of Tony's existence, the muted rhythm of his life now put into question. We might wonder if that other story, the strange and mysterious one, hinting at itself beneath the familiar one that Tony prefers to tell himself, will yet become explicit.

We have barely begun the second part of Tony's narrative, and we suddenly seem seeped in secrets. Adrian's diary, the second document originally attached to the letter, is mysteriously missing, and Mrs Ford's bequest of 500 pounds is indeed strange. Although the tone of Tony's narrative telling appears, as always, controlled and cool, conversational, Tony is again moving back into territory of repressed memory; a river shift, a possible shock wave, could again emerge. Perhaps a crime has been committed.

Sarah Ford is also apparently "a woman of mystery" (73) in a world where, as Margaret once claimed, there are "two sorts of women" (72): those with "clear edges" and those who imply mystery. But whether Mrs Ford's "mystery" is based primarily on Tony's inability to understand her, or simply a façade, a manipulative technique for ensnaring men, is as problematic for us, as readers, as it is for Tony as he wrestles with the implications of the letter he has received. Perhaps she is a genuine mystery, a secret even unto herself.

Is Tony manipulating us, as well, we might wonder, or is he enacting through his narrative a mystery that he himself is authentically working to understand? Is it the clear-edged commonality of his conversational tone that keeps us at a convenient distance from understanding, or is it our own ordinariness that blocks us from glimpsing the mystery, from experiencing the uniqueness of Tony's own life?

Veronica is another mystery, having taken Adrian's diary (as we soon discover), an important clue, we assume, to solving the mystery. In pursuit, Tony seeks out Veronica's brother Jack, gets advice again from his ex-wife (the clear-eyed Margaret): "Cash the cheque, take me on a budget holiday, and forget it" (84), and inevitably, as if by necessity, like one pursuing his destiny, then turns back, "Straight to the matter of Miss Veronica Ford" (89). As Tony says, she is "the puzzle," the enigma that "you want to solve" (90)—that "you" being us as well as Tony himself.

When Tony contacts Veronica about the documents, her first words in reply (appearing on his computer screen) are "blood money" (89), an enigmatic reference to her mother's bequest of 500 pounds (why did she send him the money?). She eventually follows up with a short fragment of Adrian's diary filled with mathematical formulas and abstract speculations about human relationships and the limits of responsibility. At the end of the fragment, though, Adrian interestingly turns from equations to narrative, leaving a cliffhanger: "Or we might try to draw the responsibility more narrowly and apportion it more exactly. And not use equations and integers but instead express matters in traditional narrative terminology. So, for instance, if Tony. . ." (95). It is that "narrative terminology"—"so, for instance, if Tony"—that seems to arouse Tony.

Reading the fragment, Tony is not driven to further speculation, the logic of formulas or abstraction, but to an immediate existential experience, a sensuous wave of feeling, an overwhelming sense that "Adrian was present in the room again, beside me, breathing, thinking" (95). It is not what Adrian has said, but something in his saying, his breathing, the rhythm of his thinking, the presence of his voice that seems now to move Tony, the return of Adrian from the grave, we might think, the ghost of Adrian,—in other words, "the exact opposite of the normal condition of life" (95). "He made you feel you were his co-thinker, even if you said nothing" (96), Tony claims, evoking a strange sense of companionship, "a sense of unease, of unrest" (97). Through the language Tony is now using, we sense the voice of Adrian doubling for Tony's own telling, a moment in which Tony has become the stranger that he is.

It is difficult not to recall Tony's witnessing the Severn Bore, the unsettling reversal of nature, the mysterious and otherworldly phenomenon that for a time, but only a short time, overwhelmed Tony's sense of what he was, the shock wave that, unlike some of his mates, he did not chase after with his torch beam, preferring to stay on the bank of the river in the dark. For an instance, he has glimpsed again the gap between what he is and who he might be: "So, for instance, if Tony hadn't been Tony" (97).

Still in pursuit, Tony meets with Veronica on the Wobbly Bridge across the grey Thames, "the direction of its flow disguised by a stiff wind exciting the surface" (3). She claims that she has burnt Adrian's diary, but gives Tony another document in a sealed envelope and then quickly leaves. (If this is not a crime story, it is surely a mystery that we are experiencing.) Not surprisingly, Tony now waits to open the envelope, pouring "an extra glass of wine" (104) at home in the evening before examining its contents. He is as cautious with us as he is with himself. Hesitant, he reads the salutation, "Dear Adrian," recognizing the letter as the one he sent Adrian "all those years ago" (104), now right underneath his nose.

Tony is thinking about us, and before continuing with his narrative, he offers us now further philosophic considerations, reviewing the thematic issues that he has been pondering throughout his narrative so far. Stepping back from the flow of his experience, he is clearly hoping to provide a context for the body of the letter he is about to read to us.

"How often do we tell our own life story?" Tony asks. "How often do we adjust, embellish, make sly cuts? And the longer life goes on, the fewer are those around to challenge our account, to remind us that our life is not our life, merely the story we have told about our life. Told to others, but—mainly—to ourselves" (104). Much earlier Tony had given us an account of this letter, referring briefly to it, especially its supposed emphasis on his opinion that "Veronica had suffered damage a long way back" (46). He had told us then that both Adrian and Veronica "were now out of my life forever" (46). That was his judgment at the time, but the letter before him now seems to undercut that judgment, open neural pathways, unexpected memories, that challenge his earlier account of himself, that call for adjustment, embellishment.

As readers, we too, need to step back at this moment in the narrative. As Tony has just suggested, we know little about his real life, only the story he has told us (and himself) about that life. If Adrian and Veronica have, in his judgment, been out of his life for the last 40 years, they have nevertheless dominated his story so far. In fact, the body of the letter, which he will offer to us in a few minutes, occupies as much space in his narrative as his initial account of his 40 years of marriage and divorce with Margaret.

The letter, close up, right under our nose when Tony presents it, is, as Tony admits, ugly, a poisonous letter, insulting both Adrian and Veronica, vile in its accusations, reckless in its bitterness and advice, not what we might expect from someone who wants "peaceableness" and relief. It expresses Tony's curse on the two of them, that Time will have its revenge, "unto the next generation and the next" (105), that Veronica suffers from "damage a long way back" (105), and that Adrian should "check things out" (106) with Veronica's Mum.

Placed in the narrative at this moment, the letter, filled with possibilities, opens a linguistic space for Tony (and for us), looping as it does back through what Tony has said and remembered, and forward into Tony's ongoing shaping and reshaping of the story he is telling. Resonating with biblical injunctions, psychological probing, philosophic speculation, and hope embedded in jealousy and fear, the rhythm of the letter hints at beginnings and a sense of an ending. Yet, the letter is simply a moment in time, something that happened once in Tony's life, a linguistic space now free from the life of its author except as that life is shaped into the story that the author is telling us: "I reread this letter several times . . . All I could plead was that I had been its author then, but was not its author now" (107). It is as if Tony is and is not Tony. Is it the life or the story that we are pursuing? Or both? As readers, we might wonder if it is what Tony has been previously or who he is now that we desire to discover, that we are working on as his narrative continues to move back and forth, demanding our ongoing attention: "So, for instance, if Tony hadn't been Tony" (97).

Like Tony's narrative as a whole, the letter is not a fixative but a solvent, changing the flow of memory, reversing its course, taking it in other directions. As Tony indicates: ". . . rereading that letter of mine, feeling its harshness and aggression, came as a profound and intimate shock" (117). It sets him wondering: "I wondered why Veronica had bothered to answer my email"; "I wondered if Veronica had punished Brother Jack"; "I wondered if her words were simply a politeness"; "I wondered if I'd been awkward, pushy, selfish" (110). Tony claims a "general remorse" (109) about his whole life, a remorse whose "chief characteristic is that nothing can be done about it" (117), but he also wonders if "remorse can be made to flow backward," even be "forgiven" (117). He claims that he "gave up on life, gave up on examining it" (109), but yet, we, too, might wonder, wonder at the intensity of his self-examination now. If life is "the accumulation, the multiplication, of loss, of failure" (113), as Tony claims, then perhaps it is his telling of his story, his ongoing account of himself, our listening to him, our working on his telling, that will redeem him (and perhaps us as well).

With the letter in mind, Tony is in pursuit of himself, but whether he has genuinely embraced the Socratic dictum "to know thyself," or simply wants corroboration that he will be well-thought of—"remember me well" (118)—is unclear. Anxious, he seeks comfort and support from Margaret who, understandably frustrated by his behavior, finally tells him that he is on his own (116). The only witness he has left is Veronica, and us, if we are still listening.

Life is much more complicated than we might imagine, Tony now reminds us, as he turns back once again to the "long buried details of that distant weekend with the Ford family" (122). Previously unacknowledged fragments of that extraordinary time long ago, somewhat routine and ordinary at the time, vividly appear close-up now, right under Tony's nose (and ours), raising endless questions and possibilities. They are fragments of a buried life, unearthed now, each one carrying with it a potentially mysterious story: Mrs Ford flipping the broken, cooked egg into the waste bin (is there a story here of birth, sex, abortion, damage done or to be done?); Brother Jack addressing Mrs Ford as "the Mother" (is there a hint at the Oedipus Complex here; the mother sleeping with the son; some kind of incest, foul play?); Veronica backing Tony against the wall of his bedroom, kissing him on the mouth, whispering into his ear, "Sleep the sleep of the wicked" (is there seduction here or even a hint of rape; violation of sexual boundaries; a wicked step-mother or step-daughters or step-sons?); Tony "forty seconds later . . . wanking into the little washbasin and slucing my sperm down the house's pipework" (was Tony simply self-absorbed, masturbating in private that weekend, dreaming about Veronica, or did he affect the whole house, change the family somehow, initiate—directly or indirectly—sexual relations with the Ford family?) (123).

Are these fragments to be taken at face value, as ordinary and discrete moments of a life, or are they now clues helping us to detect the secret embedded in the story of that life? If these fragments were his life then, his experience as they happened, they are dream sensations now, emerging into awareness through his language, his telling us. They are as fanciful, and as real, as Mr Ford's guided tour through Chiselhurst that weekend long ago. When Tony remembers that moment in the car with Mr Ford, he checks on Google Earth to observe those village touchstones again, but he cannot find them now, and the Ford's house doesn't "seem to exist anymore" (123) either (if it ever did). We might wonder if it is the story or the life, the tick-tock of time or the silence between the beats, or both, that account for the complications and complexities, the ambiguities and paradoxes of mortal existence.

Aroused by the dream sensation, memory fused with desire, we are with Tony as he suggests another meeting with Veronica. It is reasonable to question Tony's motives; he questions them himself. Has he genuinely acknowledged the Socratic notion that the unexamined life is not worth living or is he simply hoping that he can leave Veronica with a final and positive memory of him: "remember me well?" (118). Is he looking to the past or to the future? Is he in pursuit of a secret, grappling with the enigmatic mystery, the uniqueness of himself? Or is he seeking the missed rendezvous of a relationship that could have been, the romance of a time lost 40 years ago? Perhaps he is on a journey for something even further back—the trauma of birth itself and the sense of an ending that such trauma brings with it? Or is he seeking corroboration for the familiar, the story of his life that he likes to tell himself, "the account that stands up" (127), the contentment and peaceableness of a life lived at a distance from itself?

When Veronica and Tony meet, to Tony, Veronica looks both "twentyish and sixtyish at the same time." On her wedding finger, she wears "a red glass ring" (126). She is mysterious, perhaps manipulative, endlessly enigmatic. Tony tells his story to Veronica, the familiar one, the one about his 40 years of marriage and children, divorce and retirement, the peaceable version that he likes to tell himself. When he is done, Veronica gets up, not telling her story. She leaves without "divulging a single fact, let alone secret about herself" (127). Tony has not really divulged much of anything either.

Veronica's absence, the remembrance of her leaving, triggers in Tony another wave of excitement in his narrative, though. He now recalls that Veronica was indeed with him that singular night at Minsterworth. He was not alone on the bank in the dark, but with her then in quest of the Severn Bore: "Alone, she and I talked about how impossible things sometimes happened, things you wouldn't believe unless you'd witnessed them for yourself" (130). It is another shift in the deep flow of memory, an impossible moment that nevertheless happened, astonishing and singular: it is as if Tony was "alone" then but yet talking with Veronica, a dream sensation. The memory calls up "a new sympathy" (131) in Tony, beyond abstract logic or judgment: "All I can say is it happened, and that it astonished me" (131). It arouses desire in us, as readers, as well: eros and thanatos, and the conflict between them.

Looping back and forth, from the present to the past, from the past to the present, Tony has now opened the future to new possibilities, made the future into a more hopeful question. Astonished, he desires still another meeting with Veronica, a rendezvous, which could end with "a full sense of reward" (132). Tony might yet become the Tony that he dreamed about, the life that he did not live.

Veronica agrees to meet again at "an unfamiliar Tube station" (132), unknown territory for Tony. At the station, Tony first sees her as an apparition, "a particular shape and a way of standing" (134). When she moves, he follows, as if pursuing a phantom. She gets in her car, says little, drives recklessly, until they arrive at a typical but unrecognizable London neighborhood. If Tony is baffled, as we are, Veronica, by contrast, seems to have purpose and direction. She wants Tony to look, to focus, to pay attention. He is a necessary part of the story, even if he does not understand the story or what is right underneath his nose.

Tony sees a group of five people walking along the pavement in the heat: a man in heavy tweed, looking "like someone with an obscure function at a circus or fairground"; two other men, one with a "black moustache" and "rolling gait," the other with "one shoulder much higher than the other"; a fourth (echoes of Adrian), "tall and goofy," with glasses holding the hand of the fifth, "a plump, Indianish woman" (136). Behind the group, strange but familiar, Tony now spots another man, in shorts, young, with an open-neck shirt, perhaps "the shepherd" (136).

If Tony anticipated a rendezvous with Veronica, a meeting with a sense of an amorous ending, he has instead encountered another beginning, a missed opportunity, a dream-like glimpse of damage way back. It is as if the other story that we had anticipated way back in the narrative is finally starting to crest, the story that Tony has hesitated to tell himself, having preferred the version that protected him against such necessity, that ordinary version that "stands-up," that allows him to keep both feet safely on the fixed ground. Referring to the unfamiliar group he has just seen, Tony asks Veronica, "What's wrong with them?" She quickly replies, "What's wrong with you?" (137). He doesn't get it, but perhaps we, as readers, can.

Sitting inside the enclosed car, Tony witnesses Veronica out on the open street, engaging in familiar discussion with this "care-in-the-community" (137) group. The tall goofy fellow, "the fourth," good naturedly shouts out to her as she begins to leave, not calling her "Veronica" but by a different name: "Bye, Mary" (139). Then Veronica furiously drives off with Tony, recklessly aiming at speed bumps, finally responding to what Tony had asked her before they encountered the group: "Yes, we did go to Minsterworth together. There was a moon that night" (140). As readers, we might wonder if Veronica is also thinking about missed opportunities, but, like Tony, we might sense it is, in any case, too late now for a rendezvous. With Tony, we want instead to ask Veronica: "Why did that goofy chap call you Mary?" (147). Veronica refuses to answer, though. With Tony, we are on our own.

Back at home, Tony again begins "to address what had happened" (141). Not just now on the street, but throughout his whole life. He seems to know something else about Socrates now. "Who was it said that the longer we live, the less we understand?" (143), he questions, wondering, we assume, whether wisdom arrives through the pursuit of knowledge or through the recognition that we know little of significance, or both? It is as if the question, not the answer, gives purpose and direction, drives us on. Not knowing why we want to know what we cannot know, we desire the solution to the mystery just beyond our grasp.

Why did Veronica bring Tony to that street? That is the only question that Tony claims to care about now, as he obsessively returns to that same street, waiting for "something perhaps even a solution to . . . surface" (146). After three weeks, "the lopsided man and the chap with a moustache" (147), familiar figures to him now, arrive in the local pub, and then are escorted out. Tony bides his time, observes and witnesses. Sitting alone, he waits, pensively, for the time to be right, for a meeting to happen. One night it does.

In the pub, we are with Tony, as he heads to the bar to get a drink. On his way, as if by indirection, he encounters the group: "The gangly bloke was now in front of me and as I was about to make my way past I stopped and looked at him properly . . . I could sense he was keen to turn his back again. But instead, he did something unexpected. He took off his glasses and looked me full in the face. His eyes were brown and gentle" (149).

"I'm a friend of Mary's" (149), Tony says to him, first causing a smile and then panic, the gangly bloke, "the fourth," shuffling away, clearly disturbed. A few minutes later, the caregiver and Tony talk, at the bar, about the brief encounter, Tony apologizing and then explaining:

"I met him once before with Mary when she came over one afternoon."

"Then you'll understand," the caregiver replies. "Won't you?" (149)

As readers, we don't understand, but Tony thinks he does: "And the thing was, I did. I didn't need to talk to the badge man or the male carer. Now I knew" (150).

If "the gangly bloke" has caught Tony by surprise, we, as readers, might also be surprised, not by what has happened, but by Tony's response to it, his insistence that he now understands, that he gets it, that he now knows. We cannot tell what it is that he knows, but we might take his word for it, trust what he says, although for the moment, we don't get it, even if he does. Is it what he has seen that evoked the truth, whatever that truth might be? Or rather is it what we, as readers, have experienced so far through his linguistic telling that manifests the truth, which reveals the mystery that we are all seeking? Or is the truth in the gap between the two (the experience and the telling), the gap that keeps us all in pursuit?

Tony pauses again in his narrative, hesitant and self-conscious, realizing that we, as readers, need further explanation. How does he know what he claims to know? Why don't we know it, too? "I saw it in his face," Tony tells us. "If the face contradicts the speaker's words, we interrogate the face" (150). The face tells Tony that this "gangly bloke," about 40 years old, is indeed "Adrian's son" . . . the color and expression, the pallor and underlying structure, "the eyes conveying an evident truth" (150). Yes, an evident truth for Tony, but not for us. We cannot see Tony's face; we cannot interrogate it the way he claims to have interrogated the face of Adrian's son.

Yet, Tony insists that he saw the truth of the matter in the face, close up, right before his eyes. And he felt it. If it is a dream sensation, it is his dream, his truth, his experience alone, an experience that he is now sharing with us. It happened, whether we accept his judgment about it or not. It is his story to tell, and he is telling it to us. We need to pay attention. For Tony, this gangly bloke is the damaged offspring of Adrian, the original "fourth," the one who first appeared as such back in his school days.

This glimpse of a truth (if we can call it that) brings Tony a renewed feeling of remorse, as if he has been bitten for a second time by his own doing, cursed by his own words from a long way back now returning to haunt him, especially his words from the letter he sent wishing specific evil on Veronica's and Adrian's "innocent foetus" (151). Those words now create in him "a shiver of the otherworldly" (151), another visitation from the burial plot.

Was this what Tony was pensively waiting for in the pub: the arrival of his other story, the one buried beneath the ordinary one? Not the version that he likes to tell himself, but the unintentional story, the other one, the one that is always there, whether we acknowledge it or not, the "otherworldly" one that can emerge as a shock wave, unexpectedly, carrying, as Tony now puts it: "the unshiftable truth of what had happened" (151). For the moment, we might suspect that what Tony has glimpsed in the gangly bloke's eyes is his own strangeness, the doubleness that he also sensed in the voice emanating from Adrian's diary, the strange otherworldliness he experienced at the Severn Bore, a kind of vulnerability and sublime terror, an acknowledgment of the complexity of his own mortal being, the wonder of it all. At least, this is our feeling of the narrative as Tony is telling it to us now. Not what he has said, not his conceptual intention, not what he thinks he knows, but the unintentional sense of the matter, the contingencies, what he cannot grasp—the rhythm of eros and thanatos, the conflict between them, arousing desire to press on.

Tony turns once again to memories of Veronica, recalling her now with empathy that we have not felt before from him, empathy shrouded with a mood of melancholy and damage done, a sense of loss for a commitment never experienced, a "dim fantasy" (152) never actualized. Out of that sense of loss, Tony asks us to fantasize with him what has happened. We sense that he is providing answers to questions he has not asked, knowledge that he does not know, but what he believes: Veronica had become pregnant by Adrian, had given birth to a son, had sacrificed her life for that son, until, after a terrible struggle, she "allowed this son to be taken into care" (152). Tony exhorts us: "Imagine what that must have felt like. Imagine the loss, the sense of failure and the guilt" (152). For the first time, he seems to be putting himself in Veronica's place, caring for her, rather than defensively judging her: "And I'd expected her to hand over Adrian's diary? In her place, I'd probably have burnt it too, as I now believed she had done" (153).

Having rethought Veronica's life and character, recontextualizing her in terms of his story, it is not surprising that Tony next returns to Adrian, "the fourth," the original one who had through his death, we have assumed, sanctioned Tony's telling at the start, Tony's "philosopher friend . . . whose noble gesture reemphasized with each passing decade the compromise and littleness that most lives consist of" (153). Believing that he has now stabilized Veronica's place in his life, Tony will go back now into his past and "deal with Adrian" (153). If he believes that he can close this part of his life off, though, grasp the "secret" of Adrian, we need also to note that such a grasp is always as much an opening as a closing, a beginning as much as an end. It is only a sense of an ending that we can hope for.

If Adrian had not been Adrian, the one with moral courage, the singular one who grandly refused the existential gift of life, then who would he be? "One who had got his girlfriend pregnant, been unable to face the consequences, and had 'taken the easy way out' as they used to put it" (153),

Tony now insists. Perhaps Adrian's story is not extraordinary, strange, and unique after all, but ordinary, average, even banal. He is a version of Robson, someone "afraid of the pram in the hall" (155). At least, this seems to be Tony's judgment of Adrian at the moment, a judgment that sentences Adrian to ordinariness, the reversal of what we thought we knew about him. It stabilizes Tony for the time. We might wonder, though, whom Tony is really judging here, and how long such stability can hold. Like Tony's own story about himself, there is inevitably another story about Adrian, one already seeping through the boundaries of such judgment. It is not the judgment, though, but the telling of the judgment, the flow of it, that moves us forward, that demands our attention.

In conversation with us, Tony has been pursuing himself through his narrative, becoming other than himself through this linguistic exchange as unsettling as that process has often been. If he cannot permanently grasp "the secret" that he has been seeking, he has nevertheless opened himself to himself (and to us). In terms of his narrative, he now acknowledges the pain that he has spent so much time avoiding: "a hurt inflicted at long last on one who always thought he knew how to avoid being hurt and inflicted for precisely that reason" (155).

Out of that pain, ironically the cause and the effect of his attempt to repress that pain from the beginning—to create a version of the story of his life devoid of pain—he now writes an "Apology" (155) to Veronica, the best he can do: "It wasn't as good as I'd wanted, but at least I meant every word of it" (156). Given his commitment to us, and his apparent honesty, we need to listen to him. He still doesn't get it (as Veronica says in her reply to him), but we can sense now that his story is what he knows of his life, even if that life didn't happen the way he has told it. He is, "Exhausted, emptied out" (157). It is our life, as much as his, that through his story, we have been pursuing.

With Tony, we return again to the pub, waiting for something to arrive. "And then, just like that, the five of them came in . . ." (159). The case worker approaches the table, wants to talk to Tony about Adrian, not the father but the son, the gangly bloke, the innocent foetus, the damage done.

"Your presence upsets him," the case worker explains. "Do you mind me asking who you are?" (160).

It is an impossible question to answer, but Tony identifies himself as an old friend of Adrian's father and his mother Veronica (called by her second name "Mary" by their son). His response makes sense to us. Even if he does not really know who he is, we understand what he is saying. After all, we have inhabited his story. The case worker doesn't understand it at all, though. His story is different.

"Mary isn't his mother. Mary's his sister. Adrian's mother died about six months ago. He took it very badly. That's why he's been . . . having problems lately" (161).

Another dramatic reversal, the final shock wave for Tony, it leaves us shaken as well. In response, Tony can only eat another chip from his plate at the table, comment on its taste, wish everyone good luck, leave "twice the normal tip" (162), and depart the pub. It a baffling revelation, remarkable and unexpected. For Tony, though, it seems inevitable.

The linguistic narrative now calls us home, where Tony claims that he understands it all, that he gets it. The meaning of Adrian's formula in his diary—B, A (1), (2), S, V—is "obvious now." The baby (B) born to Adrian (A1 and Sarah (S), the mother of Veronica (V), is the "damaged child," and Anthony (A2) (the name Adrian used when he waited to call Tony to seriousness) is part of this remarkable "chain of responsibility" (162). As Tony sees it, he has located himself at last within that chain, placed himself in the world, knows who he is. We might doubt the validity of his reading of Adrian's formula, question the certainty of his judgment, but he has no doubt. "I knew I couldn't change, or mend anything now" (163), Tony tells us. His story has become a tragedy, his life a dream, his destiny fulfilled.

We need to question his summing up here at the end, his certainty and final judgment of things, not his honesty, though, not the telling, but the tale now told. "There is accumulation. There is responsibility." And, as Marshal said at the beginning, and Tony tells us again at the end: ". . . beyond these, there is unrest. There is great unrest" (163).

If there is a sense of closure for Tony, a summing up, a judgment, there is, for us, as readers, ongoing desire, an unsettled overflow urging us to return to the narrative itself, discover what we might have missed, what we do not know. If we have glimpsed ourselves in the depth of Tony's linguistic narrative, we are compelled to go back into it again, and again, to acknowledge what we cannot know, the mystery that urges us on. It is our own responsibility, as readers, as human beings, to take that risk, to meet that ethical demand that Tony's telling has placed in our path. If we care about ourselves, we will care about him, and we will return to our own "real life" journey with him in mind.

11

The Future of Linguistic Narrative

In Gary Shteyngart's *Super Sad True Love Story*, the 24-year-old Eunice Park is astonished to see her 39-year-old boyfriend Lenny Abramov (the last of the long-form readers) engaged in what we would call "deep reading." She explains it this way on Globalteens (an advanced Facebook) to her good friend Precious Pony: "Anyway, what kind of freaked me out was that I saw Len reading a book. (No, it didn't SMELL. He uses Pine-Sol on them.) And I don't mean scanning a text like we did in Euro Classics with that Chatterhouse of Parma I mean seriously READING. . . . I was going to teen my sister but I was so embarrassed I just stood there and watched him read which lasted for like HALF AN HOUR, and finally he put the book down and I pretended like nothing happened. And then I snuck a peak and it was that guy Tolsoy he was reading . . . I thought Ben was really brain-smart because I saw him streaming Chronicles of Narnia in a café in Rome, but this Tolsoy was a thousand pages long BOOK, not a stream, and Lenny was on page 930, almost finished" (Shteyngart 144).

Eunice is what Marc Prensky (2001) has called a Digital Native. She "verbals" in Digital, majored in Images (and minored in Assertiveness— where Professor Margaux used to call guys like Lenny a mensch, "a real human being"). By contrast, Lenny is a Digital Immigrant (as Prensky would say), someone who grew up with books but now finds himself surrounded by screens, consumer sensation, data streams, the spectacle of electronic circuitry masquerading as public transparency.

We can understand why Lennie reads, but we might wonder why Eunice admires him for doing it. For her, books are smelly objects, reminders of a decaying past. She is embarrassed that her boyfriend is so old. It's as if she is dating a dinosaur. But yet, even for her, there is something admirable about what Lenny is doing. What is it?

We can call it "the risk of reading." Eunice senses that reading opens Lennie to an alternative possibility, the unknown and dangerous territory of himself. Reading Tolstoy, Lennie is engaged with something other than the consumer rhythm of mobile devices which Eunice knows all too well, Lennie is willing to risk the adventure of deep reading. He'd like to glimpse the secrets of his mortal self. And, despite her distractions, Eunice would like to do that as well.

We usually don't think about reading as a particularly dangerous journey, but Lenny is a dangerous man, and Eunice knows it. Unlike Joshie, the Media king in Shteyngart's story, Lenny might appear weak and anxious, vulnerable and strange, but he is a real human being. It is as if when reading, Lennie is embarrassingly naked, open to himself and to others, seeking love and responsibility. In the world of hyper-sensation that Eunice lives in, the power of the Media king might provide a temporary means of survival, but reading linguistic narrative preserves the remnant of an ethical life, the possibility of knowing who you are.

Deep readers like Lenny may very well be at the end of a long tradition, but it is not one that he is willing to give up. For Lenny, that tradition stretches back through his Russian family (Chekhov is his favorite author) and through his Jewish heritage (the People of the Book). Near the end of the novel, he changes his name to Lenny Abraham, suggesting, in part, his resonance not only with the first patriarch of the Hebrew Bible but also with the ongoing sense of being a man on a difficult journey, not lonely or bored in the world of screen visibility, but an ethical human being courageously committed to the long-form of linguistic narrative, the story that he is helping to create.

Lenny is not the last man on earth to read a book, but he puts us on alert. If the book culture vanishes, deep reading might disappear as well. Deep reading is always risky, but our great desire for love and responsibility, a genuine human desire, seems enriched by such reading. It is in anguish that Lennie reads, sad with the desire to discover the truth of his life; yet, he is called by his reading, by the stories with their promise of love and responsibility.

Lennie reading might remind us of the famous scene that Augustine tells about his own experience of reading. Like Lennie, he, too, was filled with high anxiety, on the edge of endless distraction. As he tells us in his *Confessions*: He was "weeping the most bitter sorrow of my heart." Then he suddenly ". . . heard a voice from some nearby house, a boy's voice or a girl's voice, I do not know; but it was a sort of singsong, repeated again and again. 'Take and read, Take and read'." The linguistic rhythm of a human voice, no matter a boy's or a girl's, called him to return to the Bible that day. Responding to that voice, he picked up the Bible, opened it to a passage and read: "I snatched it up, opened it and in silence read the passage upon which my eyes first felt." It might seem at first to be a random act, but it proves otherwise. Once finished reading that passage, he has no need to read further: ". . . it was as though a light of utter confidence shone in all my heart, and all the darkness of uncertainty vanished away" (Augustine 159–160). The Book had read him as much as he had read the Book in that miraculous moment, and his life was forever changed.

But Augustine was not done that day, although he closed the Book that had opened to him. Rejuvenated, Augustine did what all great readers do. He returned to "real life," eager to share his reading experience with another: ". . . I closed the book and in complete calm told the whole thing to Alypius and he similarly told me what had been going on in himself, of which I knew nothing" (Augustine 160). Reading that day allowed Augustine an intimacy not just with himself but also with his good friend Alypius. Called by an ethical demand to read, he responded to that call, and then returning to "real life," engaged in ongoing conversation with others. It was an act of love.

In modern times, such intimacy and love still cannot be reduced to data or information, quantified or numbered. It can be palpably experienced, though, through the exchange of language, through the telling of linguistic narrative. It is not primarily the content of what is said, but the telling, the giving that makes the difference.

Augustine and Alypius believed that such intimacy was sanctioned ultimately by God, as if He were summoning them to Him. Today, by contrast, we often believe that it is death that sanctions and summons. As Walter Benjamin famously put it: "Death is the sanction of everything that the storyteller can tell. He has borrowed his authority from death" (Benjamin 94). We admire the courage of the storyteller, the one "who could let the wick of his life be consumed completely by the gentle flame of his story" (Benjamin 108–109). But, as Eunice knows, we also need to admire the reader whose life is also rejuventated because, he, too, had the courage to commit himself to the story.

The storyteller is the stranger that we, as readers, often encounter in the best novels. As Benjamin says, the novel is not "significant . . . because it presents someone else's fate to us . . . but because this stranger's fate by virtue of the flame which consumes it yields us the warmth which we never draw from our own fate" (Benjamin 101). It is, in other words, "the hope of warming" our "shivering life with a death" that we read about (or experience by closing the book at its completion). That hope allows us to continue on, grants us the freedom to pursue the necessity that summons us.

Death sanctions stories now, but it is intimacy and love that we find in the telling of the story, an irreducible act that cannot be separated from our death. The story calls to us, and we meet its ethical demand to respond. It carries its own risk. It serves as an invitation delivered through the gift of language, and we need to open ourselves to it. As Benjamin indicates, it is not "the epic side of truth" that we encounter in modern linguistic narrative, but "a new beauty" (Benjamin 87), one that has more to do with the care of our mortal self and others than with grasping an abstract immortal truth. That "epic side of truth" we now acknowledge is beyond our grasp.

*

It is difficult to imagine that the rich layering of human experience given to us through literary narrative, the desirous language calling to us as readers or listeners, can be surpassed (or even duplicated) by continuous exposure to images rapidly flashing across electronic screens. Linguistic telling offers a glimpse of the interior like nothing else can, a way into the depth of ourselves and others, and the possibility and promise of return. It challenges us to locate ourselves in the world and gives us an embodied sense of temporal movement and direction within that world. It puts us at risk, but it also holds out the promise of the future.

The speed and power of mobile devices often seem to pull our bodies out into the nodes of the electronic network. Fascinated by images on the screen, it is as if we become disembodied, losing our sense of interiority, turning ourselves inside out, until we are emptied of ourselves. We outsource our memory and give up our desires to the screen that appears to know more about our desires than we do. Our online behavior increasingly becomes our offline behavior. Through our online profiles, we become a reduction of ourselves, forgetting the irreducible complexity of our identity, the unknowable destiny that makes us human and unique, the secret that we used to pursue. Instead, we increasingly exist as a representation, a copy, an avatar, an image deleting who we are. By contrast, linguistic telling turns us back toward the pursuit of the undefinable secret of ourselves. Think of it this way: Language is human; digital is electronic.

If that sounds like a cartoon rendering of the screen culture, oversaturated as it is by images, we might nevertheless agree that such a culture works to mask our vulnerability, to protect against our mortality, to silence what cannot be silenced, death itself. It makes little demand on us to acknowledge imperfection or the irreducible and baffling complexity of mortal life. As a culture driven by data and information, it minimizes the kind of human experience that draws its meaning from a belief in the duration of time and human sentiment, which requires the past and the future to make the complexity and ambivalence of human life significant. As Benjamin suggests: "The value of information does not survive the moment in which it was news. It lives only at that moment; it has to surrender to it completely and explain itself to it without losing any time" (Benjamin 90). If Benjamin saw the beginning of the problem in the mechanical age of reproduction, we can see it in its most extreme form now, in the digital age of the screen, the endless now without context or shape, without past or present, without duration, endlessly streaming data and information to keep us distracted.

"Story is different," as Benjamin said. "It does not expend itself. It preserves and concentrates its strength and is capable of releasing it even after a long time" (Benjamin 90). If it does not carry any longer "the epic side of truth," it does convey something more than data or information: a rhythm of mortal life, eros and thanatos, intimate desire and death—a glimpse of something that we cannot fully know, something more that we genuinely desire to know. It is that "something more" that we seek when we leave our "real life" and enter a book, and, when closing that book, it is that "something more" that we seek when we return to our "real life" inspired by the story we have read. As linguistic beings, we are always in the company of other human beings who also use language. As readers, we are always in the company of the story teller: "A man listening to a story is in the company of the story-teller; even a man reading one shares this companionship . . ." (Benjamin 100).

*

There is nothing simple or easy in the journey into and out of linguistic narrative. It is a complex and difficult process, not user-friendly, but risky and irreducible, not safe and secure, but dangerous. We collect data and information to make things easier, to fix problems. But linguistic narrative does not pretend to offer answers; it puts us, as human beings, into question, and, in an important sense, it questions itself. As we have seen from the opening of *Genesis* onward, the narrator of the story, shaping his experience through language, can neither articulate the beginning of Creation or the End that has not yet arrived. In any account of ourselves, in fact, it seems as if our narrative is always incomplete, imperfect, demanding not only the other to listen but desiring that other to continue the story we have offered. We need the other through the telling of stories in a way that information never seems to need anyone.

Stories remind us of what endures in the human world and what makes the world human: the precariousness of our lives, our vulnerability, our commonality as imperfect human beings. By contrast, in the distraction of each flickering instant, information and data pull us away from ourselves, set themselves up as sovereign, as if they are all-knowing gods in that instant. As Lennie Abramov suggests, he might worship his screen, especially "the fact that it knows every last stinking detail about the world," but his books are unique, they are different. That difference makes all the difference. His books "know the mind of their authors" (Shteyngart 78), as Lennie, the deep reader, says.

We learn from Lennie that it is not just story but also language and voice that is at stake in the world of mobile devices, Google glasses, and screen culture. He knows the author's mind because they (authors) not only speak to him, but they speak for themselves. By contrast, we might be reminded, the icons on the screen—Siri, for example—only seem to talk to us; they never talk for themselves. It is the vulnerable human voice shaping language into story that carries the author's mind to the reader, the authentic and intelligent energy of that voice, the rhythm of its singularity and its mortality, its hint of death that we respond to. This is why Joshie (the media king) warns Lennie to get rid of his books: "Those thoughts, these books, they *are* the problem, Rhesus . . . You have to stop thinking and start selling. That's why all those young whizzes in the Eternity Lounge want to shove a carb-filled macaroon up your ass. . . . You remind them of death. You remind them of a different, earlier version of our species . . . There'll be plenty of time to ponder and write and act out later. Right now you've got to sell to live" (Shteyngart 66–67). But for Lennie, neither selling nor imaging opens a way into the capacious world of human understanding. It is, first and foremost, through language that we, as human beings, can know the world as world, can live in it and celebrate it, rather than manipulate it, as if we were gods that could survive it.

The rich texture of mortal life is threatened by the clickety-clack of mobile devices. When Lennie walks down Grand Street toward the East River Park in his "trendy old man's getup" (Shetyngart 53), he gives us a glimpse of that rich texture, what Joshie and the posthuman sensibility in general are losing with their belief that electronic know-how will lead to immortality: "I celebrated the teenaged mothers from the Vladevk Houses tending to their children's boo-boos ('A bee touched me, Mommy'!). I relished hearing language actually *spoken* by children. Overblown verbs, explosive nouns, beautifully bungled prepositions. Language, not data. How long would it be before these kids retreated into the dense clickety-clack apparat world of their absorbed mothers and missing fathers?" (Shteyngart 53). The joy and the anguish of language, the overflowing desire of its vulnerable rhythm, keeps us alive and binds us, as linguistic beings, to each other. Our attempt to shape our mortal experiences through language, our ability to offer our stories to others, to tell what needs to be told, gives "real life" its meaning.

Granted, as linguistic beings, we cannot finally make explicit the secret of our mortality, neither our origins nor our end. Both the beginning and the end lie beyond the threshold of what can be fully articulated. This is what Judith Butler suggests in her exciting book *Giving an Account of Oneself* when she writes: "If I try to give an account of myself, if I try to make myself recognizable and understandable, then I might begin with a narrative account of my life. But this narrative will be disoriented by what is not mine, or not mine alone. And I will, to some degree, have to make myself substitutable in order to make myself recognizable. The narrative authority of the 'I' must have to give way to the perspective and temporality of a set of norms that contest the singularity of my story" (Butler 37).

But Butler is not quite correct when she implies that it is the "the narrative authority" of the "I" that sanctions stories. As Benjamin has said, it is not the "I" that drives stories, but death. Death excites the telling, arouses the desire that overflows that "perspective and temporality of a set of norms" (Benjamin 94). That is what becomes the gift to us, as readers, allows us to continue on. Through this rhythm of call and response, the mortal rhythm of an ethical life, we glimpse that "singularity," the "singularity" that we all, each in our own unique way, share as vulnerable and precarious human beings. That is what Lennie Abramov was listening to on Grand Street the day he walked there enchanted by the language of children while in his "trendy old man's get up" (Shetynart 53).

There is no "narrative authority of the 'I'" anymore than there can be a speaker without a listener, or a writer without a reader. As Butler well knows, such understanding takes us to the heart of human relations and the ethics of linguistic narrative. That "I," never sovereign, never stands alone. "I am my relation to you" (Butler 81), as Butler puts it: Not "I am in relation to you" but "I am my relation to you." It is as if the linguistic telling makes us who we are and who we are not. It is not a question of "selling to live" (as Joshie told Lenny)—an illusion of immortality, but rather dwelling within language, language which lives as a call and response to the other, until death overtakes us.

As Butler says: To tell the story of oneself is "an action in the direction of the other, as well as an action that requires an other, in which an other is presupposed. The other is thus within the action of my telling; it is not simply a question of imparting information to an other who is over there. On the contrary, the telling presupposes an Other, posits and elaborates the other, is given to the other, or by virtue of the other, prior to the giving of any information" (Butler 81–82). It is not information or data that keeps us alive, though, but the linguistic telling that allows us to acknowledge the other, the difference that we care about, the relationship that makes us who we are.

Despite what Butler implies when she insists that we become "dispossessed" when giving an account of ourselves, we are really never in total possession of ourselves. Speaking and listening, reading and writing, are precisely what we need to meet the ethical demand required to be a "human being" (at least in the traditional sense of that term). In this regard, the gift of language is our invitation to discover who we are. To open ourselves to that gift is a risk as necessary to take as the journey of mortal life itself.

*

To read deeply is always a risk. We are not primarily seeking information or data when we read linguistic narrative, but daring to enter the unknown territory, the other (who is also ourself and not ourself), the one that puts us into question. As Butler claims: "Perhaps most importantly, we must recognize that ethics requires us to risk ourselves precisely at moments of unknowingness, when what forms us diverges from what lies before us, when our willingness to become undone in relation to others constitutes our chance of becoming human" (Butler 136). At such moments, we are bound to a strangeness that moves us, a possibility that we have not acknowledged before. As readers, we are vulnerable, shaken up, humbled, but yet desirous, aroused by the warmth of the story itself (as Benjamin said), an alternative possibility that we carry back with us into the "real world" as the book is closed.

What we carry back into "real life" is not information or data—that which does not "survive the moment in which it was new"—but the linguistic telling that "concentrates its strength and is capable of releasing it even after a long time" (Benjamin 90). Information consumes itself in the instant; linguistic narrative germinates within us. Language contributes to this difference, evoking memory and desire through a process that takes place at the depths of ourselves and the world.

Lennie Abramov knows this, expressing it in rich elegiac tones in his last diary entry. Walking again on Grand Street, mid-October, "a gust of autumnal wind" kicking its way down the street, he notices a tired old Jewish woman who looks up "at the pending wind" and says only one word: "Blustery." It is not the image of the woman or the experience of the wind that moves Lennie, but just the one word, "a word meaning no more than a 'period of time characterized by strong winds'." The word catches him by surprise, reminding him of "how language was once used . . . its capacity for recall" (Shteyngart 304–305).

In the age of mobile devices, such linguistic experiences are rare even for Lennie, but this particular encounter takes him deep into the interior of himself (as if he is "deep reading") and then to a return to Grand Street and the woman in front of him. It evokes a genuine human exchange. As he writes in his diary: "Not cold, not chilly, blustery. A hundred other days appeared before me, my young mother in a faux-fur coat standing before our Chevrolet-Malibu Classic, her hands protectively over my ears . . . The streams of her worried breath against my face, the excitement of feeling both cold and protected, exposed to the elements and loved at the same time" (Shteyngart 305). The word itself—"blustery"—heard on Grand Street that day loops back through time and his body, allowing him to open a moment of vulnerability and love, a moment that endures, a temporary stay from death. Then Lennie is back to the present, carrying the emotions of the past with him, extending the complexity of those emotions across time and generations: "'It is blustery, ma'am', I said to the old co-op woman. 'I can feel it in my bones.' And she smiled at me with whatever facial muscles she still had on reserve. We were communicating with words" (Shteyngart 308). For Lennie, it is an act of love, offering hope for the future.

The screen culture is intensely visual, celebrates speed and power, promotes public exposure, privileges quantitative data and statistics, technical rationality and information. It can be distracting and addictive. By contrast, literary narrative promotes a slow and meditative rhythm, invites self-reflection, favors interiority and an irreducible complexity.

It is puzzling how sensitive and thoughtful critics can draw the conclusions they do. How can Andrew Piper, for example, compare the ethics of reading to the ethics of looking at Facebook? Piper agrees that "Reading books . . . teaches us to relate to that which we cannot fully know" but then he claims that "There is an entanglement to social networking that is as meaningful as the book's pedagogy of mental distance, that I can never in the end fully know you" (Piper 43). If Piper is claiming that we can never fully know another person, it is difficult not to agree with him. (This book makes a similar point.) But to claim that the "entanglement of social networking" is "as meaningful as the book's pedagogy of mental distance" seems off on several counts. When we read a book, the relationship between the "I" and the "you" is grounded (or groundlessly grounded) in language (the linguistic unconscious): by contrast, when we look at a digital screen, the relationship is grounded in the image (the optical unconscious). When we read a book, we encounter language, become self-reflective, discover a difference within the rich and ambiguous texture of the telling, and it is the irreducible complexity of the relationship that baffles and moves us. With a digital screen (Facebook), we look at it, and become absorbed by it (or become voyeurs), fixed by the reduction of the profile, the information that consumes us.

Piper claims, "Beneath the bookish face was nothing but an unsettling void. Beneath the digital face lies instead the graph, the new optical unconscious" (Piper 38). Piper's "nothing but" sounds like an "only," suggesting that somehow the digital face (or screen) offers something more valuable than the book. But, for us, the contrary is closer to the mark. Looking through the "bookish face," we might arrive at the threshold of Piper's "unsettling void" (or Conrad's "horror" or Lacan's "Real" or the "abyss" or "death" or perhaps Augustine's God). But, whatever that "unsettling void" is, as ungraspable as it seems, it resonates with some gravity that cannot easily be denied. We can still sense it through the words, the language of that bookish face, when we read. As Maurice Blanchot once suggested, reading is "a joyful, wild dance with the 'tomb'" (Blanchot 98). It is a "lightness," but it never lacks "gravity" (as grave as that gravity might be).

By contrast, beneath the digital face, we find "the graph," (or "algorithms" and "numbers"), the bits and bytes of the optical unconscious. It is as if we are seeing ourselves without the possibility of the other. It is not the ungraspable mystery of life that we seek on the digital screen, but the thrill that leads to boredom, the reduction of ourselves, that we endlessly grasp.

In the book culture, genuine human desire had a lot to do with love and responsibility, our desire to be responsible for the other human being before us, our desire for the love of the other. If thanatos was at the bottom of life, then eros was in dialectical relationship with it (at least as long as we lived). At its best, literary narrative invites us as readers to engage (or reengage) with the experience and implications of that capacious dialectic, a complex movement that opens to the possibility of love and responsibility and reminds us of our vulnerability, the necessity of death itself. It is possible that images streaming across the digital screens can offer us something like this, but unlikely. The digital screen leaves little, if any, time or space for self-reflection. The online face is, as Piper suggests, too close, and the sense of the duration of time itself is lost. Even the storyworld that we enter through the screen (often in video game format) seems to displace our human desire for the rhythm of love and death in favor of the rhythm of winning and losing, the rhythm of the market economy. We get points for killing our opponents, praise for how fast we manipulate the closed image of ourselves, rewards for how quickly we destroy the icons that stand in our way. In such situations, there is no empathy for what we manipulate, no time to acknowledge the irreducibility of the other, only a violence, a misplaced sensation, the instant gratification of winning.

*

Finally, we need to question the so-called freedom that hypertext offers us, the apparent ability to free the reader from the linear sequence of print culture. This kind of praise for the boundless fluidity of screen culture seems off the mark as well. Linguistic telling requires a reader to interact with the language, to help create the story that is told. Its rhythm is not simply a linear progression, but an ongoing looping, back and forth, an attempt to stabilize and destabilize, reveal and conceal. It creates an indirect pathway that the reader experiences and helps to create. The reader turns away from "real life" to enter it, and then returns to "real life" when it is finished.

To believe that the reader is imprisoned by a book culture, that such a reader is locked into the writer's linear plotting is to mistake the surface for the depths of the reading experience. Because a reader of hypertext can choose his own ending for a narrative, become the writer of what he is reading, is no doubt a kind of freedom, but such freedom has more to do with procedural literacy than with verbal literacy, and it seems to devalue the ambiguity and depth of language itself. As Gregory Jusdanis remarks: "It is simplistic to argue that because print compels readers to move from left to right and beginning to end somehow jails them. Such a position represents the (printed) text as a fixed entity, a move reminiscent of the way theorists in the 1970s and 1980s conceived of 'closed texts'." Such simplicity confuses "surface reality" with "hermeneutic freedom" (Jusdanis 108). Such confusion is typical in the digital age. In fact, we might wonder if the fluid hypertext, which seems to make it nearly impossible to experience the same text more than once, is anything more than information, news that consumes itself in the instant. It is an endlessly running flow that never stops. It is best considered mere hallucination.

Literary narrative can change lives because it has depth and lasts. Unlike information, it can be experienced more than once, because each time there is another surprise. It reveals and conceals, opens and closes. We sense satisfaction when we finish a book, and yet it germinates within us. That is part of its gravity and value. Even when we read the same book again and again, each reading can still be a "unique reading," as Blanchot claims: "Each time the first reading and each time the only reading" (Blanchot 91). That is not because the text is fluid and ever-changing, but because it is bound and yet forever bounding. If it gives us comfort, a sense of home, it is also risky and dangerous: it holds out the promise of discovering our singularity. That singularity is not what some in Silicon Valley like to call a Virtual Reality Heaven, though, a perfect place created by the belief in the speed and power of digital technology; rather it is the singularity of our unique and mortal human self, the imperfect self that we desire to know even if we cannot quite know it. It sends us on the journey of our life. It demands that we keep reading until it is too late. Until then, though, literary narrative remains essential for reckoning with our basic experiences of mortality and desire. It helps us to know the strangeness of our own contingency, and the contingency of our relations to others. As linguistic beings, we cannot live deeply without it.

Bibliography

Augustine, Saint, *Confessions*, edited by Michael P. Foley, translated by F. J. Sheed, Indianapolis, IN, Hackett Publishing Company, 2006.

Benjamin, Walter, *Illuminations*, edited by Hannah Arendt, translated by Harry Zohn, New York, Shocken Books, 1969.

Birkerts, Sven, *The Gutenberg Elegies: The Fate of Reading in an Electronic Age*, New York, Ballantine Books, 1994.

Blanchot, Maurice, *The Station Hill Blanchot Reader: Fiction & Literary Essays*, edited by George Quasha, translated by Lydia Davis, Paul Auster, and Robert Lamberton, Barrytown, NY, Station Hill Press, 1999.

Bloom, Harold and David Rosenberg, *The Book of J*, New York, Vintage Books, 1990.

Boman, Thorleif, *Hebrew Thought Compared with Greek*, translated by Jules L. Moreau, New York, W.W. Norton & Company, 1970.

Brooks, Peter, *Body Work: Objects of Desire in Modern Literature*, Cambridge, MA, Harvard University Press, 1993.

—, *Reading for the Plot: Design and Intention in Narrative*, Cambridge, MA, Harvard University Press, 1984.

Burke, Michael, *Literary Reading: Cognition and Emotion: An Exploration of the Oceanic Mind*, London, Routledge, 2012.

Butler, Judith, *Giving an Account of Oneself*, New York, Fordham University Press, 2005.

Carr, Nicholas, *The Shallows: What the Internet is Doing to Our Brains*, New York, W.W. Norton & Company, 2010.

Cavell, Stanley, *The Senses of Walden: An Expanded Edition*, Chicago, University of Chicago Press, 1992.

Conrad, Joseph, *Heart of Darkness*, edited by Paul B. Armstrong, New York, W.W. Norton & Company, 2006.

Foucault, Michel, *The Birth of the Clinic: An Archaeology of Medical Perception*, New York, Vintage Books, 1994.

French, Warren G., *J. D. Salinger, revisited*, Woodbridge, CT, Twayne Publishers, 1988.

Gadamer, Hans-Georg, *Truth and Method*, London, Sheed and Ward, 1975.

Heidegger, Martin, *Poetry, Language, Thought*, translated by Albert Hofstader, New York, Harper Perennial Modern Classics, 2013.

Jusdanis, Gregory, *Fiction Agonistes: In Defense of Literature*, Stanford, CA, Stanford University Press, 2010.

Kass, Leon R., *The Beginning of Wisdom: Reading Genesis*, Chicago, IL, University of Chicago Press, 2003.

Lacan, Jacques, *The Language of the Self: The Function of Language in Psychoanalysis*, translated by Anthony Wilden, New York, Dell Publishing, 1975.

Lanier, Jaron, *You Are Not a Gadget*, New York, Alfred. A. Knopf, 2010.

Lawtoo, Nidesh (ed.), *Conrad's Heart of Darkness and Contemporary Thought: Revisiting the Horror with Lacoue-Labarthe*, London and New York, Bloomsbury Publishing, 2012.

Levinas, Emmanuel, *Totality and Infinity: An Essay on Exteriority*, Pittsburg, PA, Duquense University Press, 1969.

MacIntyre, Alasdair, *After Virtue: A Study in Moral Theory*, Notre Dame, IN, University of Notre Dame Press, 1981.

Miles, Jack, *God: A Biography*, New York, Vintage Books, 1996.

Newton, Adam Zachary, *Narrative Ethics*, Cambridge, MA, Harvard University Press, 1997.

Pagels, Elaine, *Adam, Eve and the Serpent: Sex and Politics in Early Christianity*, New York, Vintage Books, 1988.

Piper, Andrew, *Book Was There: Reading in Electronic Times*, Chicago and London, University of Chicago Press, 2012.

Prensky, Marc, "Digital Natives, Digital Immigrants Part 1," *On the Horizon*, Vol. 9, No. 5, 1–6, 2001.

Roehmer, Michael, *Telling Stories: Postmodernism and the Invalidation of Traditional Narrative*, Lanham, MD, Rowman & Littlefield Publishers, 1995.

Salinger, 1957 letter quoted at http://dangerousminds.net/comments/ salinger_on_why_catcher_will_never_be_a_movie.

Shelley, Mary, *Frankenstein*, edited by J. Paul Hunter, New York, W.W. Norton & Company, 2011.

Steiner, Wendy, *The Colors of Rhetoric: Problems in the Relation between Modern Literature and Painting*, Chicago and London, University of Chicago Press, 1982.

Stoltzfus, Ben, "*The Old Man and the Sea*: A Lacanian Reading," in *Hemingway: Essays of Reassessment*, edited by Frank Scafella, New York, Oxford University Press, 1991.

Virilio, Paul, *The University of Disaster*, translated by Julie Rose, Cambridge, UK, Polity Press, 2010.

Vizenor, Gerald (ed.), *Survivance: Narratives of Native Presence*, Lincoln and London, University of Nebraska Press, 2008.

Waxler, Robert P. and Maureen P. Hall, *Transforming Literacy: Changing Lives through Reading and Writing*, United Kingdom, Emerald Group Publishing Limited, 2011.

Weinstein, Arnold, *Recovering Your Story: Proust, Joyce, Woolf, Faulkner, Morrison*, New York, Random House, 2006.

Wolf, Maryanne, *Proust and the Squid: The Story and Science of the Reading Brain*, New York, HarperCollins Publishers, 2008.

Wood, Michael, "A World without Literature?" *Daedalus*, Winter 2009.

Texts cited for commentary

Barnes, Julian, *The Sense of an Ending*, New York, Alfred A. Knopf, 2011.

Carroll, Lewis, *Alice's Adventures in Wonderland*, New York, Dover Publications, 1993.

Conrad, Joseph, *Heart of Darkness*, Mineola, NY, Dover Publications, 2009.

Hemingway, Ernest, *The Old Man and the Sea*, New York, Simon & Schuster, 1995.

Kesey, Ken, *One Flew over the Cuckoo's Nest*, edited by John Clark Pratt, New York, Penguin Books, 1996.

Palahniuk, Chuck, *Fight Club*, New York, Henry Holt and Company, 1996.

Salinger, Jerome David, *The Catcher in the Rye*, Boston, MA, Little, Brown and Company, 1991.

Shelley, Mary, *Frankenstein*, New York, New American Library, 1965.

Shteyngart, Gary, *Super Sad True Love Story*, New York, Random House, 2010.

The Holy Bible, New International Version, NIV, 1973, 1978, 1984, 2011 by Biblica at www.BibleGateway.

.

Index